STAY HOME

Housing and Home in the UK during the COVID-19 Pandemic

Becky Tunstall

P

First published in Great Britain in 2023 by

Policy Press, an imprint of
Bristol University Press
University of Bristol
1–9 Old Park Hill
Bristol
BS2 8BB
UK
t: +44 (0)117 374 6645
e: bup-info@bristol.ac.uk

Details of international sales and distribution partners are available at
policy.bristoluniversitypress.co.uk

British Library Cataloguing in Publication Data
A catalogue record for this book is available from the British Library

ISBN 978-1-4473-6588-4 hardcover
ISBN 978-1-4473-6589-1 paperback
ISBN 978-1-4473-6590-7 ePub
ISBN 978-1-4473-6591-4 ePdf

Cover design: Robin Hawes
Front cover image: Stocksy/Jakob Lagerstedt
Bristol University Press and Policy Press use environmentally responsible print partners.
Printed and bound in Great Britain by CMP, Poole

Contents

List of figures, tables and photos

Figures

Tables

Photos

Acknowledgements

Many thanks to all the hundreds of thousands of individual people who gave up their time to respond to the many surveys and research projects upon which this book is based, both before the pandemic and in its midst, and to the researchers who planned and carried out the work and published its results. Particular thanks are due to the thousands of people who responded to the final open-ended question in the birth cohort studies surveys on COVID-19, with the often very personal and powerful comments which so enrich this book, and to the Centre for Longitudinal Studies, University College London, which provided access to the data.

Many thanks also to all at Policy Press and those who read drafts of the book and contributed essential improvements, including Peter Kenway, Liz Richardson, Shaggy Shadbolt, Helena Tunstall and Policy Press's two anonymous reviewers.

Finally, thanks to my mum and dad, Sylvia and Jeremy, for keeping me in house and home, answering my questions and listening to my answers.

1

COVID-19, housing and home

The pandemic 2020–22

National government instructions to citizens, 2020

Stay home, stay at home – UK
Restez chez vous – France
Stai a casa – Italy
Quedate en casa – Spain
Bleib zuhause – Germany
Blijf thuis – The Netherlands
Zostan w domu – Poland
μένω σπίτι – Greece
A sta acasa – Romania
Zustat doma – Czechia (formerly the Czech Republic)
Ficar am casa – Portugal

On 31 December 2019, a cluster of pneumonia cases was reported by the Wuhan Municipal Health Commission in China. These cases were to be identified as a novel coronavirus, to be named SARS-CoV-2 or COVID-19 for short. On 30 January 2020, the World Health Organization (WHO) reported almost 8,000 confirmed cases worldwide. Most of these were in China, but 18 other countries had already been affected.[1] The first people to be diagnosed with lab-confirmed COVID-19 in the UK were a mother and son in York on 30 January 2020. Concern grew, and in the week to 28 February, the FTSE 100 lost 11%, its worst week since the Global Financial Crisis (GFC) in 2008.[2] On 3 March, day 33 of the UK pandemic, a person who had tested positive for COVID-19 in the UK died – the first of what were to be over 164,000 deaths in the UK and among the more than six million worldwide by March 2022.[3]

The COVID-19 pandemic was a very rare event. Over a compressed time period, it involved almost everyone in the world. Almost everyone has had to **stay home** for at least some time. Everyone has a story, and each story forms part of the whole picture.

The next day, on 4 March 2020, I was at a meeting in Brussels with civil servants and academics from around Europe. The other UK invitees had not turned up because their universities had suddenly stopped them from travelling because they were unsure if their insurance would be valid. As we left, I avoided handshakes and said, half-joking, that this might be my last trip abroad for a while – the continental Europeans joked back, assuming I was referring to Brexit. (Seven months later, we all met again, on Zoom, to allocate money for research on COVID-19.) On day 37, a friend and I were enjoying a weekend in Bridlington in Yorkshire. Arcade staff had placed in prime position a grabber machine in which the only prize was toilet rolls, a satire on the sudden shortages of these items in supermarkets. On day 40, Nadine Dorries MP, a junior Health Minister, tested positive for coronavirus.

On day 42, when 489 people tested positive in the UK, and individuals with symptoms (although not their households) were first asked to **stay home**, I had chills, violent shakes and sweats, and a temperature well above the 37.8°C COVID-19 threshold. I could not get through to my GP. The NHS 111 recorded message and website were only interested in recent arrivals from Italy, the Far East and Iran, with no options for people who had been elsewhere, even though the first case of person-to-person transmission had been identified in China seven weeks earlier[4] and COVID-19 had been known to be in the UK for six weeks. There didn't seem to be a way to speak to a real person. (It later became clear that thousands and possibly tens of thousands of people in the UK had the virus by this point and community transmission was well under way.) There had already been days of official advice against going to Accident & Emergency departments with symptoms, and there seemed to be no way to get hospital care, short of calling 999 or collapsing in the street. There also seemed to be no way to get a test unless you had somehow made it to hospital. (Testing outside hospital and contact tracing stopped on 13 March.)[5] The next day my doctor offered me antibiotics. (In June, I paid for a private antibody test, which showed that I had had the virus at some point earlier in the year.)

That week, as for millions of others, my work diary went blank. Some 1,000 people in the UK had been tested and found to have COVID-19. On day 43, Jeremy Hunt MP, Chair of the House of Commons Health and Social Care Select Committee, looked frightened as he appeared on the BBC's *Newsnight* programme and expressed concern about delays to the already-planned lockdown, about limited testing and about the idea of herd immunity.

By day 45, 100 people who had tested positive in the UK had died. On day 46, almost seven weeks into the outbreak in the UK, Prime Minister Boris Johnson advised people to "avoid" pubs and restaurants.[6] On day 47, Sir Patrick Vallance, the government's Chief Scientific Adviser, told a committee of MPs that keeping the number of UK deaths below 20,000 would be a "good outcome".[7]

On day 48, the Eurovision Song Contest was cancelled. The Glastonbury Festival was cancelled. Filming stopped on *EastEnders*. My university moved to compulsory home working for all vulnerable people and all other staff for whom it was possible. On day 49, I stepped out on a tentative (in hindsight reckless) trip to the swimming pool, awkwardly passing a man mending the lift in my block and edging round people on the pavement. The pool staff were cleaning with power hoses, and I overheard a lifeguard saying that she wouldn't be able to pay her next month's rent – she had been a good tenant for three years and just wasn't sure of her income. She said if we had to **stay home**, she would probably go back to Spain with her children.

On day 50, the Prime Minister announced that pubs and restaurants (and swimming pools) must close that evening and not reopen. He urged people not to visit their mothers on Mother's Day that weekend[8] and announced that the full first UK 'lockdown' would start on day 53. On that day, 23 March 2020, Johnson told the 28 million people watching him on TV: "I must give you a very simple instruction: you must **stay at home**."[9]

The next day, a friend who had had mental health problems called. He had been **staying home** for 24 hours and was finding it hard.

Photo 1: A note I found on the street outside my block of flats, East London, April 2020

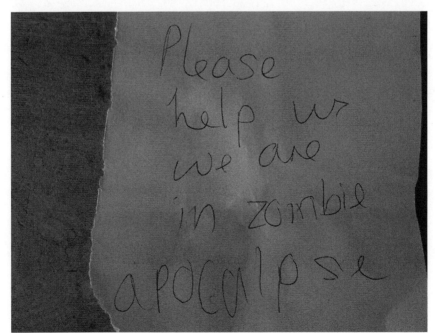

What kind of event or process was the pandemic?

Everyone on earth has views about the pandemic. Most observers recognise that it was unprecedented and multi-dimensional, but it has been seen through several different frames.

Unprecedented in scale and danger

In the variants known to date, COVID-19 itself is not as transmissible or fatal as some other diseases.[10] Other Public Health Emergencies of International Concern had been declared by WHO in the 2010s, in West Africa, in Brazil and in the Democratic Republic of the Congo (DRC). However, with COVID-19, almost all 7.7 billion people in the world were exposed to a transmissible, dangerous and initially untreatable disease at almost the same time.[11] Farrar with Ahuja pointed out that Western countries 'had not seen deaths from untreatable infectious diseases for many years'.[12] As early as January 2020, the total potential impact was compared by doctors in *The Lancet* to the 1918–20 worldwide Spanish flu pandemic, which killed tens of millions of people.[13] During the second wave of the pandemic, the UK death toll overtook British civilian deaths in the Second World War and by 2022 was of the same order of magnitude as the deaths of British forces in 1939–45.

Measures to prevent deaths and the side-effects of these measures were also unprecedented.[14] The lockdown in Wuhan city from 23 January 2020, which involved 11 million people, was at that time the biggest ever recorded quarantine,[15] but was soon outdone many times over by simultaneous lockdowns around the world. The UK's Coronavirus Act 2020 of 26 March was described as 'the most authoritarian new law since the Second World War'.[16]

Multi-dimensional

The pandemic was a health crisis, but the public reaction and measures to control it immediately made it a crisis for other aspects of physical health, mental health, education, work, business, the economy, incomes and living standards.[17] It has been described as: 'The biggest upheaval to the global order since the Second World War.'[18] There had never been a simultaneous reduction in economic growth in almost every country in the world,[19] and the International Monetary Fund (IMF) described the pandemic as 'a crisis like no other'.[20] The support to UK employees and businesses announced in March 2020 was 'the biggest ever state intervention seen in peacetime'.[21] As it progressed, the pandemic resulted in the worst UK recession since records began in 1955, with a 25% drop in gross domestic product (GDP) in January–March 2020.[22] GDP in 2020/21 was 4.8% lower than in

4

2019/20, which wiped out 17 years of growth and took the economy back to the size it was in 2003,[23] The Bank of England's pandemic 'quantitative easing', or buying UK government and non-financial corporate bonds, totalled £450 billion by November 2020[24] and amounted to about 25 years' worth of affordable housing budgets for England.

This book takes a multi-dimensional approach to housing and home and their relationship with COVID-19, as influences on physical and mental health, as elements of living standards, as sites of care and support, and as contributions to the economy.

A test of resilience

Like other shocks, the pandemic can be seen as a test of societal and housing system resilience.[25] An international comparative study of pandemic response said 'the pandemic found and revealed pre-existing weaknesses in the body politic, exploiting and aggravating them … in the health, economic, and political systems'.[26]

The Lancet Public Health argued that the pandemic 'is a test of political leadership, of national health systems, of social care services, of solidarity, of the social contract'.[27]

In a conservative definition, a 'resilient' system is one which can absorb shocks, and can 'bounce back' and continue to provide the same outcomes. In a more progressive definition, a resilient system can bounce back to produce equivalent or even better outcomes, without 'scarring', or lasting negative effects.[28] However, when the pandemic arrived, the UK's economy and housing system (and those in other countries) had not yet fully recovered from the 2008 GFC. And what is included in 'the system'? It has been argued that in housing systems, 'the dominant political economy, selected institutions, and to an extent, existing home owners and speculative investors are privileged in resilience policy'.[29] There is also a question about who or what provides resilience. In 2020, Welsh housing professionals discussing the pandemic said 'poverty undermines our ability to build resilience'.[30] Some have argued that preventing shocks is more valuable than being able to survive them and that resilience requires building back 'better' or more equitably.

A spotlight on inequality

Many commentators, researchers and members of the public have argued that the pandemic has highlighted inequalities in health, employment, income, domestic work and unpaid care, and many other areas of life, including in housing. For example, economist Joseph Stiglitz said the pandemic has 'laid bare deep divisions'.[31] The Carers Trust said that it has 'exposed many of the inequalities that have existed long before the pandemic'.[32] Gavin Smart, CEO of the Chartered Institute of Housing said "the story of the unequal impact of the pandemic is the story of long-standing dimensions of inequality in our country and in our housing system".[33] However, many have argued that the pandemic has not only exposed but has also increased pre-existing inequalities and created new ones, for example, between those who could work at home and those who could not. A report from the US think tank the Brookings Institution said 'inequality was bad and the COVID-19 pandemic is making it worse'.[34] UK Chief Scientific Advisor Patrick Vallance said "this virus feeds off inequality and feeds inequality".[35] It has also been argued that recovery plans to date do not compensate for pandemic inequalities, and may exacerbate and embed them.

A turning point?

Commentators are divided over whether the pandemic marks a historic inflexion. Has pandemic shock caused pre-existing trends to pause, reverse or change direction, or will they continue as before once the worst is over? Tooze described the pandemic as a 'turning point',[36] but Preece et al described it as a temporary break in urban rhythms.[37] Burchardt said it could be a 'new Beveridge moment', but it might also be 'a crisis which will wash away'.[38] The pandemic's effects inevitably overlapped with those of pre-existing developments. For example, social landlords in Scotland commented:

> The COVID-19 pandemic came at a time when [social housing] was responding to other major disruptive events: the Grenfell disaster … increasing risk of cyber-attacks; the emerging social and economic fall-out from Brexit; and the impact and implications of climate change.[39]

The pandemic's effects will also blend into the effects of developing and future events, like the rising cost of living.

An unfinished experience

This book was completed in early 2022, when the UK was coming out of a third wave of infections with the Omicron variant which had peaked with almost 300,000 recorded infections a day, the highest number to date. Several major impacts of the pandemic – on work, education, household finances and relationships – gradually waned from April 2020 to the end of 2021, but had not gone away (Figure 1.1).

The full impact of long COVID-19 and effects on mental health, education, employment and the economy are yet to come and yet to be understood; some of the effects of the pandemic will linger and become part

Figure 1.1: Proportion of adults saying the pandemic was affecting key areas of life, Great Britain, April 2020–November 2021

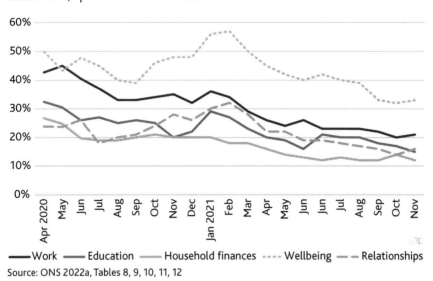

Source: ONS 2022a, Tables 8, 9, 10, 11, 12

of a new normal. There might be further peaks in infections and deaths, and is it likely that there will be other pandemics or other global shocks.

Nonetheless, many key issues and much important evidence had emerged by 2022. This book aims to provide an analysis and synthesis of the state of knowledge up to this point, which will be of value whatever comes next.

The pandemic, housing and home

In the 2010s, many felt that the UK housing system was in 'crisis', and it was described as 'dysfunctional' and 'broken' even by government ministers and departments.[40] Suddenly in 2020, the unsatisfactory system became the official national refuge. The most important policy used to control COVID-19 infection and spread in the UK – and all around the world – was for large proportions of the population to '**stay home**'. Home was also used as a place for 'isolating' those who might be infectious and for 'shielding' those at high risk. This resulted in mass changes in the way in which homes were used, experienced and perceived. In May 2020, a woman aged 62 responding to a COVID-19 survey said "my life has been compressed into home"[41].

However, some commentators have said that homes are the highest-risk environments for infection,[42] putting the wisdom of '**staying home**' in doubt. When in May 2020, the London Borough of Newham had the highest COVID-19 death rate in the country, alongside a history of widespread overcrowding, a politician from the area declared "this is a housing disease".[43]

In addition, **staying home** not only meant working at home and studying at home, but also created a new category of dependence at home for 'shielders' and 'isolators', and disrupted patterns of inter-household and at-home care and support. It meant that hundreds of thousands of people spent months worrying about housing costs and potential repossessions, and for some the meaning of home changed to being a place of confinement, anxiety or overwork. The pandemic also provided an unfortunate natural opportunity to learn about the UK housing system under unique pressure, including its flaws, its inequalities and its resilience.

However, housing and home are only commented on briefly in most of the existing book-length studies of the pandemic in the UK (Horton 2020; Farrar with Ahuja 2021; Calvert and Arbuthnott 2021; Tooze 2021) and in the House of Commons Health and Social Care Committee and Science and Technology Committees' joint investigation into the pandemic (HSC/STC 2021a).

This book focuses on housing and home. It charts experiences, taking a special interest in inequalities in housing and in pandemic impact, between income groups, ethnicities, tenure, household types and regions. It explores the extent to which the UK housing has proved resilient, and factors that contributed to housing system resilience, whether social, institutional or political.

The key questions

The book asks the following questions:

1) How prepared was the UK housing system for the COVID-19 shock?
2) How big was the impact of the pandemic on household, housing and home?
3) Were household and home implicated in COVID-19 infections and deaths?
4) Did household and home affect the impact of COVID-19 restrictions and supports?
5) Has COVID-19 altered the pre-existing inequalities in and caused by the housing system?
6) What can be learnt from the pandemic about the housing system, household and home?

The book focuses on private households, where most UK residents live. It covers the UK, with some exploration of differences between the nations and regions, and some comparisons to other nations. It focuses on housing, household and home as being of interest in their own rights, and also as cross-disciplinary lenses for learning from the pandemic to date. It covers the impact of COVID-19 on the size of the population, the number and type of households, changes in the amount of time and home and daily life at home, and the impact of the pandemic on the meaning of home. It explores the risk of infection at home; the experiences of shielding and isolating at home, being sick at home and caring for others at home. It also covers the impact of pandemic restrictions on work, income and paying for housing; the knock-on impact on housing security and homelessness; and the impact of the pandemic on the housing market. However, readers requiring detailed analysis of policymaking, working at home, home schooling, childcare, diet and exercise, domestic tasks, personal relationships and domestic abuse will need to turn to specialised sources.

The book introduces new analysis of qualitative data on the impact of the pandemic from the five British birth cohort studies (see Appendix). These studies follow people born in 1946, 1958, 1970, and 1989/90, and both people born in 2000–02 and their parents, with regular surveys throughout their lives.[44] In 2020, the cohort members had their 74th, 62nd, 50th, 31st and 18th–20th birthdays (many of those turning 50 noted that they were not able to celebrate). All the studies had extra surveys in 2020 and 2021 asking people about experiences during the pandemic, which were administered online. At the end of the surveys in May 2020 and in February/March 2021, respondents were asked an open question:

> Express in your own words the main ways the coronavirus outbreak has affected your life and/or your loved ones so far, and what you think the effects might be in the future. You can write as much or little as you like, and cover any topic you choose.[45]

This book uses the responses to this question. It also draws on the wealth of ongoing data gathering and special research carried out in 2020 and 2021 by the Office for National Statistics (ONS), the NHS, the Department for Work and Pensions (DWP), the Department for Levelling Up, Housing and Communities (DLUHC, from September 2021) and its predecessor the Ministry of Housing, Communities and Local Government (MHCLG), the Department of Health and Social Care (DHSC), the Institute for Fiscal Studies, the Resolution Foundation and others. Many of these studies switched at short notice from face-to-face to online questionnaires, and had smaller sample sizes than in normal times, or were created rapidly. Nonetheless, they are extremely valuable sources. The book also makes use of the burgeoning literature available by the start of 2022.

What the book argues

This book argues that the significance of household and home in the pandemic has been overlooked. Household and home were central to the impacts, experiences, inequalities and lasting effects of the COVID-19 pandemic in the UK (and elsewhere) in terms of infections, illnesses and deaths, and all the other health, social, psychological and economic effects. The book demonstrates that many people had homes that were not suitable for **staying home** in, or for effective shielding and isolating. This had tragic consequences for some individuals, unequal effects on some groups, and likely lasting effects for the housing system and society.

By 2022, the predicted negative effects of the pandemic on unemployment, house prices and transactions, and the growing wealth of home owners had already 'washed away'. A predicted 'tsunami' of repossessions had not emerged and homelessness was at 'normal' levels. Attention was turning away from COVID-19 to inflation, the cost of living and the war in Ukraine. However, this book argues that a large fraction of national resilience to the pandemic, including the prevention of infections, arrears, homelessness and destitution, was provided by households, families and friends, at considerable financial and personal cost. Emergency housing, care for the sick and adult social care had been further 'familialised'. Pre-existing housing problems of overcrowding, quality, unaffordability and insecurity had worsened. In addition, millions more than before were working at home, awaiting healthcare at home, experiencing mental health problems at home and caring for others at home, many with little support, and in homes not designed for these purposes.

2

UK households and homes before the pandemic

UK households

Introduction

The 'household' is an important concept in social science, policy and daily life across the world, and the term has already been used many times in this book. It combines ideas about residence with production, consumption and sharing, for example, of income, food and care. SAGE, the Scientific Advisory Group for Emergencies, was convened to advise government on COVID-19 in January 2020. It said that households are

> sites of social relationships informed by cultural values ... they are part of a network of support structures of kin and care work, which carry risks of transmission, but which are also crucial to weathering economic and social shocks.[1]

The concept of the 'household' took on heightened importance during the pandemic because it was used as the basic unit for regulating social interaction, initially through guidance, and then by law (see Chapter 3).

What is a household?

The 'household' is often taken for granted. A review of over 2,000 international articles using household data found that 97% did not define the key unit.[2] However, there are multiple potential definitions, and UK housing policy, benefits policy and statistics each use the term differently. In practice, from the very earliest modelling by SAGE, COVID-19 research and policy has used and taken for granted the standard UK statistical definition of a household. The ONS definition of a household is 'one person living alone, or a group of people (not necessarily related) living at the same address who share cooking facilities and share a living room, sitting room or dining area'.[3] This includes households that have more than one home (for example, a holiday home) and where some of household members stay in a different home on a temporary basis. In addition, a person can be a member of more than one household simultaneously. However, it is difficult for survey categories to capture this complexity. Potential alternatives to relying on 'households' include self-identifying key contacts. The adoption of 'bubbles' in June 2020 reflects this idea.

Demographers note that 'the household as defined by survey statisticians may bear little resemblance to the social unit in which people live'.[4] The home, household and most important support relationships do not match up exactly in many or even most people's lives. People may visit a home as frequent day or overnight visitors, and spend considerable continuous and cumulative time there, without meeting 'household' definitions. For example, 'sofa surfers' 'may or may not' be identified as current or temporary household members or 'hidden households' in household surveys.[5] The ONS definition says that when a household member has lived elsewhere for six months or more, they have left the household.[6] However, for young adults, 'leaving home' and moving from one household to another can be an extended, backwards and forwards process. Household definitions based on sharing meals and spaces miss out on other important resources and experiences people share: money, time, care and support. Many relationships, important for sharing and happiness, such as those between grandparents and grandchildren, often or even usually cross household boundaries.[7] Difficult cases raised early in lockdown included children whose parents lived apart but shared care, students and non-cohabiting sexual relationships. In May 2020, Professor Neil Ferguson, a member of SAGE, was forced to resign from the body after a visit to his home from someone he was in a relationship with, but who was not a member of his 'household'.[8] Some epidemiological research focusses pragmatically on the 'network of close contacts', ignoring the boundaries of family and household.

Most UK surveys disaggregate data by 'households' and a limited number of household types. The term 'household reference person' (HRP) refers to one person in a household, like the term 'head of household' which it has replaced. This person is the legal owner or tenant, or where there is more than one, the one with the highest income, and then the oldest.[9] It represents an attempt to simplify typologies by describing the household through the characteristics of this person.

Private households in the UK in March 2020

In 2019, the last pre-pandemic data, there were 27.8 million private households in the UK. Looking at households, 29% of UK households had one member and 71% had more than one member. A total of 35% of households had two members, 15% had three, 14% had four, 5% had five and 2% had six or more. Looking at individuals, 12% of all people lived alone and 88% lived with others. A total of 29% lived with one other person, 20% in a household of three, 10% in a household of four, 4% in a household of five and 2% in a household of six or more.[10]

In 2019, 37% of people in the UK lived in a couple with dependent children, 25% of lived in a couple with no children, 12% lived on their own, 9% were in a couple with non-dependent children, 7% were in a single-parent family with dependent children, 4% lived in a single-parent family with non-dependent children, 3% lived in households with two or more unrelated adults (for example, house-sharers) and 2% lived in households with more than one family – for example, a young adult couple and the parents of one member of the couple living together.[11]

People who are living in large-scale institutions or who have no fixed residence are not included in the definition of and data on 'households'.[12] They include people in care homes, hospitals, accommodation for single military personnel, prisons, immigration removal centres, students in halls of residence, boarding schools, religious communities, tied accommodation, caravan sites, hostels for homeless people, as well as people in B&Bs, 'sofa surfers' and people sleeping rough. In 2011 in England and Wales, 216,000 people lived in care homes, 150,000 in nursing homes and another 206,000 in other medical or care institutions.[13] This book does not address their pandemic experiences directly, but it is essential to note that people in care homes and other communal accommodation were not only particularly badly affected by COVID-19 infections and deaths, but were also under some of the strictest and longest-lasting **stay home** restrictions.

UK homes

Introduction

The traditional late twentieth-century aim of UK housing policy has been to provide 'a decent home, for all, at a price within their means', as part of promoting living standards.[14] In March 2020, the UK housing system was succeeding on the first part of this aim for almost all, but failing on the second part for significant minorities. In addition, substantial proportions of the population did not have adequate private, work or state protection from the impact of income shocks on their housing security, and the resilience of key organisations in the system had been weakened by austerity.

UK homes in March 2020

High satisfaction but inequalities

In 2019/20, 57% of 'household reference persons' (HRPs) in England were very satisfied with their homes and 33% were satisfied. Thus, a total of 90% were satisfied. This was a marked improvement on the 84% recorded ten years earlier[15] and was among the highest figures in the 28 European Union Member States (the EU 28).[16] However, rates were lower for HRPs of overcrowded households (65%), Black HRPs (74%), social renters and lone parents (78%), private renters (83%), HRPs aged 16–24 (85%), and Pakistani or Bangladeshi HRPs (86%).

Good and improving physical quality for most

In March 2020, most UK residents had good-quality homes. In 2018, 83% of households in England had 'decent' homes (which were safe, weathertight, warm, and with reasonably modern kitchens and bathrooms). This was a marked improvement on the 67% recorded ten years earlier.[17] In 2018, 90% of homes in England had no serious health and safety problems, such as cold or risk of falls, also a marked improvement on ten years earlier. In addition, while there were gaps between the rates for people on higher and lower incomes, they were not big, and changed little between 2008 and 2018 (Figure 2.1).

The differences between the rates of housing leaks, damp or rot between people on low incomes and others were smaller than in most other EU countries.[18] Households with minority ethnic HRPs and social renters, disadvantaged by many other measures, were in fact slightly more likely than average to be in a 'decent' home.

Because people on low incomes in the UK are generally protected from exposure to poor housing conditions, researchers have suggested that the UK housing system may be the 'saving grace' of its otherwise relatively ungenerous welfare state.[19] People on lowest incomes generally have the worst health and lowest life expectancy, but some parts of the UK healthcare system follow an 'inverse care law', by which people with the most health

Figure 2.1: Proportion of households in non-decent homes, by income quintile, England, 2008–18

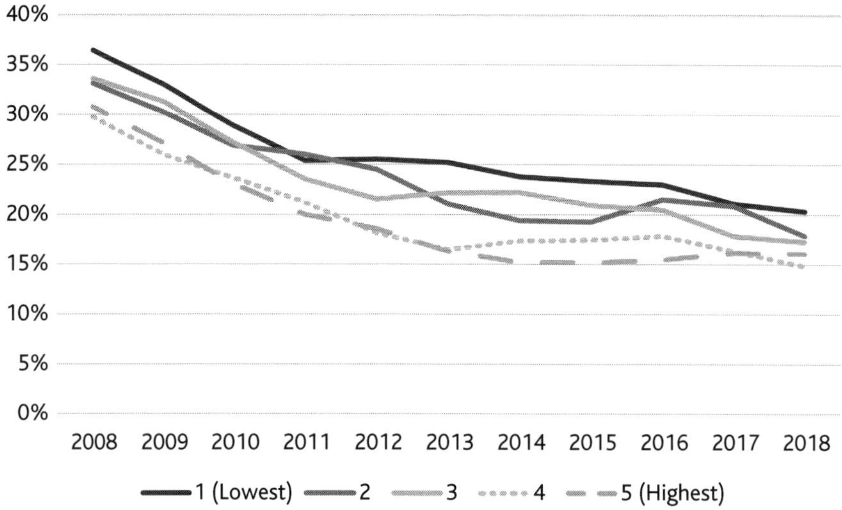

Source: DLUHC 2021d, Table DA3203 (SST3.4)

need have the least healthcare or resources devoted to them.[20] The UK housing system provided only a weak case of this law, as people on lower incomes (and who were likely to have more health needs) generally had similar quality housing to the average. However, to combat health and other inequalities, 'appropriate care' would mean ensuring people on low incomes and in worse health had housing better than average.

Tenure change

From 1990 to 2011/12, the largest tenure in England was mortgaged ownership, followed by outright ownership, social renting and then private renting. However, the proportion of households in mortgaged home ownership peaked as long ago as 1991. From then, it fell continuously, while private renting rose. In 2011/12, private renting overtook social renting, and in 2012/13, outright ownership overtook mortgaged ownership, making outright ownership the largest tenure in England, followed by mortgaged ownership, private renting and lastly social renting. After this, the private rented sector stopped growing (Figure 2.2).

Tenure trends reflect changing individual choice and constraint, in turn driven by changes in employment, incomes, savings and access to credit, and in economic institutions and economic and housing policy. In short, social housing has declined due to policy – the Right to Buy and limits on replacement building. Mortgaged ownership has declined because prices

Figure 2.2: Proportion of households in different housing tenures, England, 2000–2019/20

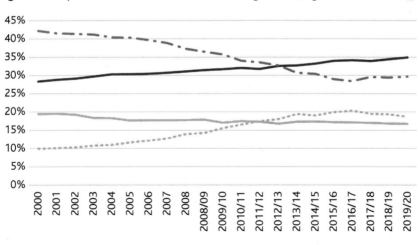

Note: Shared ownership, making up about 2% of households, is included in mortgaged ownership
Source: DLUHC live tables, Table FT1101

have risen and more potential new buyers are unable to secure deposits and mortgages or to service mortgages. Private renting has grown because potential buyers meanwhile need somewhere to live, and because being a landlord has proved an attractive investment or pension in a time of rising prices and weak returns elsewhere. Policy played a role, and the trends for mortgaged ownership and private renting changed in 2016/17 when the tax treatment of buy-to-let mortgages changed. Outright ownership has grown as earlier generations of mortgaged owners have aged and – joined by a smaller group of wealthy people – have paid off their mortgages.

The value of housing and housing policy

Owned homes have two values to their owners: firstly, as somewhere to live and as an important element of living standards; and, secondly, as an investment, which can supplement the owner's income or that of their friends and family.[21] The investment value has become more significant, as house prices have risen, and households and businesses found new ways to extract and use equity. This enables the idea of 'asset-based' welfare as a supplement and alternative to state welfare, for example, in pensions.[22] However, it creates increased individual and systemic risk – the increased financialisation of the US housing market was partly responsible for the 2008 GFC – and inequalities within ownership and between tenures.

Housing has a second value for government too: as an indicator of economic performance and as a tool of economic policy. In 2019 a total of 5% of UK GDP was linked to moving home.[23] Economists have argued that 'the British obsession with booming housing markets as a symptom of economic health is absurd'.[24] However, UK governments generally assume that rising house prices, home building and moving (particularly by mortgaged home owners and first-time buyers) have big multiplier effects on employment and economic growth.[25] The UK government's approach to housing within its pandemic policy was based on the idea that the housing market could be used to combat pandemic unemployment and recession. A Welsh housing professional observed in 2020 that 'Westminster wants to focus on the demand side, [the] Welsh Government wants to focus on the supply side'.[26]

In addition, the UK government had a direct interest in home buying and prices through property tax, including stamp duty on home sales which brought in £8.4 billion in England and Northern Ireland in 2019/20,[27] and its ownership of a 20% stake in the total £16.1 billion value of Help to Buy purchases.[28] The loss of taxable household income and unemployment creates significant costs for central government. However, the financial costs of hardship, rental evictions and homelessness fall on local authorities and households, and the impact of housing problems on health costs is gradual and diffused, and falls on the NHS, local authorities and households.

Home life before the pandemic

Surveys based on minute-by-minute diaries show us how people use time.[29] In 2014/15, patterns varied markedly between individuals, but on average British adults spent 8 hrs 53 mins a day sleeping and resting (mainly at home), and 4 hrs 37 mins on free time and socialising (partly at home). They spent 2 hrs 30 mins on paid work (usually not at home) and 2 hrs 27 mins on unpaid housework (at home). They spent 1 hr 23 mins on travel, 31 minutes on unpaid childcare (mostly at home), 19 minutes on keeping fit, 16 minutes on gardening and DIY (at home), 15 minutes on paid work at home and 8 minutes on study (see Figure 4.4).[30] Thus, even before the pandemic, people already spent over two-thirds of their time **staying home**, if the time-intensive activities of sleeping and resting are included.

On average, people spent 43 minutes more per day sleeping in 2014/15 than they did in 1975. There was little change between 1975 and 2014/15 in the time spent at work, in full-time education and commuting by people of working age. However, in 2014/15 it was more educated rather than less educated people who did the longest hours when paid and unpaid work were combined.[31] In 1975, home was a distinctively, although by no means entirely, female sphere, and women's lives were distinctively, although only partly, home-based. However, by 2014/15, the gender differences had almost disappeared. Women were on average at home for about 17 hours a day compared with 16 for men. Women's lives had changed dramatically since data began in 1975, with a higher proportion in paid work, and more time spent doing it, meaning that about two more hours a day were spent outside the home. Meanwhile, men had experienced a similar but less widely recognised shift, doing less paid work and spending about two more hours a day at home.

Homes are sites of paid and unpaid work, as well as leisure and rest. Unpaid services provided at or from home were worth an estimated £1.3 trillion in 2016 (at 2020 prices)[32] (Figure 2.3). The type of unpaid work with the highest total value was travel from the home (walking, driving or using public transport alone or with others), followed by childcare and some types of housework.

In 2014/15, men devoted the largest part of their extra time at home since 1975 to leisure, but were also spending extra minutes on sleeping and resting, washing, personal care and eating, and domestic tasks, including cleaning, washing clothes, cooking, and childcare. Like men, women were spending more time on sleeping and resting and on childcare than people four decades earlier. However, in contrast to men, women spent less time on domestic tasks, personal care, eating and leisure at home. For example, women reduced their time on housework and cooking

Figure 2.3: Gross value added of unpaid household production, UK, 2016, £ billions, 2020 prices

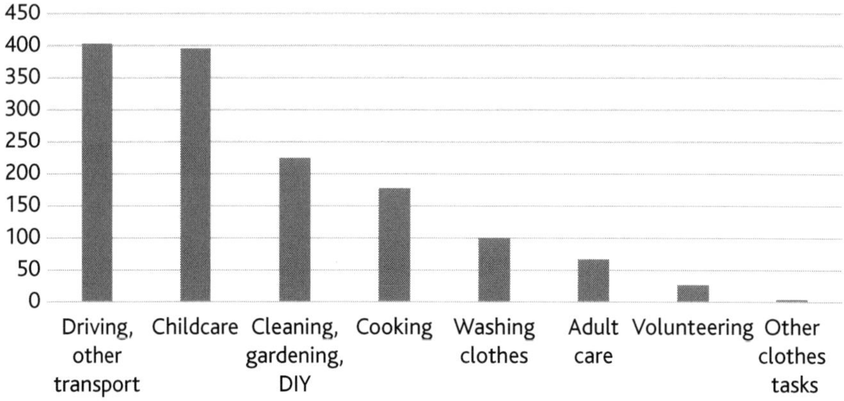

Source: ONS 2018

from 189 minutes a day in 1975 to 109 minutes in 2014/15, while men increased their time on these activities from 22 to 48 minutes per day in the same timeframe.

Alongside the increased in time on paid work for women 1975–2014/15, the biggest change is not extra male domestic task time, but the fact that domestic work is being done quicker, less often or not at all. This is probably a gain for people of all genders, because in 2015 diarists rated housework as the least enjoyable way to spend time, apart from school homework and looking for a new job. The shrinking of housework has been enabled by homes, their gadgets and fittings (and by the use of electricity).

In 2014/15 people were spending more of their time at home on enjoyable things and were also enjoying these things more than in the past. Both sexes were spending more time on childcare, and playing with children was rated as enjoyable (although childcare was not). Many home-based activities, including playing with children, cooking, DIY and sleeping, were rated as more enjoyable in 2014/15 than they had been in 1986, perhaps because they were seen less as essential, money-saving unpaid work, and more like leisure or hobbies, as complements to paid work for both sexes. Meanwhile, activities away from home, notably both paid work and voluntary work, were rated as less enjoyable over time.

However, gadgets, outsourcing and plain neglect cannot be used to get round some types of unpaid work at home, particularly the nearly half a trillion pounds-worth of unpaid adult care carried out per year (see Figure 2.5). Homes, their layouts and fittings did not always assist with the tasks of caring for children and disabled adults at home, which were growing over time and fell heavily on a minority of households.

Housing crisis?

Crisis?

Throughout the 2010s, although most people in the UK were well housed and satisfied with their homes, the UK housing system was described not only by campaigners and opposition politicians, but also by government and ministers as 'dysfunctional', 'broken'[33] and suffering 'persistent market failure'.[34] One key concern was the decades-long relatively low rate of new home building, contributing to high house prices and difficulties for first-time buyers. However, there were other causes of high prices, like low interest rates and low property taxation. In addition, there were also high costs and insecurity in private renting, low rates of new affordable home building, long queues for social housing, and high numbers of rough sleepers and homeless families.

The housing 'crisis' in the 2010s was not a crisis for all. It did not affect outright owners, mortgaged owners with affordable mortgages and secure jobs, and social renters with secure tenancies and stable incomes (even if their incomes were generally low). The housing crisis affected young people and new households on low or moderate incomes without savings or family help, looking for decent homes at a price within their means, in any tenure, not just home ownership. It affected private renters and some poorer mortgaged owners with unaffordable homes, people on low incomes receiving housing benefit which did not pay their full rent, and people who were homeless or in temporary accommodation. Households with lone parents, children, Black, Bangladeshi and Pakistani HRPs, and those in London and other high-cost areas were more affected.

Growing inequalities in space

In 2019/20, 70% of households in England had at least one more bedroom than the required by the official 'bedroom standard', 25% had the 'right' number of rooms, and 3% did not have enough rooms and were 'overcrowded'.[35] The bedroom standard is not generous, requiring people aged 10–20 of the same sex to share rooms,[36] and does not meet public expectations.[37]

A total of 87% of home owners in England had one or more spare rooms, compared to 50% of private renters and 36% of social renters. The proportion of social renters with a spare room reduced slightly from 40% in 2008/09, and the proportion of private renters with a spare room also reduced very slightly, while the proportion of home owners with a spare room grew, so inequality between tenures increased.[38] Using a different measure, in 2018, 62% of people in the top income quintile in the UK had a spare room, compared to 42% in the lowest income quintile, with a slight reduction in inequality 2008–18.[39]

Figure 2.4: Proportion of households overcrowded, by tenure, England, 1995/96–2019/20

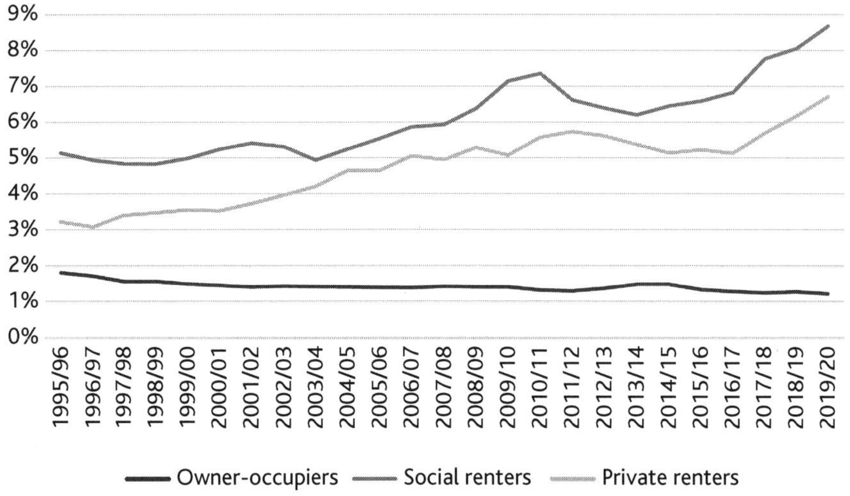

Owner-occupiers ——— Social renters ····· Private renters

Note: Data are for a three-year average ending in the given date
Source: DLUHC 2021d, Table FT1421

In addition, the proportion of households which were overcrowded was increasing, and there were very marked and increasing inequalities in overcrowding by tenure and income (Figure 2.4). Using different data, in 2018, the proportion of UK people in the highest income quintile which were overcrowded was 1%, compared to 10% in the lowest quintile, with no change in inequality 2008–18.[40]

High costs for a large minority

Housing is often defined as 'unaffordable' when households must spend 30% or more of their income on rent or mortgage payments.[41] Using this definition, in 2019/20, 17% of UK households had unaffordable homes, double the proportion of 20 years earlier. In 2019/20, housing costs made up on average 32% of private renters' incomes, 27% of social renters' incomes and 18% of owner occupiers' incomes.[42]

Over 1994/95–2017/18, housing costs grew by 37% for people in the lowest income quintile, compared to 1% for the top quintile.[43] From 2002/03 to 2015, increasing housing costs wiped out all the income gains for more than half of working-age people.[44] In 2019/20, 18% of people were in poverty before housing costs, but 22% were in poverty after housing costs were taken into account.[45] For children, 21% were poor before housing costs and 30% after. In London, the figures were 16% and 27%.[46] A total of 16%

of people in the UK were paying 40% or more of their income on housing, compared to an average of 10% for the EU.[47] People on low incomes, renters, lone parents, one-person households and young people were most affected.[48]

Over the 2007–18 period, UK house prices grew by 23%, again much higher than the average for the EU.[49] 95% mortgages become scarce after the GFC, meaning buyers had to find substantial deposits. In 2019/20, 47% of first-time buyers in England used loans or gifts or inheritance from family as part of their deposit.[50] In contrast, affordability improved for mortgaged owners after the GFC due to lower interest rates. Affordability worsened for social renters in England, as government required real rent increases over the 2001–16 period, and after four years when they were required instead to reduce rents, increases began again from April 2020.[51] Private rents increased above inflation until 2017, but then reduced.[52]

Insecurity and worsening homelessness

Since 2010, the UK has experienced sharp increases in both 'statutory' homelessness and rough sleeping, which were concentrated in England. The numbers of households in England, mainly families, who approached their local authorities and were accepted as legally owed help ('statutorily homeless')[53] increased from 40,000 households in 2009/10 to 57,000 households in 2018/19, or by 42%.[54] Use of temporary accommodation by councils for homeless households increased from 48,000 households in 2010 to 92,000 households in 2020 or by 92%.[55] However, homelessness had reduced in England over the 2000s and reduced in Scotland in the 2010s.[56] The National Audit Office attributed increases in England in the 2010s to shortages of affordable housing and to housing benefit reductions after 2012.[57]

From 2013, local authorities in Scotland were required to 'secure' housing for all homeless households, including 'non-priority' applicants like single people without special needs. From 2017, these people were eligible for some help in England, but only 'relief', such as advice,[58] and the total numbers receiving help to prevent or relieve homelessness in England actually reduced after 2017. According to the *Homelessness Monitor*, 'the explanation … is … funding constraints'.[59] English local authorities' spending on homelessness fell from £2.8 billion in 2008/09 to £2.0 billion in 2017/18 or by 29%.[60]

Snapshot figures for numbers of people sleeping rough in England increased from 1,768 in 2010 to 4,266 in 2019 or by 141%.[61] When people sleeping in cars and tents, squats and non-residential buildings, hostels, unsuitable temporary accommodation and 'sofa surfing' are included, the numbers of homeless people increased from 120,000 in 2010 to 153,000 in 2017 or by 28%.[62] In 2017 the Conservative manifesto promised to end rough sleeping by 2027, and in 2019 they moved the deadline to 2025.[63] This was not unachievable: the Major and Blair governments had broadly kept similar pledges.[64] The key was sufficient – in other words, much-increased – funding. Over the 2017–19 period, the number of rough sleepers reduced by 11%, from 4,784 to 4,266,[65] but was still well above the 2010 figure. In March 2020, ending rough sleeping by 2025 looked unlikely.

UK homes and health

When infectious diseases were the principal threat to life expectancy, housing was at the centre of public health risks and initiatives. During the 1918–20 epidemic of influenza, people with 45 ft^2 of living space per person had ten times the rate of illness than those with 78 ft^2.[66] However, by 2017, communicable, maternal, neonatal and nutritional diseases accounted for just 6.8% of all UK deaths (compared to 58% in Sub-Saharan Africa).[67] Nonetheless, the physical environment, including housing, is recognised as one of the determinants of health, alongside the social environment, behaviour, individual genetic inheritance and pre-existing conditions.[68] Overcrowding, damp and mould, cold, indoor pollutants, infestation, accidents at home, homelessness and unaffordability affect physical health.[69] In the 2010s, the impact of poor housing on health cost the NHS £1.6 billion a year (at 2020 prices).[70] Polluted air cost £22.5 billion annually, and housing health and safety risks cost £1.6 billion annually (at 2020 prices).[71] In 2017/18, deaths were 49,000 higher in winter than summer, partly due to cold housing.[72] This was equivalent to the death toll in the UK's first COVID-19 wave (Chapter 3). A total of 800 people died sleeping rough in England and Wales in 2019, at a mean age of 46.[73] The potential impact of housing on mental health, through stigmatisation, stress and anxiety, is being increasingly recognised.[74] In 2016, the cuts in the Local Housing Allowance (LHA), the local maximum amount of housing benefit people in private renting could claim, were estimated to have caused 26,000 extra cases of medium-term mental ill-health in Great Britain, due to money worries.[75]

There are marked and long-established inequalities in health and life expectancy between income groups, ethnic groups and areas in the UK. Housing tenure is strongly correlated with illness and mortality because it acts as an effective summary of social advantage. Housing inequalities are implicated in these health inequalities, and housing policies could have done more to tackle them.[76] However, as Tooze said 'shot through … with scandalous inequalities, the common order of death is accepted as such'.[77] In 2020, three years after the tragic fire at Grenfell Tower in 2017, remediation work at similar risky buildings was not complete and arguments over who should pay for work continued.[78] In 2019/20, 5% of all HRPs in England did not feel safe at home because of the fear of fire, with higher rates for people in high-rise flats (21%), social renters (10%) and people of minority ethnicity (8%).[79] This indicated the problematic state of housing safety and public health in general in March 2020.

The remaining effects of the GFC from 2008

In March 2020, in some ways, the UK economy and its housing system were still recovering from the GFC.[80] After 2008, average real incomes were depressed and did not start to increase until 2014/15.[81] Mortgage lenders reduced their exposure to further risk by reducing the number of high loan-to-value mortgages available, making access to home ownership difficult for people without personal or family savings. Average UK house prices declined by 18%, from a peak of £190,000 in 2008 to £155,000 in 2009, and did not get back to the pre-GFC level until 2014.[82] At the start of 2008, the Bank of England base rate was 5.25%, but as the crisis developed, it was reduced repeatedly, and by March 2009 was just 0.50%. It remained at this level for seven years, until a further reduction to 0.25% in 2016, after the referendum vote to leave the EU. From 2017, the Bank of England started increasing the rate, which went back up to 0.75% by 2018.[83] Lower interest rates favoured mortgaged owners, but harmed savers. The Bank also carried out 'quantitative easing', which also had the effect of supporting house price increases, while again making entry into home ownership more difficult. The 'Help to Buy' government bridging loan policy was introduced in 2013 as a temporary response to help people with limited savings, but in March 2020 was still operating.[84] By March 2020, 273,000 households in England had received Help to Buy loans,[85] with a total value of £16.1 billion, making it the biggest housing policy of the 2010s.[86] Help to Buy supported 21% of the net additions to the housing stock over 2013/14–2018/19 and added about 0.4% to the home ownership rate in England in 2019.[87] However, it helped mainly those on middle incomes and played some role in increasing prices.[88] In 2018, the aim was to phase the policy out by 2023.

In 2008, both the UK mortgage finance and house building industries were reliant on continuing growth. They had little resilience to the credit crunch and the crisis which followed it, and had to be supported by the government. In some senses, the UK political, economic and housing systems were more 'resilient' to the income and GDP shock from the pandemic in 2020 than they had been in 2008, because of the experience gained then and because of changes made afterwards. In 2008, the Bank of England and UK central government were prepared to act quickly and dramatically to support the economy and to maintain jobs. Employees were prepared to accept short hours and pay in order to support jobs. After 2008, regulation of lending was restructured and risk management increased. Mortgage lenders had realised that repossessions and forced sales meant losses and depressed prices overall. Developers reduced their exposure to debt and risk from land price changes. The government shared some of their risk through the Help to Buy programme. The long period following the GFC with low interest rates combined with low wage growth and relatively low economic growth also meant that the housing system was operating in a different economic context, resulting in a long period of 'caution and relative stability' for housebuilding.[89] It has been suggested that post-crisis regulation had aimed to make a stronger system rather than a more resilient one, by making institutions "too strong to fail".[90] In addition, one lingering result of the GFC was that the UK government perceived the emergency role of housing policy as a tool for emergency economic policy rather than as a source of public health, living standards and wellbeing.

Continuing austerity from 2010

In response to the GFC, the 2010–15 Coalition government made substantial cuts to public expenditure, and this continued under the 2016-19 May government, and, to a lesser extent, the Johnson government from 2019. The IMF and numerous commentators have argued that the UK government had other, and potentially better, options in response.[91] Housing lost more than almost any government spending area, as in earlier periods of spending constraint, partly because stopping capital spending is easier than cutting revenue programmes. Over the 2009/10–2014/15 period, UK central government capital funding for home building and improvement in all tenures was cut by 54% in real terms,[92] and in 2019/20 was lower than at any time since the late 1970s.[93] Over the 2009/10–2015/16 period, revenue budgets for local authority spending on housing, including homelessness services, housing with support for vulnerable people and regulation of the private rented sector, were cut by 44% in real terms, before rising again to a level in 2019/20 that was still 25% lower than ten years before (Figure 2.5). Spending in the other UK nations also reduced.

From 2012, there were two exceptions. From 2019/20 to 2022/23, £55.1 billion was budgeted for home ownership, compared to £9.1 billion for various types of 'affordable' rental housing. Spending on housing benefit grew until 2016, when it began to fall due to the reductions in eligibility and rates under welfare reform from 2012. Overall, government spending shifted from renters to owners[94] and from new and improved homes to consumer (and landlord) subsidy via housing benefit.

Commentators have argued that austerity reduced the capacity and resilience of organisations that were to be key in the pandemic response, including local authorities, the care system, public health and the NHS.[95] Farrar with Ahuja said

> thanks to a decade of austerity, the world's 5th richest economy [was] so woefully poised to respond ... the running down of public health in the decade before 2020 helped to turn what would have been a serious challenge into an ongoing tragedy.[96]

A senior DHSC source told Calvert and Arbuthnott that "we were doomed by our incompetence, our hubris and our austerity".[97] A Downing Street advisor told them "pandemic planning became a casualty of the austerity years".[98] The Institute for Government said:

> Public services were ... weakened after a decade of budget pressures in which quality declined, staff became more stretched, buildings were poorly maintained, and vital equipment went unbought.[99]

On care, the King's Fund said 'many key indicators already going in the wrong direction before the pandemic struck'.[100]

The emerging effects of Brexit

The referendum vote to leave the EU in 2016 and the process to the end of the transition period in January 2021 had substantial impacts on the economy and thus on the housing system, before and after March 2020, including the devaluation of the pound in 2016, falls in stock values, disruption to trade and changes in migration. The vote resulted in a return to extremely low interest rates. At the start of 2022, the Office for Budget Responsibility (OBR) predicted reduced long-run productivity, exports and imports, employment and net migration, compared to what would have been the

Figure 2.5: Total UK government revenue expenditure on housing and community amenities, England, 2000/01–2020/21, £ billions, 2020/21 prices

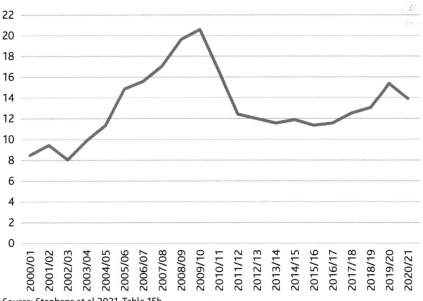

Source: Stephens et al 2021, Table 15b

case had Brexit not happened.[101] In October 2021, the OBR reported that the pandemic would have a long-term 'scarring' effect on GDP of 2%, but the impact of Brexit on the economy would be twice as large as the impact of COVID-19.[102] Like the pandemic, Brexit is an unfinished experience.

Resilience

Introduction

Overall, UK households and the UK housing system were not well prepared for infection risks, **staying home** and mass income drops. A substantial minority of households were poorly prepared, with few or no savings, limited eligibility for state help and limited potential help from social networks. Although no one knew this might be valuable, many people did not have the right homes for isolating, shielding, working or studying at home. Many UK organisations that were to be very important in the pandemic – the NHS, the care system, local authorities with their public health, care and housing functions, charities and community organisations – had lost resilience due to austerity, were already operating under strain and did not have the spare capacity or funds to provide resilience without compromising service quantity, quality and timelines. In addition, the welfare safety net had frayed. However, the housing market was probably more resilient (at least in the conservative sense) in 2020 than it had been before the GFC.[103]

Household income, savings and wealth in March 2020

In March 2020, a minority of the UK population had very low income and low living standards. In 2019/20, 17% of UK people were in relative poverty (with an income below 60% of the median) when measured before housing costs, as were 22% after housing costs. In 2019/20, 8% of the UK population, and 13% of children, were 'food insecure'.[104]

The total number of households experiencing destitution in the UK at some point in 2019 (being unable to afford two or more of six essentials or with an income below 40% of the median), and also using voluntary sector and local authority crisis services, was an estimated 1.1 million households, with 2.4 million people.[105] Another measure based on low income estimated that 1.4 million UK adults were destitute in 2017 and 2.0 million were in 2020 (excluding destitution due to COVID-19).[106]

In 2018, 37% of households in the UK were unable to meet an 'unexpected but necessary' expense of £800 (one month's housing costs for many). This was higher than in France, Germany, Belgium, the Netherlands, Czechia (formerly the Czech Republic), Poland and smaller EU nations. The types of UK households most likely to have difficulties were lone parents with dependent children (78%), households in poverty

(60%), households with three or more dependent children (52%), and one-person households aged under 65 (43%).[107] (A 'dependant' child is aged up to 16, or up to 18 if in full-time education). In 2019/20, 45% of households in England had no savings at all.[108] In March 2020, 20% of UK adults (or 10.7 million people) had 'low financial resilience', which was defined as having low or erratic income, low savings, being over-indebted, or having missed credit payments.

In 2016–18, people in the highest income quintile in Britain had a median net wealth (including housing, pensions and savings) of £868,000, while those in the lowest quintile had £41,000. Different rates of home ownership were largely responsible, but, in addition, mortgaged owners saved a median £4,500 a year, outright owners £2,100 and renters just £400.[109]

The relationship between housing and the labour market

Most households pay for their housing mainly through income from employment, although benefits, pensions, investment income, family and inheritance are also important. For outright owners, this was income earned in the working and economic conditions of the 1980s or before, but for others, it is current earnings. In March 2020, housing and living standards were more closely linked to the current labour market situation than ever before.[110] In November 2019–January 2020, 77% of UK working-age adults were in paid work, the highest since the data series began in 1995/96, mainly due to increasing female employment and dual-earner households. Economic inactivity and unemployment were at record lows.

While people in all tenures experienced these trends, employment patterns continued to vary between tenures, reflecting the routes into them. Overall, in 2019/20, 62% of HRPs in England were in work, 38% were not working. 28% were retired, 2% were looking for work, 1% were studying and 7% were disabled or caring. Mortgaged owners need income to access and pay a mortgage, and 92% of mortgaged owner HRPs in England were working, while 77% of private renting HRPs were working. Access to social renting prioritises those in housing need, including those unable to work, but nonetheless 45% of social renting HRPs were working. Most households arrive in outright ownership over time, after paying off a 25- or 30- year mortgage, but 36% of outright owners were working.[111]

Housing tenure and security

Outright ownership provides secure, largely free housing, although some owners have low incomes or reduced physical capacity and find maintenance difficult or costly. High rates of outright ownership protect some people from the effects of low income and small pensions, especially in older age.

Mortgaged home ownership is secure if buyers can keep up mortgage payments. The number of claims, orders, warrants and repossessions against mortgaged owners peaked in 2009 after the GFC, at almost 60,000 repossessions per year in the UK,[112] and then fell sharply as lenders were encouraged into 'forbearance', and owners were encouraged to relinquish homes before court action. Just 2,000 owner households were repossessed in England and Wales in 2019.[113] Fewer than one in ten claims resulted in repossession, and the process took eight months on average.

From 2012, council landlords in England were no longer required to offer 'secure' or lifetime tenancies, which had been standard since 1980, and councils and housing associations could offer two- to ten-year tenancies instead. From 2016, landlords were no longer allowed to offer new secure tenancies.[114] Many landlords also started to use one-year introductory tenancies for new tenants, before granting a longer tenancy. In practice, social housing was secure if tenants could pay rent and avoid anti-social behaviour.

Private renting was the least secure tenure. In England, private landlords could require tenants to leave, even if they had paid their rent and not infringed the tenancy agreement. These so-called 'no fault' evictions were the biggest immediate cause of homelessness in England in 2019/20. About a quarter of moves by private rented tenants were forced in some way,[115] often resulting in worse housing and material conditions.[116] Legislation in 2016 in Scotland provided open-ended tenancies and ended 'no fault' eviction.[117] In 2019 the UK government promised to end 'no fault' eviction in England, but this had not happened by March 2020. In combination, 31,000 renting households were repossessed in England and Wales in 2019.[118] About one in five claims resulted in eviction, and the process took four and a half months on average.

The housing safety net

The UK welfare state provides a 'safety net' of funds and services to protect people from falling into destitution when they lose their incomes, health, relationships or housing, and don't have savings, private insurance or family or friends to help them. The safety net includes benefits for when people cannot find work or become old or disabled, some of which are means-tested, a health system free at the point of delivery, and means-tested care. It also includes a 'housing safety net' to protect people from overcrowding, sub-standard housing or the streets. This is made up of:

1) housing benefit;
2) social and other affordable housing;
3) protection for some homeless people;
4) (arguably) high rates of outright ownership; and
5) regulation of housing quality.

This safety net was substantially weakened during the 2010s.

The UK's housing benefit system is unusually widely-accessible compared to those in other countries.[119] In 2019/20, 20% of private renters in England claimed housing benefit (usually as part of Universal Credit), as did 56% of social renters.[120] In the past, housing benefit met all the rent of those on low incomes (such as out-of-work benefits). However, since 2008, reforms have broken the link between rent and benefit levels, creating a large group of people facing 'shortfalls'. From 2008, private tenant claimants have received a local maximum housing benefit, the LHA, initially set at the median (50% percentile) rent in the area, regardless of the claimant's actual rent. In 2012, LHA was reduced to the 30th percentile. In 2016, it was frozen, and began to reduce in real terms,[121] and by 2020, on average it only covered rents up to the 13th percentile.[122] The overall benefit payable to working-age households was capped, regardless of actual costs and needs. The cap was reduced in 2016 to £20,000 a year (£23,000 in London, and £15,000 for single adults), and then frozen, affecting households in high-rent areas and those with several children most. Also in 2012, the 'bedroom tax' meant that the level of Housing Benefit paid to social renters with a 'spare room' according to the bedroom standard was reduced by 25%. The proportion of social renters in England with a spare room had started to decrease before 2012 and continued to fall afterwards. Benefits policy is set by the UK government, but the reform was not applied in Northern Ireland, and the Scottish government chose to fund this shortfall. From 2017, Child Tax Credit and UC only gave extra money for the first two children in a family, affecting larger families.

Claimants with shortfalls between UC and rent must pay rent from income intended for essential living costs such as food and utilities.[123] For every hundred households with a shortfall, an estimated 4.4 extra households became homeless, approached their local authority and were provided with temporary accommodation.[124] Because of concerns about delays and arrears, in 2015, only 48% of private landlords were willing to let to a working housing benefit claimant and only 28% to a non-working one.[125] In 2020, discrimination by landlords against benefit claimants was ruled illegal, but continued to occur.[126]

The UK also has a relatively large social housing sector and one more targeted on people on lower incomes than in many other European counties.[127] However, security of tenure has been reduced (see earlier) and affordability has reduced. There have been rent increases for existing homes, and the development of new homes at traditional social housing rents, which are 50–60% of market rates,[128] has been suppressed. From 2011, government subsidies could be used to build 'Affordable Rent' homes to be let at 80% of market rent, and these homes rapidly became the main form of new sub-market rented homes.[129]

In 2019/20 outright ownership was the biggest tenure in England, providing a home for 35% of households in England. Although they pay repairs, utilities and council tax costs, outright owners have no rent and mortgage, which – barring major repairs and inflation – generally means it is a low-cost tenure and in effect subsidises incomes and pensions. However, in 2019/20, 15% of outright owners were in poverty even after housing costs were taken into account.[130]

The UK homelessness safety net was not weakened during the 2010s, and indeed was strengthened in Scotland and Wales, but its effectiveness was limited by funding restrictions.

The family safety net

When welfare states are categorised, the UK is usually described as 'liberal', with a bigger role for the market in the welfare mix than the intermediate conservative or corporatist regimes (such as Italy, France and Germany), and the most 'decommodified' social democratic regimes (such as Sweden).[131] Empirical studies have suggested that the UK has become more liberal over time, with a greater role for markets in welfare over the 1980s and 1990s.[132] Italy, Spain and Greece have been described as 'familial' systems, with a big role for family resources in the welfare mix. However, family and informal unpaid provision form a significant and underrecognised part of the UK's welfare system too, particularly in terms of income maintenance, care and housing.

In 2019, 19% of UK residents aged 19–34 lived with their parents,[133] and for single people without children the figure was 66%.[134] The proportion with their own households was higher in low-cost areas and ranged from 32% in the North East to 22% in London. The number of 'hidden' or potentially separate households grew by about a third between 2008 and 2018.[135] In 2018/19, 7% of households in England contained at least one person who wanted to form their own household but could not afford to do so, totalling 1.6 million individuals.[136] This 'family tenure' houses more people than shared ownership. Family and friends also played an important role emergency housing and preventing homelessness. A total of 29% of the people who could not afford to form their own household, or about half a million people, had children with them, so would have been eligible for statutory homelessness support if their family had not stepped in. A woman aged 62 said "my sister in law (with a skunk habit and psychosis) and her autistic son became homeless, they came to live with us the weekend before lockdown. It was really tricky".

In 2018/19, 2% of households in England had had someone living with them in the past year who would otherwise be homeless, sometimes known as 'sofa surfing', totalling 541,000 households and more individuals.[137] The numbers in emergency accommodation provided by families and friends dwarfed the 92,000 households in local authority-provided temporary accommodation in England in 2019/20[138] and the 57,000 households who were accepted homeless by local authorities in 2018/19. Homelessness statistics only record the prevalence of familial provision when it breaks down. In 2019/20, 35,000 or 24% of households assessed by local authorities as owed 'prevention' of homelessness and 39,000 or 28% of the households assessed as owed 'relief' in England became homeless because friends and family were no longer willing to house them.[139]

The pandemic and pandemic policy in the UK

The pandemic in the UK

Introduction

In the UK, the COVID-19 pandemic had three waves of infections and deaths between January 2020 and the start of 2022. 'Age-standardised' death rates were among the highest in Europe, although relatively lower in the second and third waves. Many sources have described the UK pandemic in detail, and discussed whether deaths, illness, hardship and expense could have been prevented.[1] This chapter focuses on the developments key to understanding the links between the pandemic and housing and home.

The beginning

In hindsight, the earliest known test-confirmed case and death from COVID-19 in the UK was that of Peter Attwood of Chatham, who died on 30 January 2020 aged 84. The fact that he had COVID-19 was only discovered from later testing of a sample and was reported on 5 March.[2] His daughter believed he caught the infection from her, because she had COVID-like symptoms on 15 December 2019. This would make her the first likely case in the UK and her father possibly the first case of household transmission in the UK.[3]

The first UK lab-confirmed cases of COVID-19 recognised at the time were two people in York tested on 30 January 2020, who had travelled from China and had minimal symptoms. On 6 February 2020, a man tested positive in Brighton, again with minimal symptoms. He had caught the infection in Singapore, and infected people in France and the UK. Within days, the SPI-M subcommittee of SAGE thought there was already sustained transmission in the UK, which was later confirmed. A UK citizen on the *Diamond Princess* cruise ship died on 28 February after testing positive, and the first known death in the UK was on 5 March.[4] There may have been many cases and some deaths before these 'firsts', which went undetected at the time. On 13 March 2020, researchers said that 'by the time a single Covid death is reported, hundreds or thousands of cases are likely to be present [in a country]'.[5]

On 3 February 2020, there were eight confirmed cases, and on 5 March, there were more than 100. A woman aged 19 said her father had been in this group, after skiing in Italy:

"He sought government advice before going, because it was beginning to get bad in Italy, but the government said it was safe to go and they would be staying 100 miles from the outbreak, yet everyone on the trip caught it."

Later modelling estimated that there were 10,000 cases in the UK by this date.[6] On 13 March, there were 1,000 confirmed cases in the UK. On 16 March 2020, Public Health England (PHE) estimated that the pandemic could last a year, could infect 80% of the population and could cause 7.9 million hospitalisations.[7] On the same day, SAGE predicted that if nothing was done, 30 times more people would need intensive care than the number of beds and that 510,000 would die:[8] They said, 'On the basis of accumulating data ... the advice from SAGE has changed.'[9] Together, these data propelled the decision to commence lockdown in the UK.

The three waves by 2022

The extent of the epidemic can be measured through infections, positive tests (or 'cases'), hospitalisations and deaths. These measures all peaked three times: in March 2020, in January 2021 and in late 2021.

The number of cases is affected by the availability of tests, which were initially only available on admission to hospital. In April 2020, just over 20,000 PCR tests (the type requiring lab analysis, and the main type until the development of 'lateral flow' self-tests) were being carried out in the UK each day, but by February 2021 the number was over 700,000. Attribution of cause of deaths also improved. Later analysis estimated that actual COVID-19 deaths in the UK were about 1.5 times higher than those recorded in the first wave, but by the second wave testing and reporting had improved (see Figure 3.7 for evidence of total deaths).[10] From April 2020, large sample surveys tracked current infections, independent of public access to tests (see Figure 3.1). The relationship between infections and deaths also changed as treatments were developed, and vaccinations and new variants arrived from December 2020.

The third wave had similar infection rates to the second wave, but, thankfully, it resulted in much smaller waves of hospitalisations and deaths (Figures 3.2 and 3.3).

The total number of deaths in England and Wales per week peaked at over 9,000 in April 2020 in the first wave and reached a similar peak in January

Figure 3.1: Estimated numbers of people in private households infected per day, averages across seven-day periods starting on the given date, England, April 2020–November 2021 (second and third waves)

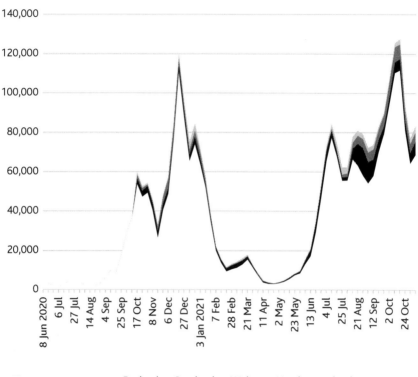

☐ England ■ Scotland ■ Wales ▨ Northern Ireland

Note: Data for Wales start in July, for Northern Ireland in September and for Scotland in October 2020
Source: Calculated from ONS 2021t and ONS 2021j

2021 in the second wave. However, in the third wave deaths remained below 1,000 deaths per week until the start of 2022 (Figure 3.3).

The difference between the actual number of deaths in any week and the average for that time of year in 'normal' years is the number of 'excess deaths'. Excess deaths in England and Wales peaked in April 2020 and again in January 2021 (Figure 3.4).

At the peak of the first wave, England and Wales had 12,000 more deaths a week than the historic average. In the second wave, excess deaths reached 5,000 a week. Deaths were about 1,000 a week above the historic average through the second year of 2021. In early 2022, deaths were below the historic average. However, there may be further excess deaths in future months or years, due to medium- and long-term effects of COVID-19 and the pandemic period.

Figure 3.2: Weekly number of patients admitted to hospital with COVID-19, UK, March 2020–November 2021 (first, second and third waves)

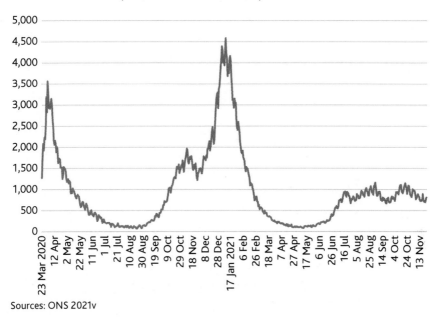

Sources: ONS 2021v

Figure 3.3: Deaths linked to COVID-19, UK, March 2020–November 2021 (first, second and third waves)

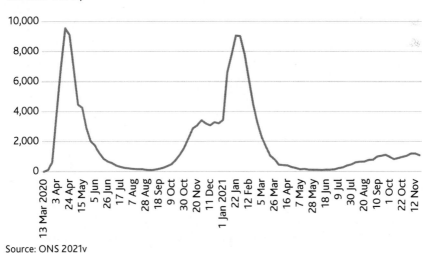

Source: ONS 2021v

Cumulative impact to date

By January 2022, surveys showed there had been about 20 million infections in the UK (including some reinfections). A total of 390 million recorded

Figure 3.4: Weekly deaths from all causes, England and Wales, March 2020–February 2022, compared to average deaths in the same week over the previous five years (first, second and third waves)

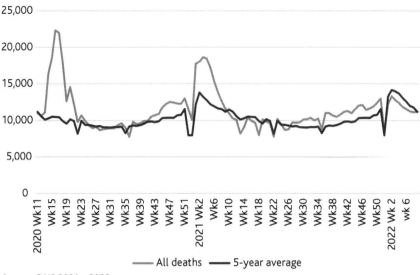

Source: ONS 2021u, 2022c

tests had been carried out (and many more went unrecorded). Over 12 million individuals, or 6% of the population, had had positive tests. Some 620,000 people had been admitted to hospital with a positive test, while 52 million people had had a first dose of the vaccine, 47 million a second and 33 million a third or booster dose. A total of 148,000 people (or 217.1 per 100,000) who had had a positive test died within 28 days of that test, while 172,000 people (or 252.0 per 100,000) had died with COVID-19 mentioned on the death certificate as one of the causes.[11] The increase in deaths was enough to reduce life expectancy at birth for women from 83.5 in 2019 to 82.6 in 2020, and for men from 79.9 in 2019 to 78.7 in 2020.[12] By June 2021, 1.5% of people or 962,000 had experienced long COVID. There may be further lost years or earlier deaths due to the long-term effects of COVID-19, or to investigations and treatments postponed or missed during the pandemic that only emerge over time, which may affect the future population.

In May 2020, relatively few cohort members mentioned deaths from COVID-19 among people they knew, but by February/March 2021, many had been directly affected. For example, a 31-year-old said "three family members have died from COVID. Six friends have long COVID"". A woman aged 50 had lost two sisters to COVID-19 and said:

"Coronavirus has had such a major effect on my immediate family and relatives and there are at least 10 of us now on anxiety/ depression medication."

Many were very angry about the number of infections, hospitalisations and deaths in the UK, and, like many professional commentators, thought some or many deaths could have been prevented.

UK pandemic deaths compared to other countries

In the first wave of the pandemic, from January to June 2020, the UK had the highest rate of excess deaths per 100,000 in Europe. When examined individually, England was in first place among European countries, Scotland third, Wales fifth and Northern Ireland eighth. In most other European countries, excess deaths were concentrated in certain areas, but in the UK, they were widespread across nations, regions and local authorities.

From July 2020, when a second wave started in many countries, other nations in Europe overtook the UK in excess deaths 'age-standardised' death rates, which take into account the fact that older populations have higher death rates in normal times. Over the January 2020 to January 2021, the age-standardised death rate for the UK was 7.9% above the average for 2015–19, but the UK came fourth after Poland, Spain, Belgium and Czechia.[13] This data includes January–February 2020 before the pandemic when there was actually negative excess deaths in the UK (the warm weather meant fewer excess winter deaths, including from cold homes). Looking at data from March 2020 to mid-2020, which excluded early 2020, included both the first and second waves, and also adjusted excess deaths by age, the UK had a total excess deaths of 18%. Again, the rate in the UK was among the highest in Europe, but the UK came fifth after Czechia, Poland, Spain and Italy. This study allowed a comparison between 103 countries, mostly in Europe, the Near East and the Americas. The UK ranked 43rd out of 103, equal to Hungary. A total of 42 of the nations had higher age-standardised excess death rates during the pandemic than the UK, with some much higher. These included many large-population counties: Peru (153%), Ecuador (80%), Bolivia (68%), Mexico (61%), Brazil (37%), Colombia (36%), Azerbaijan and South Africa (32%), Russia (28%) Chile and Tajikistan (27%), and the USA (22%). However, 60 nations had a lower rate than the UK, including some nations with much lower GDP per head and more fragile health systems, such as Cuba (1% age-standardised excess deaths), Thailand (3%), Canada (5%), Tunisia (6%), Argentina (12%), Guatemala (12%), Uzbekistan (13%), Iran (15%) and Egypt (16%). Some countries even had negative excess deaths – fewer deaths than normal – including Malaysia and Taiwan (-4%), Australia (-2%), and Japan, South Korea and the Philippines (-1%).[14] This is strong evidence that the UK could have performed better in preventing pandemic deaths.

Inequalities in infections and deaths

Introduction

The risk of infection and death from COVID-19 was very unevenly distributed across the country and the population.[15] Evidence from China in early 2020 showed that older people, men and people with pre-existing health conditions or disabilities were more at risk of death. In the first wave in the UK and in other countries, inequalities by area, neighbourhood deprivation, ethnicity and occupation also emerged. Many of these remained after adjusting for age, gender and other significant factors. Most reflect pre-pandemic inequalities in health and life expectancy. In October 2020, the SAGE subcommittees EMG and NERVTAG said that the pandemic

> is strongly shaped by structural inequalities that drive household and occupational risks ... it is essential to tailor ... measures to ... disadvantaged communities.[16]

Inequalities between regions and local authority areas

There were marked differences in the risk of infection and death between different parts of the UK. Initially, these were due to different timing of the first outbreaks, but inequalities developed due to the different local population mix, labour markets, household resources, restrictions and behaviour, and households and housing.

Cases become an outbreak when at least two linked cases have been found.[17] Using this definition, it took a further 35 days after the start of the UK outbreak on 30 January 2020 for every nation and English region to have two cases. The South East was the first, on 5 February, and Wales was the last, on 10 March. The size as well as the timing of the epidemic varied across the UK. In the first wave, London had the highest number of confirmed cases per 100,000. The second wave had an early peak in the North West and Yorkshire and Humberside, and a later peak in London and the North East.[18]

Local authorities also had varying outbreaks, epidemics with different timing and different sizes. For example, in the North East, the first local authority outbreak was in Newcastle on 5 March 2020, but it took a further 14 days for every authority in the region to be affected. On 1 June 2020, Hammond said 'areas of low infectivity could still be protected if no one outside travelled to them'.[19] However, by late May 2020, the North East had the highest rate of COVID-linked deaths of all English regions. No local measures were taken within England until the 'tier' system started in October 2020, which was a response to high infections rather than an attempt to protect low-infection areas. Wales and Scotland had tighter, more specific and longer-lasting restrictions of movement, which gave some protection to areas with lower rates of infection, but by the end of the first wave every local authority in the UK had had COVID-19 deaths.

By October 2021, the highest rates of deaths, defined as with both COVID-19 on the death certificate and within 28 days of a positive test, were in the North West, North East and West Midlands of England. However, age-standardised figures for deaths per population are the best figures to use to compare between places and populations.[20] By October 2021, the highest age-standardised rate for deaths with COVID-19 on the death certificate was in London, followed by the North West, the West Midlands and the North East of England (Figure 3.5).

The lowest death rates were in the South West of England. In February/ March 2021, a 50-year-old said "living where we do, in Cornwall [in the South West], we have been unaffected by the actual COVID-19 virus". However, they also stated: "But physically, mentally, emotionally, economically, educationally, the lockdowns are damaging us all."

Data from the Office for Health Improvement and Disparities, set up as part of the replacement of PHE in 2021, show that the inequalities in COVID-19 deaths between regions closely match inequalities in death rates

Figure 3.5: Three measures of COVID-19 deaths, by UK nation and English region, 2020–21 (first and second waves, and all three waves in Northern Ireland)

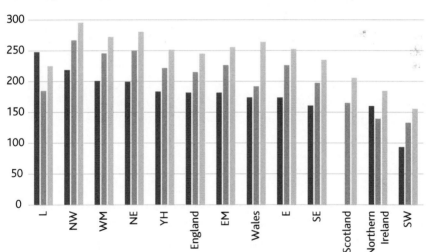

■ Age-standardised rate on death certificate   ■ Within 28 days of test   ▨ On death certificate

Note: There is no equivalent age-standardised data for Scotland. Age-standardised data for Northern Ireland are for deaths with COVID-19 to January 2021 and elsewhere to April 2021. Other data are for October 2021
Source: ONS 2021h; NIRA 2021

Figure 3.6: Life expectancy for males at birth in years, English regions, January–June, 2019–21

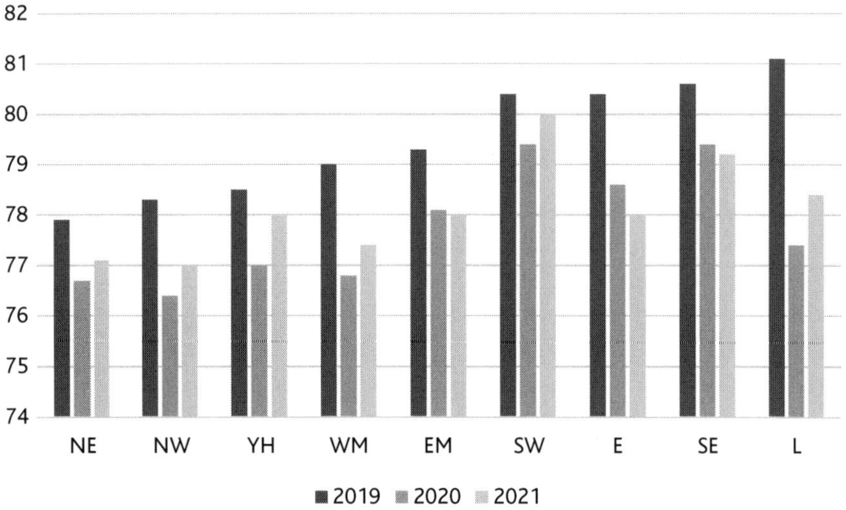

■ 2019 ■ 2020 ▦ 2021

Source: Office for Health Improvement and Disparities 2021

between regions from all causes in normal times. In 2019, the regions with the lowest male life expectancy at birth were the North East, the North West, Yorkshire and Humberside, and the West Midlands. These were also the regions with the worst COVID-19 death rates (Figure 3.6).

By 2020, male and female life expectancy at birth fell in all English regions due to the impact of COVID-19 deaths. London was exceptional because it had the highest life expectancy in 2019, but the biggest drop by 2020, reducing it to a middling position. Otherwise, the regions where life expectancy had been the lowest before the pandemic still had the lowest life expectancy in 2020 and 2021. There was no levelling up; instead, there was levelling down in the most fundamental measure of life chances: life span. In 2021, life expectancy grew in most regions, except the East Midlands, the East and the South East, but was still below 2019 levels.

The local authority with the highest age-standardised death rate in England and Wales to April 2021 was Newham in London, with a rate of 401.2 deaths per 100,000, followed by several other London boroughs. Newham's rate was more than ten times higher than that in the least-affected local authorities in England and Wales, South Hams and West Devon in the South West, which both had a rate of 31.4 deaths per 100,000.[21] In Scotland, age-standardised COVID-19 death rates for people dying within 28 days of a positive test in 2020 varied between Health Board Areas, from 191.4 in Greater Glasgow and Clyde to zero in the Western Isles.[22] In Northern

Ireland, local authority rates of deaths involving COVID-19 over the period from March 2020 to January 2021 (when the second wave was still ongoing) varied from 204.0 in Antrim and Newtownabbey local government district to 91.9 in Fermanagh and Omagh.[23]

Inequalities between neighbourhoods

By April 2021, only 13 or 0.2% of the 7,201 neighbourhoods[24] in England and Wales had recorded no COVID-19 deaths.[25] This was fewer than the 41 'thankful parishes' which lost no serving men in the First World War.[26] However, some neighbourhoods had much higher rates of COVID-19 deaths than others: those in high-risk regions, urban areas and deprived neighbourhoods. The safest type of settlement to live in in England and Wales in the first wave was a 'rural hamlet and isolated dwelling in a sparse setting', with an age-standardised death rate of 24.2 over March–July 2020. The riskiest was an 'urban town in a sparse setting' at 132.8, followed by a 'major conurbation' at 110.6.[27]

Deprived neighbourhoods had much higher rates of death from COVID, but they also did in 'normal' times. The ratio between age-standardised COVID-19 death rates in the most deprived and least deprived fifth of neighbourhoods by July 2020 was 1.3 in Northern Ireland, 1.8 in Wales, 2.0 in England and 2.2 in Scotland.[28] The ratios were greater for deaths rather than infections, which suggests that differences in the progress of the disease, due to worse resilience or care, played a role. Differences in deaths by neighbourhood in England were smaller in the second wave than the first, which suggests that there had been reductions in infections or improvements in treatments by late 2020. However, over the period from March 2020 to April 2021, there were 2.0 times as many deaths from all causes in the most deprived neighbourhoods. There were also 1.9 times as many deaths from non-COVID-19 causes (Figure 3.7). Thus, deaths from COVID-19 were only very slightly more unequally distributed than other deaths. However, they did result in increased inequality in life expectancy between neighbourhoods.[29]

Health professionals have long experience in explaining health inequalities, including differences between people in different places.[30] Simon Stephens, Chief Executive of NHS England until August 2021, said that higher COVID-19 death rates in deprived areas were due to "a combination of occupational exposures, crowded housing, prior health risk, including obesity ... and broader inequality".[31]

Inequalities in risk between places have implications for other dimensions of inequality. The worst-affected regions in the UK in terms of age-standardised death rates were London, the North West, the West Midlands and the North East (Figure 3.5). Together these areas contained 44% of the

Figure 3.7: Age-standardised COVID-19-linked deaths and other deaths per 100,000 for the most deprived and least deprived deciles of neighbourhoods, England, March 2020–April 2021

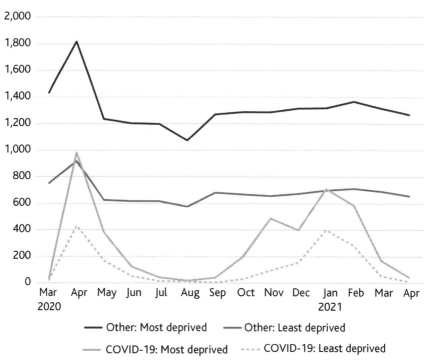

Note: The peak in 'other' deaths in the first wave is probably due to underreporting of COVID-19 deaths
Source: ONS 2021h

English population in 2020.[32] However, they contained 66% of all minority ethnicity people in 2011,[33] 60% of people in poverty (before housing costs) in 2017/18–2019/20[34] and 51% of all social housing tenants in 2019.[35]

Inequalities between age groups

Death rates for COVID-19 were much higher for successively older groups. However, death rates are much higher for older people for all causes of death and for 'normal' times (Figure 3.8). Differences in risk by age for death from COVID-19 were very similar to 'normal' inequalities.[36]

Inequalities between genders

At every age, men had higher COVID-19 death rates than women (Figure 3.8). In England and Wales, the age-standardised rate of deaths

Figure 3.8: Age-specific COVID-19 death rates per 100,000, England and Wales, 2020

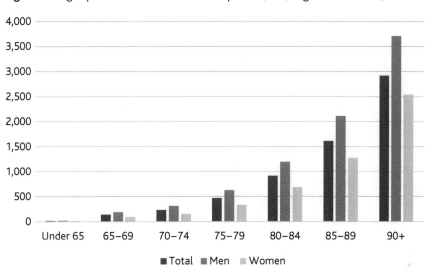

Note: Age-specific death rates are used to enable comparison between age groups
Source: ONS 2021k

within 28 days of a positive test over the period from March 2020 to April 2021 was 1,262.6 for men, and 912.8 for women.[37] Similarly, in Scotland, the age-standardised rate of death with COVID-19 on the death certificate for the whole of 2020 (including some pre-first wave time) was 137.7 for men and 91.4 for women. In Northern Ireland, age-standardised deaths rates from March 2020 to January 2021 with COVID-19 on the death certificate were also substantially higher for men.[38] Combining age and gender, in 2020 a woman aged over 65 in England and Wales had less risk of COVID-19 death than a man five years younger.[39] If a pensioner couple was made up of a man and a woman five years younger, his risk would be three times higher than hers.

Men usually have lower life expectancy than women and higher chances of death in any year. However, the gender inequality from COVID-19 was greater than the 'normal' rate, and inequality in life expectancy between the genders was higher in 2020/21 than the average for the same period in 2015–19.[40] There has been relatively little research into this inequality, and the extent to which it might be attributed to differences in pre-existing conditions, work situation, behaviour or other factors.

Inequalities by pre-existing health or disability status

After the first wave, the 5% of people with the highest predicted risks from COVID-19 infection (slightly larger than the 'clinically extremely vulnerable' group identified by the NHS; see Chapter 6) accounted for 76% of all COVID-19 deaths. People in the top 20% of risk accounted for 94% of all deaths.[41] Overall, about 80% of those who died with COVID-19 on the death certificate by November 2021 in England and Wales had one or, in most cases, more than one 'pre-existing condition', such as diabetes, high blood pressure, respiratory disease and heart disease.[42]

Over the period from January 2020 to February 2021, people with limiting long-term conditions accounted for 58% of all COVID-19 deaths, but they also accounted for 55% of deaths from all causes, so COVID-19 did not appear to increase 'normal' inequalities significantly. Over the same period, the rate of COVID-19 deaths for men in England who had a long-term condition which limited their daily activities 'a lot' was 899 per 100,000 person-years, compared to 291 for non-disabled men. For women, the disparity was 627 compared to 162.[43] However, these figures do not take into account the fact that people with limiting conditions were generally older than people without them. Again, there has been relatively little research into this inequality.

Inequalities between ethnic groups

In the first wave in England and Wales, after adjusting for age, the risk of death from COVID-19 for men of Black African ethnicity was 3.7 times higher than for White British men, while the risk was 2.6 times higher for Black African women than for White British women. The figures for people of Bangladeshi ethnicity were 3.0 higher for men and 1.9 higher for women, for Black Caribbean ethnicity 2.7 higher for men and 1.8 higher for women, and for Pakistani ethnicity 2.2 higher for men and 2.0 higher for women compared to White British people.[44] In Scotland, Pakistani and Chinese people also had higher risks of deaths than the White population.[45] The differences in death rates between ethnic groups were larger than 'normal' ethnic inequalities in mortality.

For the second wave, there are data on infection, which reflect differences in exposure to risk. Over the period from September 2020 to July 2021, the age-standardised number of positive tests per 100,000 person-weeks in England and Wales was 347.3 for people of Bangladeshi ethnicity, 343.2 for people of Pakistani ethnicity, 249.7 for people of Indian ethnicity, 224.3 for Other groups and under 200 for all other groups.[46] Further analysis suggests that inequalities in pre-existing conditions did not play a significant role in ethnic inequalities in terms of the numbers of positive tests, but inequalities in neighbourhood deprivation did.[47]

Inequalities in location, household and housing partly explained ethnic inequalities. In the first wave in England and Wales, area population density, neighbourhood deprivation and the proportion of households which were multi-generational and overcrowded (along with age, exposure to high-risk jobs and some measures of pre-existing health conditions) explained at least half the higher rate of deaths for all minority ethnic groups compared to White British people. These factors explained all of the differences for White Other, Mixed and Chinese men and for Bangladeshi, Black Caribbean, Mixed and Pakistani women. During the second wave, the same area, housing and other variables explain part of at least half of the higher death rate for Bangladeshi, Pakistani, Black Caribbean and Mixed groups.[48] However, if minority ethnic groups had had equal access to neighbourhoods with average density and deprivation, average housing space, average risk jobs and average pre-pandemic health, many lives might have been saved. If Black lives matter, Black people need improved housing, neighbourhoods and work.

Inequalities between occupations

Among those who were working outside the home, over the first and second wave (March 2020–January 2021), jobs involving contact with the public or enclosed spaces had age-standardised death rates more than 20 times the average (Table 3.1).[49] Care workers, nursing auxiliaries and nurses were among the highest-risk jobs, but again different dimensions of risk interacted. Male care workers and hairdressers had more than twice the risk of death than female ones. Male-dominated jobs had the highest death rates. New jobs became high risk in the second wave, as more people returned to workplaces.[50]

The details of the work environment and safety measures can significantly affect risk. Patient-facing NHS staff in Scotland had three times the risk of hospitalisation with COVID-19 in the first wave than other NHS staff, whose risk was close to average. From February to June 2020, the odds of hospitalisation among this high-risk group fell, reflecting improved PPE and other infection control.[51]

Another major inequality in risk was between those who could work at home during the pandemic and those who could not. This has not been explored to date. However, in the first wave, when chefs and restaurant managers were mostly furloughed at home rather than working, they did not feature among the highest-risk jobs for men.

The basics of COVID infection and disease

What was known by March 2020

Scientific understanding of COVID-19 has developed over time. However, key basic information was available in January, February and March 2020. As there were initially no treatments and no vaccines, it was clear that the only methods of control were to reduce social contacts. In late March 2020,

Table 3.1: Rates of death involving COVID-19 per 100,000 employees aged 20–64, top ten high-risk occupational categories, England and Wales, by gender, deaths registered 9 March 2020–7 May 2021

Job	Wave 1 rate (rank)	Wave 2 rate (rank)
Men		
Bakers and confectioners	597 (1)	809 (1)
Butchers	179 (2)	213 (5)
Police officers	134 (3)	266 (3)
Publicans and bar managers	127 (4)	268 (2)
Ambulance staff (not paramedics)	99 (5)	
Hairdressers/barbers	91 (6)	
Waiters	91 (7)	
Security guards	87 (8)	
Care workers	84 (9)	
Nursing auxiliary	78 (10)	
Restaurant and catering managers		233 (4)
Chefs		192 (6)
General elementary (low skilled)		164 (7)
Bank and post office clerks		159 (8)
Plant and machine operatives		152 (10)
Spas and leisure assistants		158 (9)
Women		
Hairdressers	40 (1)	64 (6)
Care workers	33 (2)	70 (4)
Social workers	26 (3=)	
National government administrators	26 (3=)	
Housekeepers	23 (5)	
Nursing auxiliaries	20 (6=)	
Childminders	20 (6=)	
Bank and post office clerks	19 (8=)	
Secondary school teachers	19 (8=)	
Nurses	19 (8=)	
Sewing machine operators		90 (1)
Café and bar managers		75 (2)
Chefs		74 (3)
Bar staff		65 (5)
Residential and domiciliary care managers		52 (7)
Security guards		50 (8)
House parents and residential wardens		47 (9)
Postal workers, couriers		42 (10=)
Food, drink and tobacco operatives		42 (10=)

Source: ONS 2021f

Note: Only jobs with a minimum number of deaths are included

UK government introduced a set of policies to prevent infections, affecting the whole population, and forming a major part of all policy introduced in 2020 and 2021. These policies, including **staying home** (which will be discussed later), were based on what was known at the time.

Fatality

- High case-fatality ratio: on 24 January 2020, *The Lancet* reported that six (or 15%) of the first 41 cases hospitalised in Wuhan had died.[52] On 24 February, the WHO reported a case fatality ratio of 3.8%, increasing with age, up to 20% for people over 80.[53] The 3 March UK national Coronavirus Action Plan said that COVID-19 had high hospitalisation and fatality rates compared to flu,[54] which has a case-fatality ratio of about 0.1%.[55]

Transmissibility

- Person-to-person transmission: on 21 January 2020, the WHO said it was 'very clear' there was 'some' human–to–human transmission.[56]
- Household and family transmission: on 24 January 2020, *The Lancet* documented household and family transmission in China.[57]
- Community transmission (transmission other than from arrivals from abroad): in the second week of February 2020, the SPI-M subcommittee of SAGE thought there was sustained transmission in the UK. On 25 February 2020, PHE said 'there is currently no transmission of COVID-19 in the community' and it was 'very unlikely that anyone receiving care in a care home or in the community will become infected'.[58] On 5 March, SAGE said that there was sustained community transmission in the UK.[59]
- Asymptomatic (and pre-symptomatic) transmission: by 20 February 2020, the experience on the *Diamond Princess* cruise ship had shown that asymptomatic transmission was possible,[60] and this was recognised in the national Coronavirus Action Plan on 3 March.[61]
- Means of transmission: early concern focused on transmission through nasal fluid or saliva on hands and on surfaces. On 17 March, the UK Health Secretary Matt Hancock said: 'Washing hands regularly for 20 seconds or more remains the single most important thing each of us can do.'[62]
- High transmissibility: in January 2020, the number of people infected by a typical COVID-19 case was estimated at 2.6–3.5, similar to estimates for the 1918–20 Spanish flu of 2.0–3.0 and more than typical flu outbreaks of 1.3.[63] The 3 March national Coronavirus Action Plan said that COVID-19 had high transmissibility, like flu, but not that it was likely to be higher than flu.[64]

How knowledge developed

In July 2020, the WHO recognised that COVID-19 could be transmitted through the air and as evidence built up, concern increasingly shifted to droplets and 'aerosols', the smallest particles which can hang in the air.[65] In addition, it emerged that risk of serious illness and death was unequal. COVID-19 itself changed over time, with the development of more transmissible and more dangerous variants, from the Alpha variant which was first sequenced in Kent in September 2020.[66] Improved infection control, testing, treatments and, from December 2020, effective vaccines became available. This increased the number of cases measured per infection, but reduced the case-fatality ratio.

The policy to limit infections and to mitigate restrictions

Introduction

There is agreement among the most substantial studies of COVID-19 policy in the UK completed by 2022 that the UK response was slow, and to some extent ineffective and inefficient. Not only in hindsight, but also on the basis of information available at the time, different decisions could have been made which would have resulted in fewer infections, hospitalisations and deaths.[67] For example, the House of Commons Health and Care and the Science and Technology committees' joint report in September 2021 described early policy as 'slow and incremental', 'wrong',[68] an 'outlier internationally'[69] and 'one of the most important public health failures the United Kingdom has ever experienced'.[70] It said that the key UK policymakers were behind a 'veil of ignorance', but that it was 'partly self-inflicted'.[71] In June 2020, Professor Neil Ferguson, a member of SAGE, said that locking down one week earlier would have prevented half of the COVID-19 deaths in the first wave, or 20,000 deaths.[72] The decision to lock down was taken not once but three times in England and in the nations (Table 3.2), and it is widely believed that there were costly delays each time. In their comparative study of national pandemic response, Jasonoff et al asked of the UK:

Table 3.2: Summary of **stay home** policies, UK nations, 2020–21

	1st lockdown	2nd lockdown	3rd lockdown
England	23 March–3 May	5 November–2 December 2020	6 January–25 March 2021
Scotland	23 March–29 May	5 January–2 April 2021	
Wales	23 March–1 June	23 October–9 November ('firebreak')	28 December 2020–13 March 2021
Northern Ireland	23 March–3 May	8 January–12 April 2021	

Source: Tatlow et al 2021

Why did a country with a strong national health service, world-class biomedical science, finely-tuned advisory structures, and sophisticated strategies for pandemic preparedness end up with one of the highest rates of ... mortality?[73]

Household and home only featured to a limited extent in pandemic policy. From May 2010 to March 2020, there were ten different UK government housing ministers,[74] and it seems unlikely that they would have been able to consider the potential housing implications of pandemics in their brief tenures. In any case, the published information on the flu pandemic wargames did not refer to accommodation for sick or vulnerable people.[75] The chief scientific advisor post at the housing ministry (the Department for Communities and Local Government (DCLG), then the MHCLG) was unfilled from 2013 to July 2019, and the new incumbent first attended SAGE in May 2021. The SAGE subcommittee focusing on public behaviour, SPI-B, was asked to address household and housing, but only as part of investigation of the relative impact of COVID-19 on different ethnic groups, and only in September 2020.[76] They produced a further report explicitly on the threat of in-household transmission, but only in January 2021, 22 months after the first **stay home** order.[77] Most of the key policies affecting households and home during the pandemic were developed in Downing Street, by the DHSC, the Treasury or the DWP, rather than by the governments of the UK nations, or the department responsible for housing in England (the MHCLG until October 2021, which was then renamed the DLUHC).

The development of UK pandemic policy

On 23 January 2020, 11 million people in Wuhan in China, where COVID-19 was first found, were told to **stay home**. This was the biggest **stay home** order the world had ever seen and was strongly enforced. Jeremy Farrar of the Wellcome Foundation, a member of SAGE, said that at this point, 'there was almost a disbelief, including from me, that [lockdown] was possible' in the UK.[78] Taiwan, a democratic capitalist state, followed. Dominic Cummings, the Prime Minister's chief adviser, said that until late March, 'the almost universal view was that it was inconceivable that we would be able to do a Taiwan-type thing'.[79] One of Calvert and Arbuthnott's sources said that after the 2016 Exercise Cygnus pandemic flu wargame explored lockdown: 'The assessment, in many sectors of government, was that the resulting medicine was so strong that it would be spat out.'[80]

On 25 February, Italy put 11 towns into lockdown.[81] On 3 March, the UK Coronavirus Action Plan, approved by the UK four nations, was launched with the first of what were to be daily televised briefings.[82] It did not refer to **staying home**, except for those with suspected or proven infections. On that day, Johnson said 'for the vast majority of the people of this country, we should be going about our business as usual'.[83] On 9 March, Italy extended its lockdown nationwide. By 10 March, Farrar said 'my attitude was changing too: if Italy had no option but to follow China, the UK would have to follow suit'.[84] On about 13 March, Dominic Cummings and Patrick Vallance appeared to switch to the idea that lockdown was necessary and urgent.[85] On 13 March, SAGE minutes said that lockdown would be hard to sustain and should not be rushed into. On 16 March, Spain introduced a national lockdown. On the same day, on the basis of frightening new data, Patrick Vallance said "SAGE advised … in essence a full lockdown".[86] SPI-M said that isolation of cases and their households and social distancing of vulnerable groups would probably not be enough to prevent the NHS being 'overwhelmed'.[87] That evening, the Prime Minister asked people to work from home and to avoid travel, pubs and restaurants.[88] On 20 March, a London-only lockdown was briefly approved at No. 10, including with the Mayor of London, before being dropped.[89] Lockdowns had started in Hong Kong, Singapore, Japan, Vietnam and South Korea.

Pre-emptive staying home

Tooze proposed the use of the word 'shutdown' instead of 'lockdown', because it implied that agents other than government could influence social and economic activity.[90] By late February 2020, there was considerable public awareness of the COVID-19 threat, speculation about lockdown and pre-emptive shutdown.[91] A man aged 62 said "having lived in Asia before, experienced SARS, caught H1N1, we recognised this was going to be a problem back in January". His family had stopped all socialising and visits outside the home except to groceries and DIY shops at that point. An NHS psychologist aged 31 said she and colleagues had asked to work at home in March 2020, but had not been allowed to do so. From January to March 2020, there were more than usual moves both in and out of hospital.[92] By 27 February, at least 14 schools had closed, despite government advice to stay open.[93] A man aged 50 said he lost work as a martial arts instructor before lockdown, as the council stopped group bookings at its leisure centres. A Jehovah's Witness aged 62 said that at their Kingdom Hall "all meetings were suspended before the government's direction".

On 11 March, the Bank of England responded to widespread concern and falling confidence by reducing its base rate from 0.75% to 0.25%, and on 19 March it reduced the rate further to 0.1%, as did the central banks in many other countries.[94] The Bank also started a renewed programme of 'quantitative easing', last used after the GFC, which would total £450 billion by November 2020.[95] A woman aged 62 said "I actually locked down ten days earlier than he [Johnson] told us to", and a person aged 50 also said that by the time of the announcement "I had already been isolating and working from home for 1½ weeks". In the week of 16–20 March, attendance at school was only 84% and shopping patterns were changing.[96] GP appointments and hospital admissions fell.[97] By 24 March, 140 social housing organisations had at least some staff working from home.[98]

This is the first example of a major element of the response to the pandemic: individuals, households and families taking their own measures to reduce risk, independent of and without the support of the national or local state, or other organisations. The psychological effects of the pandemic were also well under way. A woman aged 50 said "before lockdown I was having daily panic attacks heart palpitations etc, my anxiety was through the roof". A woman aged 50 stated "at the beginning just before lockdown I was immensely worried and didn't sleep for a week".

The stay home policy

The start of staying home

On Friday 20 March 2020, Prime Minister Johnson announced to an awe- and fear-struck nation that pubs, restaurants, leisure centres and schools would not reopen after closing that night. People were told to **stay home** as much as they could and to work from home if at all possible. On Monday 23 March, the Coronavirus Act for England and Wales, which provided the legal basis for enforceable lockdown and which had 'raced through Parliament with little amendment and scant debate',[99] came into force. The Prime Minister told the 28 million people watching on TV that night:

> "I must give you a very simple instruction: you must **stay at home**. You should not be meeting friends. If your friends ask you to meet you should say no. You should not be meeting family members who do not live in your home. You should not go shopping except for essentials like food and medicine – and should do this as little as you can. If you don't follow the rules, the police will have the powers to enforce them."[100]

This date represents the start of the UK's first national 'lockdown'. From then on, there were only four legal reasons to leave home: to go to a specified 'key' job that could not be done at home; to get food or medicine; for one hour's exercise a day; and to seek urgent healthcare. Children could not go to school (unless they were the children of key workers or were receiving support from social services).

Visits to the threshold or into a private home were only allowed to bring supplies to a vulnerable person, to deliver children between separated parents, and for essential work by carers, social workers, healthcare workers and tradespeople (at most points in the pandemic). Social visits, moving home or visiting a second home were not allowed. People could only meet one person who did not live in their household. People should keep two metres apart. The most vulnerable people should 'shield' or stay entirely at home for 12 weeks (see Chapter 6). The slogan '**stay at home**, protect the NHS, save lives', later adapted to '**stay home**', was introduced.

The development of policy

Less staying home *May–September 2020*

On 10 May, it was announced that people who could not work from home should return to work the next day, and people could exercise outdoors for as long as they wished. The UK government changed the slogan for England from '**stay home**' to 'stay alert', but the other nations of the UK did not.[101] From this point on, guidance given and rules made by the governments of the four nations began to diverge.

On 1 June 2020, a phased reopening of schools in England started with reception and primary years 1 and 6, followed by Wales from 20 June, Scotland from 22 July and Northern Ireland from 24 August,[102] although normal operation was not resumed anywhere before the summer holidays. More options to not **stay home** opened up. From 1 June, outdoor markets reopened and from 15 June non-essential retail followed suit. From 4 July, pubs and restaurants reopened, and members of two households were able to meet indoors and outdoors, and stay overnight in England.[103] 'Strong reopening messages were pushed by the central UK Government',[104] including the Eat Out to Help Out subsidy for pubs and restaurants.

Renewed staying home *September 2020–April 2021*

However, new restrictions began at the same time as reopening. Case numbers began to increase in June 2020 (Figure 3.1, 3.2). In July 2020, Leicester was the first area in England to be put under tighter restrictions than those operating across the country. On 14 September 2020, the number of people not all from one household who could meet indoors or outdoors was limited to six. On 22 September, a 10 pm curfew on pubs and restaurants in England was announced, and people were asked (but not required) to work from home if they could.[105] Deaths began to rise in October (see Figure 3.3). On 14 October 2020, a three-tier system of local restrictions was introduced in England, with more restrictions on home visits in some areas.

On 2 November, a second national four-week lockdown started in England and Wales, under similar restrictions to the first one, although schools remained open.[106] On 19 December, a new Tier 4 was created for some areas, which prohibited all indoor mixing between households. After a brief and confused hiatus over Christmas for areas in Tiers 1 to 3, in January 2021 all four nations were in a renewed lockdown.[107] Changes and variation between nations and tiers (in England) made the rules harder to remember, and surveys showed that people's awareness of the rules that applied to them reduced over time.[108]

Hale et al developed an index of the stringency of pandemic restrictions, including stay home orders, closures of schools and workplaces, suspension of public transport, travel bans and public information campaigns. UK stringency was highest at this point (Figure 3.9).

Stay home orders were lifted in March and April 2021. Policies on social distancing, mask-wearing, shielding and isolating continued after the end of the last lockdowns. However, some further restrictions were introduced in late 2021, with the third wave of infections dominated by Omicron, especially in Scotland and Wales.

Using Hale et al's index, on average from 1 January 2020 to 30 November 2021, when compared to the EU 27 nations, the UK ranked as the fifth most stringent, behind Italy, Greece, Germany and Ireland, and equal to Portugal.[109]

After two years, in Northern Ireland, all legal restrictions, including the need for COVID-19 certificates in nightclubs, face coverings, track and trace requirements and the cap on 30 people in private homes, were ended on 15 February 2022. Scotland followed on 21 March. Three days later all legal restrictions, including compulsory isolating at home for people with COVID, test and trace, isolation payments and free testing, ended in England, followed by Wales on 31 March.

Variation in **stay home** policies between the UK nations

In total, in 2020, people in Wales were required to **stay home** for 99 days, in England for 92 days, in Scotland for 68 days and in Northern Ireland for 50 days (Table 3.2).

Overall, Scotland had the highest average 'stringency' score from March 2020 to April 2021, followed by Wales, Northern Ireland and then England. Differences were certainly of political significance. They gave a high profile to the leaders of nations and to national distinctiveness itself. For example, Welsh housing professionals felt that

'in its responses to COVID-19 Welsh Government was distancing itself from Westminster ... it had grown in stature and authority over the last few months.'[110]

Figure 3.9: COVID-19 policy stringency index, UK, January 2020–December 2021

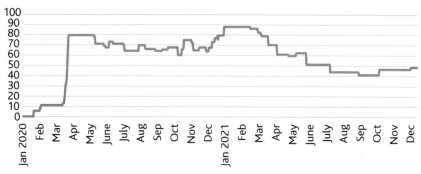

Source: Hale et al 2021

However, differences were not great, and the nations 'increased and decreased the stringency of closure and containment policies at similar times, within a similar range of stringency'.[111] In addition, the UK government retained control over key areas, including tax and benefits, most elements of national governments' budgets, and border control. England, the least stringent nation, did have higher death rates than the other nations. However, full evaluation of the impact of differences on deaths and other impacts is awaited.

People, households and time at home in the pandemic

The impact of COVID on the size of the population

Births: an acceleration of a downward trend

Between January and September 2020, there were 464,000 live births in England and Wales. This was a reduction of 17,000 live births or 3.6% when compared to the same nine-month period in 2019. There has been a long-term decline in annual numbers of live births in the UK, despite the rising total population, since at least 2011. However, the reduction between 2019 and 2020 was larger than the reduction any year except 2013 (when population fell by 23,000 between January and September).[1]

Deaths: an increase

Over the pandemic period, death rates have increased, with deaths due to COVID-19 and other excess deaths (see Figure 3.4). From January 2020 to January 2021, the average weekly age-standardised death rate for the UK was 7.9% above average, 8.5% for England, 5.8% for Scotland, 5.7% for Northern Ireland and 5.3% for Wales.[2]

International migration: a change in trend

Aburto et al said: 'Measuring migration flows is always a challenge, and the picture has become even more murky during the pandemic.'[3] Nonetheless, there seems to have been a significant change in trend. Foreign-born and non–UK citizen populations grew continuously between 2008 and 2017, and then stablished between 2017 and 2019. However, the UK's non–UK citizen population dropped by 231,000, a reduction from 9.4% of the total population in 2018/19 to 9.0% in 2019/20. The foreign-born population also fell by 240,000, from 14.3% of the total in 2018/19 to 13.8% in 2019/20.[4] The change is likely to be due mainly to out-migration, although acquisition of citizenship could have played a small role. Change was concentrated in England, in London, among people with citizenship of newer EU Member States, and who had migrated to the UK for work.

The change is likely to be partly due to Brexit, which officially took place on 31 January 2020 (see Chapter 2), and partly due to disruption to work and life caused by COVID-19.[5]

The impact of COVID-19 on the number, size and shape of households

Changes in the numbers and types of households

The number of households in the UK decreased from 27,824,000 in 2019 to 27,792,000 in 2020, or by 0.1%. This halted a very long trend of annual increases in numbers of households. The average number of people per household increased from 2.37 in 2019 to 2.39 in 2020, halting a long trend of annual decreases. The estimated number of one-person households reduced by 3.6%. The number of two-, three- and four-person households increased slightly, but the number of five-, six- and seven- or more person households reduced[6] (Table 4.1).

These changes are due to individuals moving between households and to more households dissolving than forming. Increasing household size could result in overcrowding in households without spare rooms.

Moves during the pandemic

From 23 March 2020 to 13 May 2020, moves of individuals and whole households between homes were generally prohibited. However, last-minute moves were in effect encouraged, when on 24 March, England's deputy Chief Medical Officer (CMO) Jenny Harries and UK Health Secretary Matt

Table 4.1: Number of households of different sizes, thousands, UK, 2019 and 2020

Number of people in household	2019 Number	2019 Percentage	2020 Number	2020 Percentage	2019–20 Number change	2019–20 Percentage change
1	8,197	29.5%	7,898	28.4%	-299	-3.6%
2	9,609	34.5%	9,675	34.8%	66	0.7%
3	4,287	15.4%	4,337	15.6%	50	1.2%
4	3,881	13.9%	4,095	4.7%	214	5.5%
5	1,254	4.5%	1,246	4.5%	-8	-0.6%
6	396	1.4%	377	1.4%	-19	-4.8%
7+	201	0.7%	163	0.6%	-38	-18.9%
Total	27,825	100%	27,791	100%	-34	-0.1%

Source: ONS 2021b

Hancock told people to 'make a choice and stick with it'.[7] In addition, the NHS and PHE explicitly suggested juggling people between households to reduce infection risk (see Chapter 5).

From March to June/July 2020, 1.3% of households in England moved home, only slightly below the rate for the same period in 2019/20.[8] From June/July to November/December 2020, 3.3% of households moved,[9] and from November/December 2020 to April/May 2021, 4.1% moved.[10] However, most moves appeared to be for 'normal' reasons, and only about a third of those who moved said that COVID-19 restrictions had affected their decision.[11]

In addition to whole household moves, some households lost or gained individual members, and more of these moves appear to be due to COVID-19 restrictions (Table 4.2). Bear et al said 'new multigenerational households that have formed to absorb the economic and social shocks of the pandemic'.[12]

In total, this suggests almost 1 million moves in and out due to COVID-19 restrictions in England. There were 730,000 moves in due to COVID-19 and 243,000 moves out. Among cohort members, changes in household membership were reported by 26% of those aged 19, 15% those aged 31, 14% of those aged 50, 12% of those aged 62 and 3% of those aged 74.[13] The households most likely to have had someone move in were parents with adult children, households with children, those with an HRP aged 25–34 or who was of White ethnicity. Households most likely to have had someone moved out were couples with adult children, those with an HRP aged 45–54 and those in the highest income quintile.

Table 4.2: Proportion of households experiencing change in membership, England, March 2020–April/May 2021

	March–June/July 2020	June/Jul–Nov/December 2020	Nov/December 2020–April/May 2021
Someone moved in	2.3%	1.7%	2.3%
Someone moved out	1.2%	3.3%	2.3%
Both	0.1%	0.4%	0.1%
Any move	*3.6%*	*5.4%*	*4.7%*
Moves due to COVID-19 restrictions	77% (moves in) 31% (moves out)	34% (moves in) 18% (moves out)	24% (moves in) 17% (moves out)

Source: MHCLG 2020a, Tables T31a, T32, T33; MHCLG 2021a, Tables T27, T28, T29; DLUHC 2021a, Tables T26, T27, T28

Moves to support older people

The reduction in one-person households was concentrated among the oldest people. In 2020, there were 321,000 fewer people aged 65 and over living alone than there had been in the previous year, suggesting they moved or were joined by others.[14] Older men were particularly likely to stop living alone (an 11% reduction, compared to 6% for women). In June/July 2020, slightly higher proportions of households with someone shielding had a household move than average, almost entirely resulting from moves in.[15] In February/March 2021, a woman aged 62 said she had moved in with her clinically extremely vulnerable 91-year-old mother in March 2020: "I was widowed in July 2019 so it made sense … I miss my own space and routines. I also worry about my flat."

Moves to reduce risk to vulnerable people

Members of the public identified the potential risk of infection within the household right from the start of the pandemic, ahead of policymakers (see Chapter 5). A woman aged 19 who worked in a hospital said "I have had to move out of my house due to my dad having numerous health issues and currently staying in my boyfriend's aunt's holiday cottage". A woman aged 62 who had been living with her husband who had Parkinson's, three adult children and one of their boyfriends said "before the lockdown we decided it would be sensible to separate the generations and [I and my husband] rented a v. small cottage and moved in". A man aged 19 who lived with his parents said "my grandmother is now living with us as it made practical sense as before she lived with young children". In May 2020, a woman aged 50 said all her student children had returned home and her son had brought his girlfriend "as her mother is shielding".

Vulnerable people tried to evade risk, both by moving into and out of care homes. A middle-aged woman said in May 2020 "my brother took my dad out of interim care fearing the virus outbreak in care homes". Another middle-aged woman said that her disabled mother "had been living with us (carers in every day). She went into a care home over lockdown as we felt it wasn't safe here for her".

A few households divided the home and household into two in order to separate high-risk and high-vulnerability residents. A woman aged 19 was living with her parents:

"however in a space created for guests so separate from my parents as my dad is high risk and I work in a care home in the kitchen and we have positive cases there".

Moves by young adults to parental or older adults' homes

In 2019, 40% of UK residents aged 15–34 and 27% of those aged 20–34 were living with their parents. In 2020 (including some pre-pandemic months) the proportions grew slightly above trend to 42% and 28%. Among the traditional student age group, aged 18–22, the proportion living with parents grew from 63% to 69%.[16] The number of households in the UK made up of couples or lone parents with adult children increased from 2.7 million in 2019 to 3.0 million in 2020, or by 11%.[17]

Some of these moves were university students moving from term-time accommodation for more comfortable, less lonely and cheaper lockdown study. A woman student aged 19 said in May 2020 "within a matter of days about 90% of people had moved back". Another said: "The week before lockdown my mum called … and told me she was picking me up from uni that afternoon." A 19-year-old woman student whose parents' home was overcrowded had moved in with her boyfriend and his parents "so I had a quiet place to write essays". Those who stayed behind or returned were often in sparsely filled halls or flats, and some had very difficult experiences. In February/March 2021 a 19-year-old said:

> "I was isolated in a room by myself for 4 months during the first lockdown … daily suicidal thoughts still … isolation killed more people and spirits than the virus ever did."

Young people outside the traditional undergraduate ages of 18–22 were also affected, and some moves were forced by finances. A 62-year-old said their postgraduate son had lost his part-time job, "he was unable to pay his rent and the other students he shared a flat with were in the same situation. he had to come home", and was still there nine months later. A 62-year-old woman said her 31-year-old son and longstanding partner had both moved back to respective parental homes in different countries at some emotional cost "to avoid accommodation rents". Another 62-year-old woman said her adult son had come home, "because he struggled with living alone when working from home". This process affected the housing careers both of young and old. A woman with two adult children said "I have … moved to a much smaller house as my two eldest children no longer live at home … however within two days of lockdown they moved back".

Moves into cohabitation

Just 2% of those aged 19 and 3% of those aged 31 moved in with a partner over the pandemic.[18] For this small group, lockdown appeared to have precipitated cohabitation. A woman aged 19 who had been living with her parents and granddad said "I ... moved in with my boyfriend (new relationship) very abruptly as my granddad is very high risk". Fortunately, "this has gone well". In some cases, the cohabitation was in a parental home, in effect as a 'hidden household'.

Moves out of big cities

ONS figures show that the number of households in London increased by 1.3% between 2019 and 2020.[19] However, there seemed to be some moves from London, and other urban areas, to less urban ones. In February/March 2021, a middle-aged woman said her adult daughter had returned from London "due to high number of cases in London". *Homelessness Monitor* found reduced demand for the private rented sector in London in mid-2020, which made it easier to place homeless households there.[20]

Moves to second homes

In 2018/19, 873,000 households in England or 4% of the total had a second, permanent home.[21] On 21 March 2020, the Cornwall tourist board asked holidaymakers to stay away in order to reduce the risk of infection and pressure on services.[22] Nonetheless, in May 2020, a woman said that

> "second home owners have caused a lot of concern in Cornwall and they have flagrantly flouted the laws and spoilt what is a special community here ... this is an issue that has been simmering away for years but has really come to the surface".

In May 2020, a woman aged 74 was in Spain: "we thought it would be better here which has proved correct ... no pushing or shoving ... here they obey the rules on all counts". As rules changed, moves to second homes become legitimate. By February/March 2021, a person aged 50 said they and their partner had moved to their second home outside London: "more space and freedom". Not using a second home was a big regret for many. In May 2020, a woman aged 74 said "we should be in our second home in Greece now"; her UK flat had no outdoor space because she and her husband they usually spent three months abroad each year. In February/March 2021, a whole summer later, a man aged 62 said "we have a lovely caravan 50 mins drive away which we couldn't visit last year at all".

Blocked and delayed moves

The disruption of the housing market could also affect household size and shape. A woman aged 50 said that she and her husband had divorced and were part-way through selling their home in March 2020: "This was incredibly difficult ... we suddenly got thrown together 100% of the time, at a time when my husband was dating other women." In January/February 2021 a 62-year-old woman said her husband had not been able to travel to Pakistan: "he normally stays in UK only three months a year between extended visits ... he has now been here for 14 months".

Break-up of relationships and marriages

A total of 24% of adults in couples said their relationship with their spouse or partner was better or much better over the July 2019 to July 2020 period, and 17% said it had improved over the July 2020 to July 2021 period, despite and because of the strains of the pandemic. A middle-aged woman said "strangely my relationship with my husband has improved". Another said in February/March 2021 that "my husband has liked lockdown we've become even closer".

However, 17% of adults in couples said their relationship was worse or much worse over the July 2019 to July 2020 period, and the same proportion said things were worse over the July 2020 to July 2021 period, rising to 24% for people aged 18–29.[23] Some problems emerged due to COVID-19, including financial and health worries, more time together or more time to think. A woman aged 62 said that the "forced togetherness", with her husband working at home, "has exacerbated things and made me realise we do not get on with each other". One woman reported that her husband had used key working in a near-empty office as cover for an affair with his secretary and said "there will be no end of divorces coming out of this pandemic". A woman aged 19 said that "due to the pandemic my mother has become severely anxious and has separated from my step-dad". A woman aged 31 said that she and her husband "had been arguing a lot due to extra pressures at work resulting in our separating".

Bubbles

The idea of the 'bubble', an 'exclusive social network',[24] was developed in early 2020 in New Zealand. It could involve more than one household, but was confined to a local neighbourhood. People were given 48 hours before lockdown to create their bubbles,[25] which averaged 3.6 people and 1.3 households.[26] The UK adopted versions of the idea. On 13 June 2020, one-adult households in England were allowed to form a 'childcare' or 'support' bubble, and meet and stay overnight with their chosen household. Similarly, on 19 June, one-adult households in Scotland could form 'extended groups'. Bubbles were in effect a modest extension to the definition of the home-based household in order to recognise important relationships and the provision of care and support beyond the household (see Chapter 2). The idea was later extended well beyond the household setting to groups of school students, ranging from parts of classes to whole year groups.

Being allowed to resume at least some natural informal cross-household care and support had a big impact on many people. A woman aged 62 whose mother was 97 said "this is where the restrictions have hit hardest ... support bubbles meant that I could at least share the care of our mother with my older sister". A lone parent aged 50 said: "Having practical and emotional support in the home was amazing!" All bubble members could benefit. A middle-aged woman had bubbled with her son and daughter-in-law, who both had learning disabilities: "As they have coped really well this has been lovely for us. We get out of the house to go and see someone else twice a week." Another woman aged 62, who used her bubble to home school three grandchildren three days a week, said "I thank Boris [Johnson] for support bubbles, it's given me a purpose, to heal and feel like my old self again".

Being at home in the pandemic

Compliance with advice and **staying home** *restrictions*

Self-reported adherence to laws and guidelines about **staying home** varied over time and between people, but was generally high, if not complete, and 'surpassed any of the modellers' predictions'.[27] In March 2020, 65% of people in the UK said they were sticking to the rules 'completely' and about 90% were following the rules 'most of the time'. In May/June 2020, 51% of people said they had seen others breaking COVID-19 regulations.[28] Complete compliance fell to 40% in September 2020, before rising again to 60% in December 2020,[29] as 'stringency' increased (see Chapter 3). In January 2021, 56% said they followed rules 'completely' and 96% said they did so 'most of the time'.[30]

When data were first collected, in May 2020, 81% of adults were not leaving their home other than for work, exercise, essential shopping and medical reasons (Figure 4.1). The proportion **staying home** reduced rapidly as non-essential shops, bars and restaurants opened from June 2020 onwards, before rising to a peak of 65% in the second wave. Despite the significant increase in the proportion of people who worked at home, the majority of working people either continued to work outside the home (incurring risk for themselves and their households) or were furloughed. Total hours worked dropped by 15% from 1 billion per week in December 2019/February 2020 to 0.85 billion per week in the first lockdown in March–May 2020, suggesting 0.15 billion extra hours at home. Work hours then rose gradually, and the second and third lockdowns had less impact.[31] The proportion working at home remained stable despite the reduction in restrictions between the first and second waves.

Figure 4.1: Percentage of adults not leaving their home (other than for work, exercise, essential shopping and medical reasons), May 2020–May 2021, and percentage of working adults working at home all or part of the previous week, March 2020–December 2021 (first and second waves), Great Britain

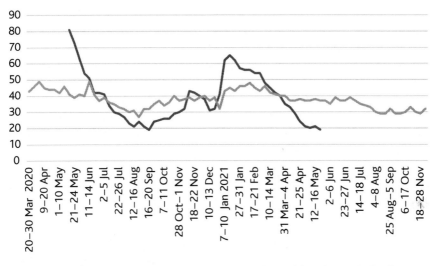

— Adults who stayed at home　— Working adults who worked at home

Source: ONS 2022a, Table 1a

There were big differences in rates of people working outside the home by employment type and region. For example, in November 2020, the proportion of people in work who were working outside the home at least some of the time ranged from 68% in the West Midlands, 67% in the East Midlands and 66% in the South West to 58% in Yorkshire and Humberside and the South East, 57% in Wales and 45% in London.[32] These differences meant that there were also differences between tenures, income and ethnic groups in the proportion of people working outside the home.

The proportion of people who broke rules on visitors and visiting private homes in the second wave was relatively low. In early January 2021, for example, only 18% of households had had a visitor in the past fortnight (Figure 4.2).

Between March 2020 and April 2021 (the first and second waves), complete compliance with **staying home** and other regulations was lower in higher-income households, among more educated people, in urban areas, among men, among minority ethnic people, among key workers and among people in good physical health.[33] In June/July 2020, 17% of people were finding it fairly or very difficult to comply with social distancing restrictions.[34] A total of 25% social renters were finding it difficult, compared to 22% of private renters, 15% of mortgaged owners and 12% of outright owners.[35] Those who

Figure 4.2: Proportion of UK households who had a visitor or visited for more than an hour, December 2020–July 2021

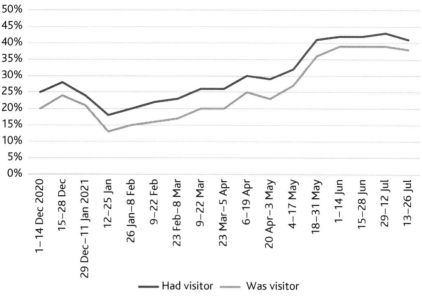

Source: ONS 2021w

were lone parents, in big cities, in London and on lower incomes were more likely to find it difficult, while those in households with younger and ethnic minority HRPs were likely to find it more difficult than average, but were more likely to comply. A woman aged 62 who worked with ex-homeless people said "I worry at work as the tenants I support keep breaking the rules and sneaking out". At a homeless shelter operating during the pandemic, staff had to 'openly rethink boundaries that were set in stone before',[36] such as enforcing bans on drinking, smoking and drugs, because of the need to help residents **stay home**.

The occupancy of homes

Overcrowding

Between 2019/20 and April/May 2021, the proportion of households in England that were overcrowded increased markedly across all tenures. The proportion of outright owners who were overcrowded increased from just under 1% to 1%, and among mortgaged owners from 2% to 4%, a reversal of the past trend. The rate for social renters increased from just under to just over 9%, a slight acceleration of the past trend (see Figure 2.2). The rate for private renters increased from 7% to 14%, a big acceleration of the past trend (although MHCLG point out that the difference between social and private

Figure 4.3: Changes in overcrowding rates by tenure, England, 2014/15–April/May 2021

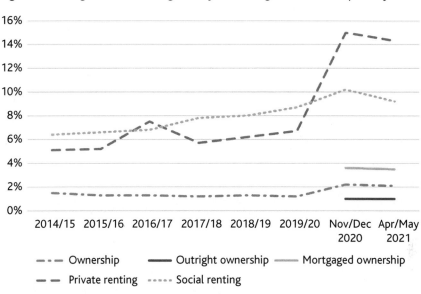

Note: data for 2014/15–2018/19 are based on three-year averages
Source: DLUHC 2021d FA1422 (S127); MHCLG 2020f, Table 1.18; MHCLG 2020a, Table T42b; DLUHC 2021a, Table T40b

renters was not statistically significant)[37] (Figure 4.3). This sudden change in overcrowding for private renters must have been due to moves. Some of the moves were choices, but some must have been due to constraints, particularly unaffordability.

The increase in overcrowding was much more dramatic for households with ethnic minority HRPs. The rate for households with minority ethnic HRPs jumped from 12% in 2019/20 to 23% in April/May 2021, while the rate for households with a White HRP grew from 2% to just over 2%. In April/May 2021, 18% of households with a Black HRP, 19% of those with an Indian HRP and 36% of those with a Pakistani or Bangladeshi HRP were overcrowded.[38] This represents a marked increase in inequality between ethnic groups.

Overcrowding increased in some English regions during the pandemic, including the North East, the East, the West Midlands and London, which had a modest increase but remained the region with most overcrowding, at 12% of households in April/May 2021.[39] The types of household for which the chances of overcrowding increased were couples with children, lone parents with adult children, and unrelated sharers. Some household types saw a modest reduction in overcrowding: households with more than one family and lone parents with dependent children. There was little change in the relative risk of overcrowding for different income groups.[40]

The proportion of all households in England with one or more spare rooms remained stable throughout the pandemic, at about 38% of households in England. However, the proportion of households with a minority ethnic HRP which had a spare room reduced from 22% in 2019/20 to 12% in April/May 2021.[41]

Time spent at home

From 23 March 2020, people in the UK were told to **stay at home**. In this first national lockdown, most people were at home for 23 or more hours a day, and 41% did not go out at all for five or more days a week.[42] In March/April 2020, the average British adult spent 17 minutes a day on travel (including walking) compared to 83 minutes in 2014/15.[43] In May 2020, a man aged 50 said:

> "I used to travel a lot for work, to Ireland every other month and to the US four times a year. ... I used to take about four foreign holidays per year. ... My world has shrunk and I rarely venture out of the neighbourhood."

A middle-aged man said "I've driven less than 10 miles in the past two months". A woman aged 62 said "I miss the world. I haven't left my ... village since 22 March". In May 2020, a woman aged 50 who continued to work in her shop which sold essentials while her husband and children worked and studied from home said she felt left out, with "so many people sharing '**stay at home**' stuff".

As 2020 progressed, people gradually went out more (Figure 4.1) and the average days spent entirely at home reduced from four to two days a week by July 2020.[44] By September/October 2020, daily travel time had increased to 28 minutes.[45] There was little difference in time spent at home by age, household type or location. However, people with lower household incomes and people with mental illness spent the most time at home.[46]

Daytime home occupancy

In June/July 2020, while most elements of the first UK lockdown were still in operation, 41% of households had at least one extra adult spending the day at home and 14% had two or more. A total of 34% had at least one person working at home. The remainder had people at home due to furlough (the government scheme to pay the wages of people unable to work due to the pandemic; see Chapter 7), new care responsibilities or loss of daycare for adults with special needs.[47] In October/November 2020, 39% of working adults were working at home at least part of the time, while 49% were working only outside the home.[48] By April/May 2021, 33% of households still had at least one and 8% had two or more extra adults at home.[49]

Lower-income households had higher proportions of economically inactive residents before the pandemic, and so were more likely to have had adults at home during the day before and during the pandemic. However, higher-income households were more likely to have extra adults at home during the day during the pandemic because they were more likely to have jobs and the kind which could be done at home. In June/July 2020, 67% of households in the highest income quintile had at least one extra adult at home during the day, compared to 24% in the lowest.[50]

From March to July 2020, most UK school children were not attending school and were studying at home. A woman aged 19 said "I am part of seven siblings … our routines have gone from 6 hours in school to 24 hours at home". After the summer holidays, from September to December 2020, schools were open, but in January–February 2021, 85% of school students were absent.[51]

Using time at home

The way people used time changed sharply at the start of the first lockdown. On average, more time was spent on sleep, free time, childcare, keep fit, gardening and DIY, and work at home. Less time was spent on work outside the home, housework, personal care, travel and study. By September/

Figure 4.4: Average minutes per day spent on different activities by adults, Great Britain, 2014/15–March 2021

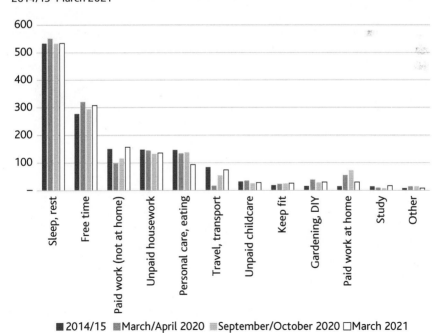

Source: ONS 2021i

October 2020, time use had reverted towards pre-pandemic patterns, except for housework and working at home, but in March 2021, increased average time working at home had persisted (Figure 4.4).

However, patterns varied substantially between individuals. For example, reductions in travel time benefited people on higher incomes most: they had spent more time on travel in 2014/15, but were close to the average by March 2021.[52] Similarly, increases in time on gardening and DIY benefited people on high incomes most: they had spent less time on these activities than those on lower incomes in 2014/15, but by March 2021 this had reversed.

The intimate geography of staying home

Introduction

In March 2020, the typical UK home was a semi-detached or terraced house, with three bedrooms, a garden and two or three residents. However, British homes varied from spacious, well-equipped houses to temporary accommodation for homeless families, or the street. Households varied from people on their own to multiple families (see Chapter 2). The demands placed on homes by the pandemic varied between households and over time. There was less change for households working outside the home during the pandemic, for those already working at home or not working, but in some there was substantial additional occupancy, as well as multiple activities at home. Production of unpaid childcare and adult care at home increased, as did cleaning, gardening, DIY, cooking and washing. Unpaid education was added, and paid work was transferred to the home, while unpaid transport services reduced. In many cases, homes took on the new role of providing safe spaces for shielding and isolating (see Chapter 6).

The ever-presence of home, and the micro-mobility available within and around it, formed a key part of the experience of the pandemic for all, especially those not working outside the home. In May 2020, a woman aged 50 said:

> "I find it is all very groundhog day, sleep, walk 5 ft to desk, eat, TV, sleep … never did I think the morning commute on a motorway was actually a great way to start and end the day … there is no downtime between work and 'what's for dinner'."

Congestion at home

Extra residents and increased daytime occupancy in many homes meant more competition for space, quiet, tables, computers and broadband. They meant more demands for cooking, washing and cleaning, more wear and tear, and the need for more management of competition.[53] A middle-aged woman said:

"Home feels slightly cramped, as my eldest daughter came home from university for lockdown. I didn't feel she could share with her 14-year-old sister anymore, so she's moved into the study downstairs and my husband's moved his work stuff into the shed. It's not a huge house for six!"

A 50-year-old woman said "children and husband at home all the time so not getting the alone time/privacy I'm used to … the house is very noisy now". A 62-year-old woman stated:

"It's felt more crowded in the house with two adult children here all the time! Son aged 30 is usually here at weekends and works away during the week but is now furloughed. Our daughter is now working from home and of course neither of them are going out in the evenings!"

Another 62-year-old woman said:

"My adult children have come home, two extras [girlfriends] … the house feels very crowded and I have moved into the smallest bedroom. … I struggle to keep the place clean and tidy, they "help" but don't see what needs to be done."

In May 2020, a woman with one child at home and two more returned adult children said the house could be "fractious" as one child's night shift conflicted with two other's online studies. In February/March 2021, a person aged 50 with a partner and three student children at home, said "living together for such a long time becomes a little more edgy". A woman aged 19 in her parental home with a total of seven people under one roof said that the biggest effect of the pandemic "was the family fighting which has been caused out of everyone being at home … I have cried a great deal despite it not being mine or my family's fault".

Staying home meant reduced costs on travel, food and leisure outside the home for many, which contributed to increased savings for some (see Chapter 7). However, extra time and people at home added to other costs. A woman aged 50 living with her disabled son said "our utilities bills have increased because we are in the house more, but our benefits haven't increased". A middle-aged woman said that having her adult children at home "has caused our financial situation to be worse". A 50-year-old woman with two student children at home said "I've been feeding five adults through lockdown one and two". A student aged 19 stated that "although I am still paying rent for my student house in Leeds, at home my parents buy all the food etc".

Kitchens

Due to greater occupancy and the constraints on eating out, kitchens were in greater use for meal preparation – for example, for weekday lunches at home. In addition, cooking served as a leisure activity for many. Some kitchens were also in greater use for dining, work and study, and household socialising. A woman aged 50 with children said "we were always out at weekends, visiting places, camping etc so that was a big adjustment, we have started cooking and eating together more". A woman aged 50 was enjoying being at home with her 14-year-olds: "we make time to sit around the table and chat. Do cooking, quizzes …". A retired man aged 62 with a working wife and son and daughter-in-law who moved in when lockdown started said "my cooking has improved". A man aged 50 whose adult children had returned home said "whilst unable to go on holiday, we have used the funds to renovate our kitchen and dining room into one social space which is amazing".

Proximity could create new routines. A middle-aged woman said:

> "My son is working from home. He sets up a work area on the kitchen table each morning. I'm … in the spare bedroom. We have lunch together and take turns to cook dinner."

Larger kitchens could also have novel uses. A man aged 62 said in February/ March 2021 "we go to dancing lessons which had had to stop, but we have resumed some online in the kitchen!". A self-employed dance teacher aged 31 had switched to doing lessons from her kitchen, but said "it's far from ideal".

Living rooms

In March/April 2020, the average British adult had 5 hrs 8 mins free time, 31 mins more than pre-pandemic in 2014/15.[54] Living rooms were in greater use for watching TV, eating and household socialising, and just passing the time. In February/March 2021, a person with a child aged 19 said "the highlight of my week is sitting on the sofa watching television on a Saturday night". Some cohort members had upgraded their living spaces with new equipment. By February/March 2021, a man aged 62 and his wife had bought a new hi-fi and TV system. A woman aged 50 said "my husband and I have paid for Netflix which has been great". However, a person aged 62 stated that "sofa sitting is extremely depressing". A woman aged 31 with a newborn baby said that she wished her child knew "there is something outside of just hanging out in a living room with your mum".

In addition, many of the extra adults working at home worked in their living room. A woman aged 19 said "both me and my flat mate work from home in the living room as our flat is small and it can get hard spending every waking minute together". A woman aged 50 said "I'm stuck in the lounge/office for most of the day/week". For some the lounge was a second-best workplace within the home. A woman aged 50 stated that "I work in the lounge as [my husband] is in the [home] office". If someone was using the living room for work, others in the household might have to be restricted. A woman aged 31 said:

"Having my husband working from home has been extremely difficult because I have had to stay in my bedroom all day, watching TV ... because of our open-plan ground floor, there can't be noise as he has meetings and calls.".

In high-occupancy households, someone might have slept in the living room before the pandemic, and any movers-in may have ended up there. In May 2020, a student aged 19 had returned to her parents' home and had to sleep in the living room: "my relationships with my family has suffered as a result". Similarly, shielders and isolators in the 41% of multi-person households which did not have spare bedrooms[55] sometimes took over the living room (see Chapter 6). In February/March 2021, a middle-aged woman said she had been isolating in the lounge since March 2020: "It's been tough being very close yet so far apart from all in my household."

Most UK homes do not have another general-purpose room, but they could provide useful work and social space. In February/March 2021 a person aged 62 said that when spring came, "I will bring my 'office' downstairs into the dining room so I can bob out into the garden between meetings". Another person aged 62 said he had been promoted "as I work in the home renovations sector which has seen a significant rise in people wanting their homes renovated in particular creating home offices".

Bedrooms

In March/April 2020, the average adult in Britain spent 551 minutes a day on sleep and rest, 19 minutes more than in 2014/15.[56] A middle-aged woman, at home with her husband, student and postgraduate student children said "we have had lots more sleep without alarm clocks going off each day which has been extremely relaxing". A man aged 50 said "I have slept better which helps with mood and patience". Some homes had more sleepers in them. A woman aged 19 had given up her 'dream job' and first independent flat to return to her parents' home: "I still continue to pay for my flat with my furlough pay while I sleep on the floor of my sister's room."

Many bedrooms were also in heavier use for work, study or retreat from the rest of the household. A woman said her 19-year-old student daughter had returned home and now had a desk in her parent's bedroom: "that causes issues in a morning if she wants to study early. Likewise if she wishes to study late". A man who had downsized after his children had left home had two adult sons back and sharing a bedroom, one "studying for his university course in my bedroom during the day … luckily there is a desk and a computer". A student aged 19 said that she was trying to get the motivation to do "10 hours plus of uni work a day at home sitting at a desk in my parents' bedroom because there is no other space for it". Some returning adult children had brought partners and some started cohabitation in former childhood bedrooms. A woman aged 50 said "my children share a room with one desk and I allocated this to the eldest one who is doing GSCEs". The younger child did her schoolwork on her bed.

Many young people spent a lot of time in their bedrooms, and for many parents this symbolised their fears about the effect of the pandemic on their sons and daughters. A woman aged 50 said her daughter was "spending her life in her bedroom". In February/March 2021, a woman aged 50 said that her 13-year-old daughter's mental health "deteriorated a lot, had to go to counselling, spends much more time in her bedroom since the pandemic, does not see or connect with her friends as she used to".

For people in shared housing, the bedroom could be the whole or main part of their home. A student aged 19 said that "it can become hard to find a reason to leave your room and I have so much less energy as I am not seeing people. We are so bored of it and feeling so hopeless".

Spare bedrooms

In 2019/20, 38% of households in England had one or more spare bedrooms, according to the 'bedroom standard' (see Chapter 2). Spare bedrooms were often turned over to work or study. A man aged 31 said "my new job was almost exclusively based in our spare room for many months". A middle-aged woman stated that "my husband has been stuck in the spare room since 20 March". A woman aged 62 said that her husband, who was a university lecturer, had been "conducting lessons and seminars online from our back room". However, some bedrooms were too small to work in. A woman aged 62 said that "my husband is in a very small bedroom for his office". Another woman aged 62 stated that her son had returned to live with her and her husband "as the room he rents in a shared house down south is too small for him to work in".

Specialised or equipped rooms

Some homes had a spare bedroom or downstairs room which had been set up as a home office or study, with a desk, a chair and a computer, which usually limited other uses. In February/March 2021, a person aged 31 said "I have a fantastic home office which has made working from home very nice". A woman aged 31 stated that "I am fortunate we had the space to make a study so I can still have the work/home separation". A middle-aged woman said "my husband works from home and this has been great for us as we have plenty of room for him to shut himself away when busy". A person aged 31 noted "I am fortunate enough to have a well-equipped home gym so I have been able to continuing exercising as normal".

Bathrooms

Greater occupancy placed more pressure on bathrooms and toilets, although more flexible schedules provided some mitigation. A 19-year-old woman student back with her parents and siblings said "in uni I had my own room and bathroom but now I have to share both which isn't horrendous but … if I want a shower I have to tell everyone an hour before". The bathroom could be a place to gain privacy. Another woman aged 19 was worrying about her mum and siblings, and said: "On rare occasions, it'll hit and I'll be in tears late at night, trying not to wake anyone up. Or in the bathroom."

Garages and sheds

Some people converted garages into new uses. A middle-aged woman with a sixth-former son keen on fitness said "we are very fortunate as we have been able to set up a home gym in the garage". Another middle-aged woman said that her husband had brought the outside work in by converting their garage into a pub, "which has been an amazing place to go at the weekend".

Garages could also be use as liminal spaces and quarantine sites. In May 2020, a middle-aged woman with a daughter aged 19 and an elderly mother said "I meet up with them both for walks and a cuppa in my Mum's garage". In February/March 2021, a woman aged 50 said she and her husband had a fridge in the garage which they used to quarantine all food deliveries and purchases for two days before bringing them inside. Many people used extra time at home to tidy up things stored in garages.

Gardens

In June/July 2020, 83% of all households in England had gardens. In March–April 2020, the average person spent 39 minutes a day on gardening and DIY, and in September–October they spent 28 minutes, well above the 16 minutes in 2014/15.[57] A woman aged 50 said "I do feel for others who may be in cramped accommodation and without a garden – it makes such a difference". A woman aged 62 noted "I have a garden and that has been my saving grace as I get outside and physically do hard work cutting hedges etc". A man aged 62 said "our large garden has never looked better and we will shortly be enjoying loads of fresh fruit and veg that I grow". A woman aged 74 stated "as long as I am in the garden, I am a happy bunny".

At least in good weather, gardens could provide some extra living space, as well as an area for leisure and gardening itself. In May 2020, a woman aged 50, whose son and his family had moved in temporarily before the pandemic and then had been unable to move out, said "I am able to get outside a lot and get some space, until the grandchildren come out to find me".

A man aged 50 commented "I wish I had a garden".

Doorsteps and curtilage edges

During the pandemic, doorways, front gardens and windows became more significant as the potential sites of COVID-safe visits between friends and relations, although these contacts were generally seen as not very satisfactory. In February/March 2021 after 11 months of restrictions, a person aged 62 said that they did see their daughter and granddaughter who lived nearby, but it was "just a quick hello over the garden wall or at the window". Another person aged 62 said "I've missed family and friends seeing them from a window is not the same as sitting having a cuppa and a chat".

Flats

In 2018, 85% of people in the UK lived in houses rather than flats.[58] Many house- and flat-dwellers felt that flats were more difficult to **stay home** in. A 31-year-old said that "the sheer boredom of having to spend the vast majority of my time stuck in a one-bed flat has been almost overwhelming and at times it has been difficult to stay positive". Another 31-year-old said: "Because I live in a flat without a garden I feel a bit trapped." Another commented "I hate seeing everyone enjoying their gardens whilst we were stuck in a flat". A woman aged 62 said that her children "have become quite depressed living and working alone in small flats". Many of the young adults who went to live with their parents during lockdown were leaving flats or shared housing behind.

Flats involve communal spaces, and potentially closer contact with neighbours. A woman aged 50 said that other residents of her block "have caused me huge distress with noise and breaking the rules". On the other hand, a woman aged 62 said the communal garden at her block allowed her to "meet people and … talk to them every day. Some are there when I need them. Especially help with my dog or shopping when I am ill".

Location

Home location changed in significance during the pandemic. Case rates and risk from disease varied markedly by region, local authority and neighbourhood (see Chapter 3). Location relative to friends and relations, who might need or provide care and support, also became more important. In February/March 2021 a 50-year-old said "my father [aged 80] lives next door so he is safe and lives a fairly independent life", but another 50-year-old and her husband said "we live 200 miles from family so that is difficult". In February/March 2021, a 50-year-old commented:

> "All my family and friends live in Essex and I am currently living in Derbyshire due to not being able to afford living in my home county. … I have only seen immediate family twice in one year and I have not seen any of my friends at all. … I have been very lonely."

The very local neighbourhood, reachable on foot, become more important, especially when travel was limited. In February/March 2021, a 31-year-old said that their flat "was plagued by a gang right outside dealing drugs, taking advantage of lockdown to engage in constant anti-social behaviour". A parent aged 31 "said "we live in a two-bed flat with no garden in a run-down area. My child is only two … [and] confined to mostly indoors as we cannot travel to nice outdoor spaces". A woman aged 50 commented: "There is nowhere interesting to walk to from our home as we live in a very built up suburb of a big city." In contrast, many rural residents commented on their beautiful, uncrowded surroundings. However, location in relation to some services became less important. A person living in Brighton said in theory they had arts and culture on their doorstep, but "now it feels as if my flat could be anywhere and I wonder why I am paying such a high rent for the privilege".

The impact of the pandemic on the meaning of home

Introduction

The concept of 'home' often refers to residents' subjective responses and attitudes to the places in which they live, including both the individual physical home and the wider neighbourhood, area or even nation. Some societies and languages use the same words for both the subjective and physical concepts, while some use different words, like 'home', 'house' or 'flat'. 'Home' can be a social or psychological concept, entirely independent of a fixed physical space. People can feel 'at home' in particular communities, and some homeless or mobile people can feel 'at home' in the world without fixed housing. Most existing literature on 'home' emphasises positive elements: when people have a secure and comfortable home of their own, they have a refuge, a place of security, control, privacy, rest, belonging, personalisation and self-realisation.[59] The literature explores factors that enable or block these positive feelings, such as lack of choice about home and household, insecurity, mobility and poor housing conditions. For many home owners, home has a second role as a form of savings and wealth, meaning choice and security, as well as a place to live.

Before the pandemic, most people in the UK were satisfied with their homes, and their homes were of good quality (see Chapter 2). However, for some people, at some times, home can be 'home horrible home'. It can be a place of constraint, unhappiness, risk and harm.[60] Some harms may be particularly associated with home, including domestic abuse, child abuse and neglect, self-harm, loneliness, mental health problems, drink or drug problems, eating disorders and negative experiences associated with chronic illness and disability. Loneliness may have a spatial dimension or may be exacerbated by spending a lot of time at home. Pre-pandemic, for some UK people, housing conditions were threats to their health; housing costs and household bills were threats to current living standards, mental health and future plans; and other household members were constraints or threats. Gurney argues that the 'dark side' of home has 'been neglected in favour of mapping and celebrating the positive attributes of home'.[61]

The challenge of the pandemic to the meaning of home

During the pandemic, homes acted as refuges from the virus. They were also places that needed to be actively protected from it. For some people, the role of home as the safe, beloved location for the most important social interactions and for pleasant, less stressful activities was enhanced by more time and new activities at home. For example, a man aged 50 said "I am a devoted Muslim ... as a family, we are closer than ever doing all our daily worships together at home". Some people may have bonded further with their homes: for example, through the increased time spent on home improvement and gardening.[62]

However, increased time at home and the multiplication of activities within the home were involuntary, and far from what most people would have chosen. Some people may have become alienated from their homes and from spending time at home in general. The special status of home was challenged by the arrival of activities, including work, study and official interactions. The pandemic led to a marked weakening of the privacy of the home through interactive video communication. Homes were not safe from the risk of infection (see Chapter 5). The constraints of **staying home**, exposure to household members and privacy from the outside world led to an increase in some types of harm at home, such as anxiety, loneliness, domestic conflict and abuse. It also led to displacement of harms such as overwork, overeating and drinking from other sites, and created new types of harm, such as undereducation, and stress from home schooling and from managing infection risk.

Changes to the meaning of home during the pandemic

It has been widely stated that the pandemic has changed people's relationships with their homes, both in the UK and worldwide. Home "came forward as a noticeable rather than taken for granted component of life";[63] "Rarely has the importance of home to each and every one of us been so clearly demonstrated".[64] However, by 2022, few studies had directly examined the impact of the pandemic on the meaning of home. In a small study of older people in Northern England, a third said their attitude to their home had changed over the pandemic, a third said it had not and a third had intermediate views.[65] A study in Turkey found that many people had ambivalent or conflicting attitudes to home during the pandemic and that instead of being a retreat from or contrast to other places or parts of life, home was omnipresent and all-meaning. One respondent said: "Nowadays home means 'life' to me."[66] This section draws mainly on the experiences of cohort members to describe some meanings of home that were unlikely to have been entirely new, but appear to have been newly salient or newly prevalent.

Positive meanings of home

Renewed appreciation – Numerous middle-aged people and those aged 50 and 62 who had comfortable homes expressed renewed appreciation of them, often remarking that many others were worse off. A woman aged 62 living with her husband and son said:

> "Our house is set over three floors with spare bedrooms, so there is plenty of space ... we also have plenty of televisions, computers, bathrooms and a garden – so none of us need to share these things ... keep thinking how lucky we are."

Home as centre for participating in the world – Some shielders who had limited mobility in normal times said they appreciated the improved access to activities online from home due to the pandemic. A disabled person said:

> "When lockdown lifts, I hope those who are 'healthy' remember how important these things were for their own sanity and sense of community so that everyone ... can continue to live a fuller life if they are stuck at home."[67]

Home as safe, or as the only safe place – An older woman said "I have continued to work at the hospital during lockdown and have valued my home environment even more when I come home".[68] For some, home became the only safe place. In January 2021, during the third national lockdown, 44% of adults in Great Britain felt 'uncomfortable' or 'very uncomfortable' about leaving their homes.[69]

Home as restorative – Some people viewed lockdown time as an unexpected opportunity to rest, to restore mental and physical resources, and to reflect and plan. A middle-aged woman who had just ended a relationship with an alcoholic partner said "while painting my ceiling I was overwhelmed with a sense of joy … each day I'm happier, calmer and less stressed".

Ambiguous meanings of home

Home as a workplace – Until the nineteenth century, home (and the fields) were the main workplaces in the UK. The pandemic led to a marked and probably lasting increase in the use of home as a workplace, and home can be thought of again as a significant site of production as well as consumption.[70]

Home as a semi-public space – Virtual communication 'has seen the continual decrease in distance between public and private space'.[71] During the pandemic, the increased use of video communication for socialising, work and official contacts such as legal cases, benefits interviews and medical appointments meant that millions of homes slipped instantaneously back and forth between private and public roles. Sounds and views of the home which residents might have preferred to have kept private were transmitted to those who would not hear or see them in normal times. Prime Minister Boris Johnson used what he had seen for political purposes:

> "for years SNP leader Ian Blackford has been telling the Commons that he is nothing but a humble crofter on the Isle of Skye. Well now … we can inspect the library or is it perhaps the billiard room of Ian Blackford's croft".[72]

Negative meanings

Home as prison – Many people referred to **staying home** as being like imprisonment. A man aged 19 with mental health problems said "my home often feels like a prison … I have been able to cope with these feelings through distracting myself but they are always there to some extent". A person aged 31 said "I am a prisoner. I exist but I do not live. Lockdown destroyed my quality of life". A woman aged 62 noted that a weekly visit to her work site "feels like day release". A man aged 62 said that **staying home** was "not what human life should be". A middle-aged woman said:

"I have suffered with sporadic anxiety when in a room with all my family ... I have spent a lot of time alone in my bedroom and have even crossed the road and sat in my car to be able to see the world from beyond my window".

Home as a site of extreme work – Many people working at home during the pandemic said that they were working more intensively and for longer hours. There were new unpaid tasks, and paid and unpaid work were combined. A woman aged 50 employed in payroll said:

"I truly don't think I have ever worked this hard and such long hours. We are so busy and inundated with queries. I have worked all day and then logged back on again after dinner and worked till 2 or 3 am on many nights."

Another woman aged 50 noted:

"Being a home schooling parent is an absolute nightmare. I am cook, cleaner, teacher, teaching assistant, midday supervisor, disciplinarian 24 hours a day, seven days a week now. It is harrowing. My mental health and wellbeing are suffering, as are my children's."

Another woman aged 50 living with her husband and four home-schooling sons said:

"I have to be a constant motivator, fitness instructor – which is laughable – cook, cleaner, carer for my mother who is unwell, mentor, counsellor. ... The only motivating factors has been the ever-present fact that they all need me to be someone for each of them. But I am exhausted."

A middle-aged woman with a husband and adult children working and studying at home said "I am servicing them with no let up, from computer repairs to food to laundry – and no thank yous". She was also working full-time as an accountant, volunteering, monitoring her ageing mother-in-law and supporting a friend whose mother was dying.

Loss of periodic quiet and privacy in multi-person homes – In normal times, home often provides a place to be alone, even in multi-person households. This meaning has been overlooked, but the impact of its loss highlighted its value. A woman aged 50 working outside the home but with a husband and three children working and studying at home said "one thing I miss is the house to myself on my days off. There is always someone round at the moment and I quite like time on my own after a busy shift".

Loss of refuge and private meaning of home due to presence of work or other activities – A shielder said "business is conducted in the realm once restricted for slumber and love".[73] A woman aged 31 who worked in domestic violence support commented "we used to be able to support each other when we were in the office together. Now we are in our living rooms listening to horrific stories all day". A woman aged 50 working at home alongside her husband and said "I find the no split between work and home difficult. My husband is now more a colleague than a spouse". A woman aged 31 working at home stated:

> "I feel trapped in the house ... at the end of the working day or later sometimes I go straight into the kitchen to prepare tea and tidy up etc. I am starting to feel the house is really small and resenting it."

Loss of meaning from events due to taking place virtually at home – The transfer of celebrations, funerals and other emotionally significant events to the domestic arena (via the limited viewpoint of a camera and screen) could rob them of some of their meaning or power. A person aged 50 said "I successful defended my PhD on 8 May. Except, I defended it in my spare bedroom, alone. No friends and family ... no party".

The role of household and home in COVID-19 infection and death

Policies to reduce the impact of household and home on infection

Introduction

The key UK policy to reduce infections told people to **stay home**, unless they were key workers and could not work from home. Social interaction outside the home and access to private homes by non-residents were controlled by law from March 2020, a move that was totally without precedent in modern times (see Chapters 1 and 3). These restrictions preoccupied policymakers, the media and the public.

However, people were allowed to and required to **stay home** with their households. In-home and in-household transmission was a major means of infection, but there was little policy or public information on means to prevent infection at home. The policy to provide self-contained emergency accommodation for rough sleepers and night shelter users was a notable exception. Private households, where 98% of UK people lived,[1] remained relatively neglected, even where they contained infected or vulnerable people.

Accommodation for rough sleepers and night shelter users

Policy on risk in the living environment developed differently for homeless people compared to that for the general population. This was due to the pre-existing work on reducing homelessness, an energetic and well-networked specialist third sector and community of experts, a pre-existing government 'tsar', the relatively small number of people involved and an element of luck.

In early 2020, homelessness charities and doctors in the UK and abroad were concerned that rough sleepers and hostel residents couldn't isolate, were particularly vulnerable and might infect others. The issue was raised on 11 March 2020 in *The Lancet Public Health*.[2] On 11 and 12 March, there happened to be a conference on homelessness and health, where UK academics, doctors and homeless non-governmental organisations (NGOs) discussed the risk of outbreaks in hostels and day centres.[3] Following this, two senior doctors with experience of providing healthcare for homeless people, Andrew Hayward and Alistair Story of UCL, brought together a team including the MHCLG, PHE, NHS England and the GLA (Greater London Authority), which was soon 'working at breakneck speed',[4] and developed a practical and affordable scheme for using hotels emptied by lockdown restrictions. The doctors said: "We were able to secure a lot of support from different agencies. ... This was achieved incredibly rapidly, over the course of about a week."[5] On 26 March, the MHCLG wrote to all local authorities in England, instructing them to move everyone sleeping rough and in communal shelters and some 'hidden homeless' people into safe places, ideally self-contained accommodation, within two days.[6] This 'Everyone In' policy was unprecedented.

A total of 5,400 people needing housing were identified initially.[7] As well as housing, residents received support to deal with other health and training needs, and plans to move on to other accommodation, including permanent accommodation.[8] Usual guidance to local authorities to provide help to single people only if they were in priority need and with local connections, and to exclude the many non-UK citizens with 'No Recourse to Public Funds' (NRPF),[9] was suspended.

The charity Crisis said that the start of 'Everyone In' was 'a landmark moment'[10] because it aimed to provide self-contained, permanent homes for rough sleepers, without any intermediate period in hostels and temporary homes. The charity Shelter said it was 'one of the most extraordinary things to have ever happened in homelessness in this country'.[11] Local authorities and homelessness charities were 'praised for rapidly rising to an unprecedented challenge'.[12] The other UK nations soon developed similar schemes[13]. By May 2020, 15,000 people sleeping rough or in hostels in England had been rehoused in self-contained temporary accommodation[14]. On 2 May, Louise Casey, former director of the Blair government's Rough Sleepers' Unit, who had already been asked to assist the Johnson government with its pre-pandemic pledge on homelessness (see Chapter 2), was switched to helping people move from pandemic accommodation into permanent housing.[15] In September 2020, 10,000 were in temporary accommodation, 19,000 had been moved on to permanent accommodation or other situations better than temporary accommodation,[16] and by May 2021, a total of 37,000 had been helped by the scheme in England.[17] However, the quality of the response varied somewhat between areas. Initial funding to local authorities specifically for 'Everyone In' was a very modest £3.2 million. A more substantial £105 million was announced in June 2020 to help provide move-on tenancies after hotels, and £160 million previously announced funding for new supported housing was brought forward.[18] English local authorities were also given a total of £3.2 billion (or in later figures £4.6 billion)[19] to support various types of vulnerable people during the pandemic.

However, a *Homelessness Monitor* report in July 2020 said that after the initial phase, there were

'ambivalent, and changing, signals from central Government about the application of the usual homelessness eligibility and entitlement criteria'.[20]

In Wales, housing professionals commented on the good partnership between the Welsh government and other agencies, but difficulties also emerged.[21] Initially, central government told English local authorities that anything they spent would be covered, but this became less clear over time. There were questions about whether people who became homeless during the pandemic, people with NRPF or without 'local connection' or 'priority need' could be helped, and whether shared accommodation could be used. In May 2020, local authorities were told to 'use their judgement' about whether they could offer move-on support to people with NRPF.[22] Later, the government said that housing homeless people in the pandemic was to continue, but was to be funded by local authorities through pre-pandemic money as part of the pre-pandemic homeless strategy (see Chapter 2). In January 2021, as a third national lockdown began in England, there were calls for 'Everyone In' to be restarted.

In early July 2021, *Inside Housing* reported that 'The government has insisted that the scheme is still operating',[23] but in June councils had been told to close 'Everyone In' hotels by the end of the month, as a condition of receiving funding to address rough sleeping. By late July in London, only two 'Everyone In' hotels remained open to provide for homeless people whose immigration status was unclear, and homelessness NGOs had moved on to post-'Everyone In' projects.[24] The chief executive of Homeless Link said "the work of the past 15 months risks being undone".[25] Nonetheless, 'Everyone In' has been seen as one of the policy success stories of the pandemic.[26]

However, most of the 153,000 'core homeless' people in England[27] (see Chapter 2), including those sleeping in cars and tents, squats and non-residential buildings, hostels, unsuitable temporary accommodation and 'sofa surfing', did not receive special policy attention. This was despite the fact they probably faced above-average infection risk. For example, 'unsuitable temporary accommodation' means whole families are in one room or are otherwise overcrowded.[28] A health visitor working with families in temporary accommodation said:

'Much of the accommodation is poor, and certainly unsuitable for self-isolation. Some families are having to share kitchens and bathrooms … with people who have drug or alcohol problems and behavioural issues.'[29]

In addition, jobs providing support to homeless people were some of the highest risk from COVID-19 death, including social workers, housekeepers, residential care managers and security guards (see Table 3.1).

A short pause on house rental, sales and moves, and construction

The housing rental market and home building activities were treated from the point of view of their contribution to the economy (see Chapter 2). The housing market was one of the first sectors to reopen in England during the first lockdown. From 13 May 2020, after just seven weeks, people were allowed to show and view homes for sale and rent, and to move house.[30] Government advice recommended handwashing, two-metre distancing, masks, appointment-only and unaccompanied viewings, and more cleaning.[31] Many agents moved viewings and meetings online. However, resident renters could not refuse if landlords wanted to show potential new tenants around.[32] While there were differences across the UK, they were modest (see Chapter 3). The housing market opened again in Northern Ireland after 12 weeks, in Wales after 13 weeks and in Scotland after 14 weeks.

Similarly, construction ceased at the start of the first UK lockdown, but in England work was allowed to restart after seven weeks, as long as sites were 'COVID-secure'.[33] Both lettings and sales, and construction activity continued through subsequent lockdowns. Property and construction roles were not among the very highest risk (see Table 3.1), but several construction roles had above-average risk.

The role of household and home in infection, illness and death

Introduction

Staying home in private households avoided exposure to COVID-19 and any other risks outside the home, but inevitably increased exposure to risks at home (see Table 5.1). Gurney pointed out that home is a key location for many harmful events and processes, including conflict and domestic abuse, accidents, problematic eating, drinking or drug use, loneliness, depression and mental illness, suicide, and overwork in paid work or unpaid housework and care.[34] **Staying home** also meant deficits in social contact, work, education, income and other activities.

In addition, while protecting from COVID-19 risk outside the home, **staying home** necessarily increased risk of infection at home. As early as 16 March 2020, in the paper that precipitated the first lockdown (see Chapter 3), SAGE said that **staying home** would increase infections at home, and that it would increase the chance that a person with the virus would infect other household members from 50% to 70%.[35]

Table 5.1: The risk effects of **stay home** policy

	Risk	Who is at risk
Regulated risk (COVID-19)	Getting infected/infecting others outside the home	Household and others
Knock-on/displaced risks	Getting infected/infecting others inside the home Harms to physical and mental health at home Other harms at home	Household

Source: Derived from Sunstein 1996

Through their role in infection, the UK's households and homes were directly implicated in the severity and unequal impact of the pandemic in the UK. If both private homes and care homes are included, it is likely that most infections leading to deaths occurred 'at home'. Home location, household composition, occupancy, and residents' roles affected risk at home. Housing conditions, housing affordability and financial situation could affect the ability or likelihood of residents to **stay home** and to avoid risk outside the home. Thus, housing inequalities contributed to inequalities in infection and death. Some of these infections and deaths, and some of this inequality could have been prevented.

Getting infected at home

As COVID-19 is an infectious disease, with a single infection event and location, establishing the links between housing and COVID-19 should in theory be easier than for the conditions which account for most modern deaths, and which have gradual and multiple causations (see Chapter 2). However, data from test centres, hospitals, and coroners on COVID-19 cases and deaths were not usually linked to information on individual housing circumstances.[36] This made it difficult to research the role of household and home in infection. In September 2020, SPI-B said:

> There is little information on household composition, ethnicity, crowding and the risk of transmission ... [and] the role of occupant behaviour.[37]

Nonetheless, professional opinion suggested very early on that home was an important location for infection. The day after SAGE's comment on transmission at home, on 17 March 2020, when whole households were asked to isolate together if one member showed symptoms, Health Secretary Matt Hancock said "it is likely that people living with others will infect each other or be infected already".[38] On 30 March 2020, *Private Eye*'s medical correspondent Phil Hammond said: 'The Chinese realised from previous SARS outbreaks that most spread occurs in family groups.'[39] On 18 May he said that because risk of infection depends on physical closeness and time exposures,

> the highest-risk environments will clearly be enclosed, with a high density of people present for long periods with poor/recycled air circulation: homes, care homes, nursing homes, planes, prisons, call centres, warehouses, factories and religious ceremonies.[40]

Mark Walport, Government Chief Scientific Advisor from 2013 to 2017, told the HSC/STC in December 2020: "A lot of transmission goes on within households."[41] In addition, a substantial body of evidence emerged from around the world and the UK over time.

International evidence on infection at home

The world's first family clusters of COVID-19 were reported on 24 January 2020, six days before the first confirmed cases in the UK. A trader at the wet market in Wuhan in China which was the first known site of infection had infected his wife at home.[42] A family in Shenzhen were infected by a family member who had been in Wuhan.[43] In February 2020, the *Diamond Princess* cruise ship became the world's biggest cluster of cases, despite passengers being confined to their cabins.[44] This provided a model of how transmission could occur among people required to **stay home** in dense conditions and with people making deliveries.

Since then, studies in China, Japan, France, Germany, Italy, the USA, Vietnam, Malaysia, Singapore, Morocco, Greece, South Korea and elsewhere showed that in-home transmission could create 'household' or 'family' clusters.[45] A systematic review found that of the 108 clusters identified by June 2020, 62 (57%) were in families (not necessarily all living together), 19 were at gatherings and conferences, five were at religious organisations and the remaining 22 were linked to neighbourhoods, transport, shopping areas, tourist sites and hospitals. This study concluded that 'prevention of infection among household members is an important strategy to contain the transmission of COVID-19 worldwide'.[46] A German study found that 'household/family members are exposed to high virus loads and therefore have a high risk'.[47] Contact tracing in the USA, Canada and Hong Kong noted that 'at least 20–50% of infections can be traced back to a household contact'.[48]

A review of household cluster studies found that once an adult became infected, on average 66% of other household members followed (the 'secondary attack rate').[49] Another review found figures of 5–30%, averaging 18%,[50] a third found figures of 6–51%, averaging 21%,[51] and a fourth an average of 17%.[52] A review of 87 studies in 30 countries up to June 2021 found an average rate of 19%.[53] This study found that transmission was more likely in households than in workplaces, hospitals and social events outside households. Studies suggested that household size, membership and housing characteristics appeared to influence the number of housing members infected by the first case.[54] Rates were higher where the first case had symptoms, for women, for adults and older household members, for spouses, in later studies when testing and research methods had improved, and for variants of COVID-19 which emerged from late 2020.[55] Rates were lower where the first person infected was isolated outside the household within five days of first symptoms appearing.[56]

UK evidence on infection at home

The first person in the UK known to have died with COVID-19, Peter Attwood, appears to have caught it from his daughter,[57] which would make him the first known case of household or family transmission in the UK.[58] Not only was there risk of transmission at home in the UK, but it appears to have been higher than has been found in international studies. Among the first few hundred confirmed cases in Britain, of those infected within the country, 51% were household members of other cases, many probably infected at home. The study concluded that 'the household [is] a high risk setting for transmission'.[59] Another early study (when testing was not widely available) found that 37% of household members of an infected person also tested positive or had symptoms.[60] Based on many more cases and much improved testing, an October 2021 study showed that 38% of unvaccinated household members of a person with the Delta variant also got infected, as did 25% of double-vaccinated household members.[61]

An international review which included the UK concluded: 'Households appear to be the highest risk setting for transmission of COVID-19.'[62] It also concluded that the UK had higher secondary attack rates than other countries and suggested this was partly due to measurement differences, but also because the UK had no out-of-home isolation of cases and weaker advice on isolating within the household than in other countries. A study in Wuhan found that after the introduction of mass out-of-home isolation of cases, the proportion of household members infected by a case reduced from 18% to 4%. Modelling suggested that **staying home** and social distancing in China reduced cases to 38% of what they would have been with no policy. However, early detection of cases and out-of-home isolation were more significant, and reduced cases to 20% of what they would have been.[63] In the UK, risk of household transmission was lower where the first case was admitted to hospital, providing a form of out-of-home isolation.[64]

SAGE began to address risk at home in September 2020, six months after people were told to **stay home**, as part of its investigation into high infection and death rates among minority ethnic people. SAGE and its subcommittees said

> interactions in a home environment may pose greater risks than public and workplace settings due to familiarity with the location and people, and a lack of clear responsibility to ensure that an environment is safe. People are more likely to relax and let their guard down.[65]

They described normal household tasks like cleaning and laundry, as well as caring for sick relatives, as 'risky'.[66]

While recall and judgements are unlikely to be perfect, home was the most likely location of infection identified by people who had been infected in England and Wales by mid-2021 (Figure 5.1). A total of 44% of all infections of under-18s were believed to have been at home, 34% of 18–34 year-olds, 36% of 35–49 year-olds, 28% of 50–64 year-olds and 30% of people 65 or over.[67] 78% of 'close contacts' passed on to NHS Test and Trace by January 2021 were household members.[68]

Figure 5.1: Where people who had COVID-19 thought they were infected, England and Wales, 2020–21

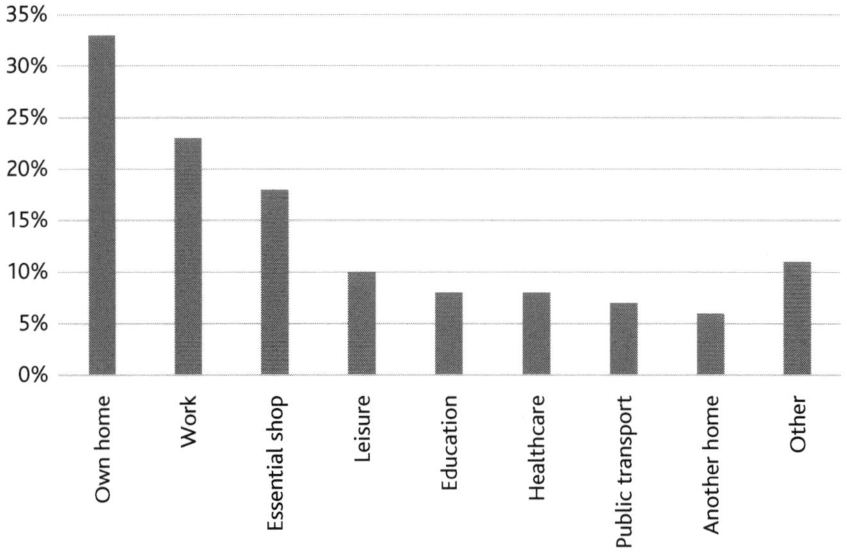

Note: Respondents could name more than one location
Source: Beale et al 2021

Photo 2: UK government public information advert, *The Guardian*, 27 March 2021

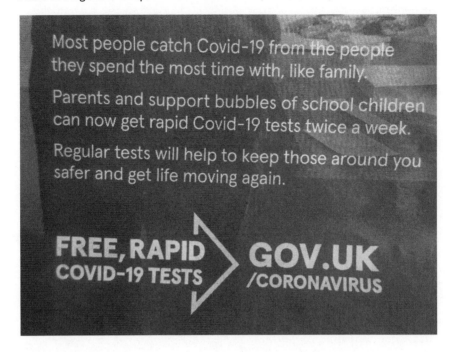

In May 2020, COVID-19 tests were not widely available outside hospital, so most cohort members could only report suspected infection. A woman aged 62 said that she thought "I had COVID-19 in December but was not diagnosed by a doctor. I gave it to my family too". A middle-aged man said he contracted the virus at work and gave it to his wife, and his mother caught the virus in hospital and "got sent home to infect my dad". A middle-aged woman commented:

> "My partner had moderate and unpleasant symptoms of COVID-19 …
> I had mild symptoms. … My son had two days of mild symptoms and
> my 83-year-old mother believes she had mild symptoms."

In January 2021, EMG/SPI-B addressed in home transmission again. They said it was 'very common' but 'not inevitable'.[69] By March 2021, in the context of encouraging take-up of home-testing to support the return of children to school, PHE adverts were saying 'most people catch COVID-19 from the people they spend most time with, like family' (Photo 2).

Estimates of infections at home and resulting deaths

UK secondary attack rates are likely to have varied over time, due to changes in time at home, variants and vaccinations. Using the October 2021 data, attack rates were between 25% and 38% in multi-person households.[70] Using the conservative assumptions that households of every size had an equal risk of initial out-of-household infection, and the same secondary attack rates, a 25% secondary attack rate in multi-person households would mean that 26% of all infections occurred at home, and a 38% secondary attack rate would mean that 39% of all infections occurred at home.[71]

By January 2022, surveys showed there had been about 20 million infections in the UK. If 26–39% occurred at home, this means that 5.2–7.8 million infections occurred at home.

If we then assume that all infections at home and elsewhere had an equal risk of death, infections at home could have caused 26–39% of all pandemic deaths. Thus infections at home could have caused 38,000 to 58,000 deaths within 28 days of a positive test by the start of 2022.

Household characteristics and risk of infection at home

According to a SAGE summary, all five large UK studies of COVID-19 risk (ONS, REACT-Imperial, Biobank, QResearch and OpenSAFELY) 'together provide compelling evidence for the independent effect of household composition on COVID-19 risk'.[72] The important household characteristics included clinical vulnerability, domestic tasks, sexual relationships, care needs and caregiving, spaces and facilities, and jobs and relationships outside the households; 'the pathways … are likely to be multiple and complicated'.[73]

Larger households

The five studies found a link between larger households and higher risk of infection.[74] In June/July 2020, 4.7% of people in one-person households had antibodies to COVID-19 (indicating that they had been infected), compared to 13.0% in seven-person households. After accounting for ethnicity, demographic characteristics, home neighbourhood deprivation, region, and co-morbidities, people in households with three to five members had a 31% increased risk of a positive COVID-19 test, a 33% increased risk of a COVID-19 hospital admission, an 18% increased risk of a COVID-19 ICU admission and a 36% increased risk of a COVID-19-linked death, compared to those with one or two members. A household size of three or more was associated with increased odds of testing positive for White and South Asian people, and increased odds of severe COVID-19 for South Asian people (see Chapter 3 on ethnic inequalities).

Overcrowding

Overcrowding is a traditional concern for public health, especially in relation to contagious diseases. Overcrowding was associated with higher national COVID-19 case rates in a wide range of countries.[75] SPI-B said that overcrowding 'increases risk of droplet and aerosol transmission within a household',[76] and EMG and SAGE said that reducing risk of infection within households 'is likely to be more challenging for people in crowded or cramped housing'.[77] People in overcrowded homes were less likely to follow lockdown rules in full, perhaps because they found it more difficult to **stay home**.[78] However, firm UK data only emerged in February 2021. After adjusting for age, sex, whether there were children in the household and the number of close contacts outside of the household in the last seven days, the infection rate for people in homes with less than one room (including kitchens) per person kitchens (which were likely to be overcrowded by the bedroom standard but could include some other households) was 2.3 times the rate for others. The authors concluded:

> Overcrowding is one of a complex interplay of factors contributing to higher levels of COVID-19 in many socially deprived and ethnic minority groups ... public health responses need to explicitly consider overcrowded housing.[79]

This link between overcrowding and infections is concerning, given the increase in overcrowding over the pandemic, especially among minority ethnic households (see Chapter 3).

People working and studying outside the household

Research and public interest has tended to focus on the dramatic increase in people working at home and furloughed at home over the pandemic, but a majority of people in work continued to work outside the home for most of 2020 and 2021 (see Chapter 3). In November 2020, 49% of working adults in Great Britain were working only outside the home, and 11% were working both at home and elsewhere (Figure 4.1). Research on infection risk by occupation has tended to focus on the risk to the employed individuals (see Chapter 3). In practice, as ONS said in January 2021, "the occupations of others in the household ... could increase exposure to members of the same household".[80]

'Patient-facing' NHS staff in Scotland had three times the risk of hospitalisation with COVID-19 in the first wave than non-patient-facing NHS staff (see Chapter 3), but other members of their households had twice the average risk.[81] The whole household of people working outside the home, particularly in high-risk roles, should have been seen as a category of vulnerability, just like infected and clinically vulnerable people and their households, who were the subject of substantial guidance, law and research (Chapter 6).

Members of the public were well aware of potential risk from work, and some made strenuous efforts to reduce it. In May 2020, a woman aged 50 who was a staff nurse said "I have felt like a lamb going to slaughter! It is scary working in a hospital in PPE then coming home to your family worrying you may pass COVID-19 on to them". A middle-aged woman said her husband had been called off furlough by his employer and "now we are very worried he may catch the virus or we may catch it. I have two auto-immune conditions so it is a very frightening time". In May 2020, a woman aged 19 commented "my mum is a pharmacist in a hospital. So we have to be really careful when she comes home". NHS and social care staff were torn between the duty to treat and duty to family, and adopted elaborate procedures to protect their households, for example, changing out of work clothes on the threshold, segregating their clothes and showering immediately.[82] However, other occupational groups, such as bakers and butchers, where evidence of risk only emerged over time (Table 3.1) did not have the information to be able to reduce risks in these ways.

Multi-generational households

The five major studies (ONS, REACT-Imperial, Biobank, QResearch and OpenSAFELY) found links between mixed-age households and risk of infection, which remained after controlling socio-demographic factors and underlying health status.[83] One study found that women aged 65 or more living in multi-generational households were more likely to die from COVID-19 than those living only with other older adults (after accounting for age, household overcrowding, geographical factors, socio-economic factors and underlying health). Older men were only at higher risk if they were living with children. Another study found that living in a multi-generational household explained 14% of the higher risk of COVID-19 death for older South Asian women, but was not a factor for older men or those from other ethnic groups. Dominic Harrison, Director for Public Health (DPH) for Blackburn with Darwen, told the House of Commons HSC/STC that if you were a confirmed case

> "and you have to go home and self-isolate in a pre-1919 terraced house with a large multi-generational family, it is almost impossible not to infect the rest of your family".[84]

Shared housing

SPI-B said that residents of shared housing 'would be most at risk of external and internal transmission',[85] because of shared spaces, surfaces and objects, and the potential difficulty involved in creating and enforcing rules in these households.[86] Shared spaces may have to be negotiated even while **staying home** and isolating. In May 2020, a woman student aged 19 in a shared house said there had been

"disagreements between a flat mate and the rest of us who live here as she was breaking quarantine and didn't understand how visiting her boyfriend was affecting everyone".

The opening of the housing market in England in May 2020 meant that potential tenants could view rooms and new residents could be moved into shared housing, even if other residents did not want this.[87] A parliamentary answer said that "during viewings, tenants of shared homes should stay out of indoor common areas. … They could remain inside their own private room with the doors closed".[88] However, after letting, they would have to share spaces with the strangers.

Flats

In 2018, 20% of homes in England were flats.[89] Access to most flats involves some semi-public shared spaces and surfaces – doors, hallways, stairs, lifts and corridors – between the shared front door and the doors of individual homes, which could pose risks. Some of these shared areas have to be negotiated even while **staying home** and isolating – for example, to put out rubbish. In my own block I have noticed the repeated confusion of people coinciding at the door of the building over whether to be polite as normal (and hold the door open for each other) or safe (to distance and let the door slam in another's face).

Domiciliary care

Rates of infection and deaths were high for people in care homes and care workers (see Figure 3.1), but also for people receiving care at home. In England, from 23 March to 19 June 2020, there were 4,500 excess deaths among those receiving domiciliary care, or 225% of the average for the same period in 2017–19.[90] This was a higher rate of excess deaths than was found in care homes in England by this point. In February/March 2021, a cohort member aged 62 said that a family member had died of COVID-19 which she had caught from her carer. People receiving domiciliary care were at greater risk of serious disease and death

because of their age and underlying health problems and because of the way care is provided. Care workers might visit multiple clients daily, and clients might receive care from multiple care workers.[91]

Reducing the risk of infection at home

Introduction

Hundreds of billions of pounds were spent on controlling infections outside of the home and mitigating the effects of these measures (Chapters 3, 6). However, a substantial fraction of all infections occurred at home. Fung et al concluded their study of household transmission:

> While preventing spread in congregate public settings is a critical first step, a full-fledged strategy for reducing transmission must also involve interventions to prevent transmission within households.[92]

However, neither the UK government nor the governments of the nations had significant policy on avoiding infection at home. They spent little on the issue, and almost all the effort and financial and other costs of attempts to reduce infection at home were borne by households themselves.

PHE and SAGE advice on reducing risk of infection in private households

From early 2020, PHE, SAGE and other agencies recognised the risk of infection in statements and guidance. However, in September 2020 SPI-B said:

> There is very little evidence regarding which mitigation behaviours are most effective at reducing transmission in the home.[93]

There was also little research into public understanding of and adherence to guidance on avoiding infection at home, other than questions on illicit visitors, in contrast to the case for measures to reduce infection outside the home. You might want to consider how many of the recommendations you were aware of and how many you adhered to. In January 2021, 22 months after the first **stay home** order, SAGE subcommittees listed ideas for preventing infection at home, which they estimated would reduce infections at home by 25%.[94] Based on my earlier estimates, this might have meant 10,000 to 15,000 fewer deaths from COVID-19 in the UK.

Right at the start of the pandemic, the WHO advised that if people with COVID-19 lived with others, they should stay in a separate room and, failing that, all household members should wear masks, distance indoors and ventilate the home.[95] Similarly, SAGE subcommittees said 'the most effective action is for the person to self-isolate within a different room'.[96] PHE recommended as follows: 'Stay as far away from other members of your household as possible', 'Use a face covering … when spending time in shared areas inside your home', 'Ask the people you live with to help by bringing your meals to your door, helping with cleaning and by giving you space', or failing this, 'take your meals back to your room'[97]; 'Use a separate bathroom from the rest of the household … [or] try and use the facilities last, before cleaning the bathroom … use separate towels'. PHE also recommended that people with COVID should '[k]eep your room well-ventilated by opening a window' and to wear 'warm clothes'. For the rest of the household, it recommended additional cleaning, separate crockery and linens for the person with COVID, not shaking laundry and using a dishwasher, if possible. It recommended opening windows and internal doors, checking vents were clear, and leaving extractor fans running for longer than usual. It advised that: 'Cleaning cloths and personal waste … should be stored in disposable rubbish bags … placed into another bag, tied securely and put aside for at least 72 hours.'[98] In January 2021, EMG/SPI-B recommended wearing glasses or sunglasses in place of goggles when tending an infected household member.[99]

Household strategies to avoid infection at home

From early 2020, many cohort members were well aware of the potential risk of getting infected or infecting others at home, particularly if the household contained vulnerable people or people working outside the home and in high-risk jobs. Many households paid careful attention to available advice and formed their own strategies to reduce risk.

A woman aged 62 who lived with her adult daughter and son-in-law and who worked in a hospital and as a bus driver said:

> "Because of the kid's jobs, I am a bit over the top with cleaning the house daily with anti-bacterial … No shoes past the hallway, and washing any post and deliveries."

Some people maintained the same discipline month after month. In February/March 2021, a 31-year-old said "I wiped all my food, keys phone etc with antibacterial wipes since April 2020". This extra cleaning required time, physical capacity and extra expense. However, Bear et al found that many people experienced 'stress and "mental exhaustion" of making decisions to keep themselves and their families safe'.[100] This extra work tended to fall unequally, especially upon women and the middle-aged women in multi-person households. SPI-B suggested that women would be at higher risk of in-household transmission than men as they carried out the bulk of care and of domestic tasks.[101]

A woman aged 62 said "I find it strange that a cleaner is allowed into your home but not your son/daughter". However, many people tried to avoid having workers in their homes to reduce risk. A middle-aged woman said her mum and dad had "let go of their [domiciliary carers] and are coping themselves as they are fearful of the virus". A middle-aged woman had arranged a cleaner for her mother, but she had halted this due to the pandemic and was "worried she is not looking after her home properly". Lodgers could provide company and income during the pandemic, but also affected privacy, space and risk of infection. A 62-year-old who still had a lodger said:

> "[He] is not washing hands regularly and is always going shopping or seeing friends, hence more arguments. I thought about giving him notice as he's my main risk of COVID-19 but I don't want to make him homeless and besides I need the money."

Inequalities in the ability to reduce risk of infection at home

Following PHE and SAGE advice would require a spare bedroom, a spare bathroom, equipment, additional labour by other household members in providing food, cleaning and washing and managing adherence to rules, and a repertoire of unfamiliar and anti-instinctive behaviours, for example, backing in and out of spaces to maintain distance, and ventilated and therefore cold rooms for sick people. In November 2020, EMG/SPI-B said:

> The ability to undertake mitigations may be affected by the physical nature of the home … (house type, available space and number of rooms, sanitary and ventilation provision, and outside space), and this is likely to be more challenging … in crowded or cramped housing or with limited facilities … Financial constraints … may limit the ability of some people to provide effective mitigations, and support may be needed.[102]

In January 2021 they referred to the 'triple burden' of people in poverty, more at risk to infections from their occupations, likely to have serious financial loss from self-isolation, and likely to have less satisfactory homes for self-isolation.[103] PHE acknowledged that: 'Not all these measures will be possible if you, or those you live with, have conditions such as learning disabilities, autism or serious mental illnesses.'[104] It also said that successful risk minimisation was not possible in households with young children, or where there was an infected or vulnerable person who needed care, or who was a carer.[105] Dominic Harrison, DPH for Blackburn with Darwen, told the House of Commons HSC/STC that, for people living in high-risk situations,

> "we are giving as much guidance and support as we can … but the ask for them is very different from the ask for the average member of the population".[106]

'Non-policies' on reducing risk of infection in private homes

In the UK, there was little policy on avoiding infection at home other than advice provided through TV statements, websites and public information adverts. However, there were several 'non-policies' on reducing infection at home: ideas for policies which were implemented outside the UK, or which were suggested by authoritative sources in the UK, including SAGE and its subcommittees.

Providing alternative accommodation for shielding, isolation and convalescence

One important UK non-policy to prevent infection at home was to provide alterative accommodation for the infected people or any vulnerable household members. The 2016 Exercise Cygnus preparation for pandemic flu presumed that hotels could be used to supplement hospital care.[107] A study of household transmission in China suggested that 'home isolation … might lead to the risk of family clusters of COVID-19'.[108] A study in Taiwan concluded:

> Large families … should be monitored when the index [first] case is found. Presymptomatic and symptomatic family members could be quarantined.[109]

On 30 March 2020, *Private Eye* said "most spread occurs in family groups and the last thing you want to do is isolate them all in a house together".[110]

In Hong Kong, holiday camps were used to isolate suspected cases from January 2020.[111] In Wuhan, suspected cases were isolated away from their households from 2 February 2020.[112] SAGE noted that by late 2020, Italy, Finland, Poland, Serbia and Lithuania,[113] the US state of Vermont[114] and New York City had provided places for people with COVID-19 to recover away from other members of their household.[115] In November 2020, Dominic Harrison, DPH for Blackburn with Darwen, said: "At some point, we may want to consider putting people up in hotels."[116] The same month, SAGE suggested that 'Practical support should be offered to allow safe isolation of individuals living in crowded or multi-generational households', which could include free alternative accommodation.[117] In December 2020, Mark Walport, former government Chief Scientific Officer, said that one way to reduce transmission was to 'take an infected person out of the household and house them in a hotel … The question is whether that sort of approach would be acceptable or not'.[118] However, a study published on 7 September 2020 had already found that isolation outside the home was indeed 'feasible and acceptable' to the British public.[119] In January 2021, EMG/SPI-B recommended the rapid offer of free isolation accommodation outside the home, especially for households with vulnerable members.[120] In February 2021, PHE recommended do-it-yourself out-of-home isolation:

> Where possible, arrange for anyone who is clinically vulnerable or clinically extremely vulnerable to move out of your home, to stay with friends or family for the duration of your home isolation.[121]

Some UK citizens did have access to isolation accommodation. In the earliest weeks of the UK outbreak, all confirmed cases were hospitalised 'for isolation rather than clinical management purposes'.[122] NHS staff who became infected were given the option to move into a free hotel for their isolation in order to avoid infecting household members, paid for by the NHS at up to £100 a night. Rough sleepers were provided with self-contained accommodation, and in London, those who had COVID-19 could be 'clinically monitored in a safe infection control environment' in a specialist hotel.[123] In 2021, the London Borough of Newham provided free isolation accommodation.[124] Newham had high proportions of large, overcrowded, multi-generational households, and was the local authority with the highest age-standardised COVID-19 death rate in the UK (see Chapter 3). Under the scheme, anyone in a household where someone had tested positive but the others were still negative and someone was older or vulnerable, or someone had to work or care outside the home, could get a free hotel room to cover the infectious period.

Isolation accommodation was never provided on a large scale in the UK, although there was substantial capacity. From March to July 2020, there were 700,000 vacant hotel rooms, and hundreds of thousands of vacant spaces in student accommodation. Some groups of hotels contacted local government and the NHS in early 2020, offering to provide convalescent accommodation to prevent discharge of people with possible COVID-19 into care homes.[125] MP Barbara Keeley said that some care providers offered potential isolation accommodation but "they received no response from the Government".[126]

Reducing risk for people in shared housing

SPI-B said that 'Mitigations and isolation may be difficult to enforce mutually' in shared homes. It recommended more advice and model 'social contracts' to set out safe behaviour. It also suggested that that 'enforcement of safe home environment rules on the rental sector' would reduce the risk to people on low incomes.[127] It also recommended emergency grants to landlords for repairs and, for example, to improve ventilation.[128] These recommendations were not acted upon.

Reducing risk for people in flats

Managers of larger blocks of flats, whether freeholders or social or private landlords, could mitigate risk to some extent through more cleaning, ventilation and advice to residents. Social landlords provided considerable advice and support to residents, which would have helped them **stay home** successfully. There was also advice on social distancing in communal spaces – for example, in using lifts (Photo 3). However, policy, implementation and practice varied. In the local authority where the photo was taken, other social landlords did not forbid or recommend against lift sharing (for example, in my block).

Photo 3: One London social landlord warns its tenants about the risk of shared spaces, January 2020

Reducing risk at work in household with members working outside the home

Non-policies to reduce risk of infection at home from work outside the home include better protection at work, assisting moves of high-risk or high-vulnerability people (see Chapter 4), and reassigning work roles for those with vulnerable household members (see Chapter 6). In a study of NHS staff in Scotland, the authors proposed that employers should 'redeploy healthcare workers from patient facing to non-patient facing roles if they *or their households* [emphasis added] are more susceptible to severe disease'.[129] Similar approaches could have been applied in other workplaces to protect employees and their households.

Resilience

Finally, SAGE also made recommendations for long-term, structural policies that would not affect the current pandemic, but might improve resilience for future shocks. It said that government should 'Pursue longer term programmes to reduce deprivation' and local authorities should be helped to 'improve the affordability and quality of social and private rental accommodation'.[130]

Being vulnerable or ill at home in the pandemic

This chapter focuses on being vulnerable to COVID-19 infection, other physical or mental health problems, or because of the need for care and support. Readers requiring detailed analysis of vulnerability to health-harming behaviours or to domestic abuse are advised to turn to specialised sources.

Shielding and isolating at home

Introduction

'Shielding' and 'isolating' were the strictest forms of **staying home** (see Chapter 3). Millions of people who were particularly vulnerable to serious illness and death if they become infected were asked to shield, initially partly to protect the NHS from having too many serious cases, and latterly for their own protection.[1] Millions more with COVID-19 or suspected of having it were asked to isolate in order to protect others, primarily people outside their household.

The high COVID-19 risk and isolation of vulnerable people in care homes during the pandemic has been widely acknowledged. However, the situation of vulnerable people shielding at home has been less recognised. Shielding alone amounted to prolonged solitary confinement, which is prohibited by the United Nations. Shielding and isolating with others was risky. Shielders and isolators became new types of dependent people, and most relied on family and friends for support.

Many people did not have the right homes for shielding and isolating. Pre-existing inequalities in housing space (see Chapter 2) worsened during the pandemic (see Chapter 4), and became more dangerous, because they affected the risk of transmission at home (see Chapter 5). People on low incomes, of minority ethnicity and tenants were disadvantaged. Shielding and isolating had personal and financial costs, which were not recognised or compensated fully or (in the case of shielders) at all. Inequalities reduced the effectiveness of shielding and isolating, and meant that some infections and deaths occurred which could have been avoided.

People at most risk from COVID-19

In March 2020, the chief medical officers of the four nations of the UK drew up a list, based on what was known at the time, of conditions likely to make people 'clinically extremely vulnerable' (CEV) to COVID-19 infection or severe disease. These conditions included reduced immunity due to cancer treatment, cystic fibrosis, severe asthma and severe chronic obstructive pulmonary disease.[2] From 22 March 2020, letters were sent to the people on the list to recommend that they should 'shield' at home. Coordinated announcements were made by the four nations' governments.

Initially, 1.5 million people were identified in England. Over the course of 2020, the list lengthened, as information about risk improved and as groups lobbied to be included. (In 2020, I was using immunosuppressant medicines because I was in remission from blood cancer. I received a shielding letter in August 2020, five months into pandemic measures, and after having had COVID-19). By the time shielding ended in September 2021, the list for England had 3.7 million names, making up 7% of the population.[3] In Scotland, the list was fairly stable at around 180,000 names or 3% of the population. In Wales, by May 2020, the list had 131,000 names or 4% of the population.[4] These lists remained significant throughout 2021 and into 2022, as CEV status conferred priority for vaccinations.

Guidance on shielding

From March 2020, people who were defined as CEV were advised not to leave their homes, even to get food and medicine. They could have visits from essential carers. If they lived with others, they should try to maintain social distancing from them at home. Shielders could legitimately refuse to work outside the home. They could get priority access to supermarkets and, via local authorities, could reach council and voluntary food and medicine deliveries, and in some cases phone befriending, to supplement what family and friends could do.

Shielding was an even more dramatic restriction on freedom than **staying home** for the general population, and it lasted much longer. Shielding rendered people housebound and dependent on others. It never became law, possibly because it would have faced legal challenge. The initial guidance was to shield for 12 weeks. On 1 June 2020, shielders were told they could leave home to meet one person from another household, and on 6 July 2020, if they lived alone, they could form support bubbles (see Chapter 4). In England and Scotland, shielding initially lasted for 18 weeks until 1 August 2020, when it was 'paused'. Then employed shielders who could not work at home were told they should return to their workplaces. Shielding restarted in England on 19 December in Tier 4 areas and then resumed nationwide during the lockdowns from January 2021. Scotland did not formally restart shielding, due to concern about the harm it could cause, preferring to aim at informed choice for vulnerable people.[5] Shielding continued in England

and Wales until 1 April 2021 when it was 'paused' again. It ended formally in England in September 2021 and in Wales in March 2022.[6]

Who shielded

Most CEV people followed guidance closely.[7] Other people also decided to shield or at least to follow more restrictive practices than recommended for the general population for at least part of the pandemic, even if they were not formally 'CEV'. In June/July 2020, 17% of households in England had at least one person who reported they were shielding, and in November/December 2020, during the second wave, the figure was 21%.[8] This would have amounted to at least 4.9 million people. These informal shielders included shielders' household members and people not on the CEV list, but at above-average risk.[9] In March 2020, the NHS listed conditions putting people at 'moderate risk', which included large minorities of the population. People aged over 70 made up 13% of people in England in 2019/20, 8% had diabetes, 6% had asthma, 4% had chronic kidney disease, 3% had severe obesity and 3% had heart failure. These people were not required by guidance to shield and did not get official support to do so, but many chose to adopt an informal form of shielding. In May 2020, a 62-year-old woman said "Having autoimmune disease ... chron's and underactive thyroid is not great in 2020." Carers UK noted 'confusion ... among carers about the meaning of shielding'.[10]

Based on the English shielding list in July 2020, 52% of all CEV people were women, despite the fact that it was known early on that men were at greater risk from COVID-19 (see Chapter 3). A total of 63% were aged 60 or over and 30% were 75 or over,[11] 23% had severe chronic obstructive pulmonary disease and 8% had severe asthma.[12] At least in Scotland, CEV people were more likely to live in deprived neighbourhoods.[13] The proportion of people defined as CEV varied markedly between regions and local authorities, probably because of different practices in identification as well as different prevalence of risk.[14] There is no medical data on the bigger group of self-reported shielders, but they had distinctive characteristics. In June/July 2020, 53% of self-reported shielders in England were women, and 32% of households with an HRP aged 65 or more had a self-reported shielder. A total of 26% of households in the lowest quintile of income had a shielder, compared to 8% in the highest quintile, while 24% of social renting households, 23% of outright owners, and 9% of mortgaged owners and private renters had a shielder.[15]

Many shielders were registered disabled or had limiting long-term conditions, but guidance and law on pandemic measures made little explicit reference to the legally protected category of 'disability'. NGOs said disabled people have been disproportionately affected by the disease itself as well as by policies introduced in response to COVID-19 ... disabled people and the staff and carers supporting them [have been] simply overlooked.[16]

Guidance and law on isolating

From a few weeks from 30 January 2020, all people in the UK known or deemed likely to have COVID-19 were isolated in hospital, even if they had only minor symptoms (see Chapter 5). Hospital isolation ended on 10 March 2020 as the 'containment' phase of the national Coronavirus Plan ended. From that point on, people known or likely to have the virus were asked to isolate at home.[17] NHS England said 'Self-isolation is when you do not leave your home because you have or might have coronavirus.'[18] Isolators could not go out for any reason, and could not receive visitors, other than carers.[19] Like shielders, isolators became dependent on others for essentials.

Policy evolved as research, testing and understanding of risk developed. On 26 February 2020, Matt Hancock said that if one household member had tested positive, the rest of the household "should go about their normal business in the normal way".[20] From 16 March, isolation was extended to ten days for people living alone,[21] where they lived with others, and 14 days for the whole household. On 28 May, NHS Test and Trace was launched in England and gradually began phoning people with positive test results and their 'close contacts' in and outside their household to tell them to isolate. Similar systems were created in the other nations. In late 2020, local tracing developed to supplement the national system.[22] In July 2020 in England, isolation was extended to include other members of any bubble, and to the households of children in a school 'bubble' where someone had tested positive. From 24 September 2020 when the NHS App was launched, isolation was extended to people 'pinged' to tell them that they had been within two metres for at least 15 minutes of someone who later tested positive. From 28 September 2020, isolating became a legal obligation, punishable with a fine of up to £10,000.[23] On 11 December 2020, the period of isolation was reduced from 14 days to 10 days for the infected person or suspected case, but remained at 14 days for household members.[24] In December 2020, people could leave isolation if they tested themselves negative on day six and seven of their **stay home**. From 16 August 2021, people who had been fully vaccinated no longer had to isolate when another household member did.[25] On 17 January 2022, mandatory self-isolation was reduced to five days, and on 24 February it was ended entirely.

Who isolated

Isolation was brief compared to shielding (see earlier). However, it involved much larger proportions of the population. By 2022, there had been

12 million recorded positive tests and probably millions of further unrecorded positive self-tests (see Chapter 3). Isolation received more political attention than shielding, partly because it involved more people, because failures in isolation affected other people in addition to the isolator and their household, and because more isolators had to interrupt work to isolate

While some people who tested positive were hospitalised,[26] at least 11 million people knew they should have isolated at home. Others may have isolated after symptoms or because they were contacts of people with the virus. From November 2020 to April 2021, NHS Test and Trace called 3.2 million people to tell them to isolate, and almost twice as many contacts.[27] In February/March 2021, a woman aged 50 said "my daughter had to isolate twice before the latest lockdown while her friends were at school". A woman aged 62 said her daughter had to isolate three times in her room in a flatshare, when flatmates who worked for the NHS, and then teacher colleagues got COVID-19. By 2022, Sir Keir Starmer, leader of the Labour Party, had had to isolate six times.

As a cancer charity told HSC/STC: "The language and communication around shielding, isolating and social distancing has been confused."[28] Self-reported 'isolators' appear to include people avoiding social contact to protect themselves as well as to protect others.[29] In April 2020, 41% of people in Great Britain said they were isolating, but the proportion fell to under 10% by August 2020 and remained at that level until at least November 2021, with only a very small increase during the second wave of infections (Figure 6.1) (see Chapter 2).[30]

For children, isolation was a majority experience. From September to December 2020, 60% of all school children in England had to take time off school to isolate. Some 7% of all school days were lost due to COVID, and for children on free school meals (a measure of low family income), the figure was 8.5%.[31]

There were big regional variations in self-reported isolation by adults, which suggested that people were responding to changing local patterns of infection and risk (see Chapter 3). For example, in June/July 2020, 43% of households in the North West had had someone isolating at some point, compared to 34% in the South East. By November/December 2020, the start of the second wave, the rate jumped to 51% in the North West and 46% in the West Midlands, but changed little elsewhere.

How shielders responded to the guidance

In May 2020, 63% of people who were CEV in England were following the (voluntary) guidelines 'completely'. A total of 65% were not leaving their homes or only doing so for exercise, while 86% were not receiving visitors, apart from carers. Before the pandemic, 28% of CEV people in England

Figure 6.1: Proportion of adults who were isolating, Great Britain, March 2020–November 2021

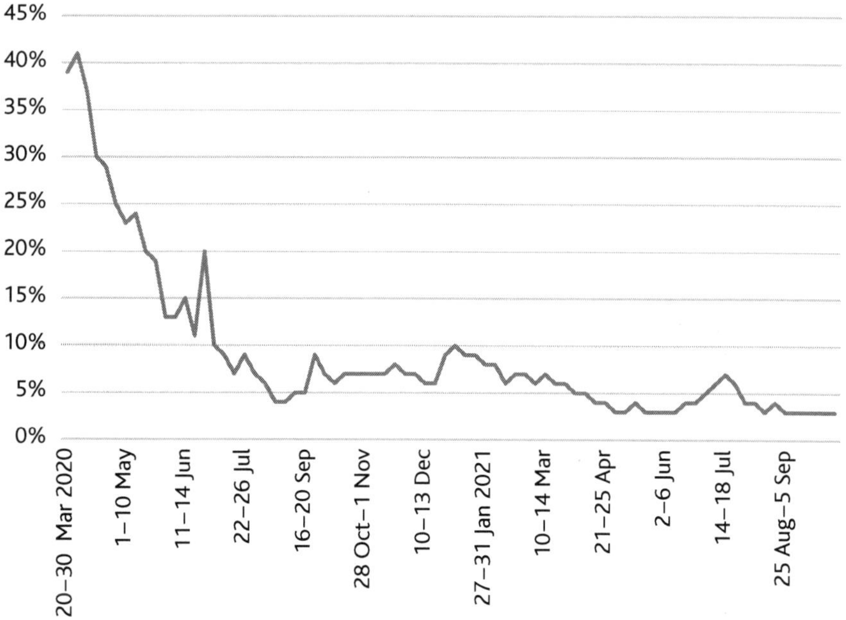

Source: ONS 2022a, Table 1a

were working outside the home. By July 2020, 10% of CEV people were working from home, while 14%, or at least 690,000 people, had stopped work. This would mean lost income for most, even if they were furloughed (see Chapter 7). Only 3% continued to work outside the home, against guidelines.[32] Some 18% of households in England where the HRPs was shielding had applied for a mortgage holiday by June/July 2020, reflecting difficulty in paying for housing,[33] compared to 10% overall (see Chapter 7).

In July 2020, when guidance had eased, 34% of CEV people had not left their home since March 2020.[34] By February/March 2021, some shielders had been **staying home** for almost a year, despite the official 'pause' in shielding. A middle-aged woman with multiple sclerosis said:

> "My husband and I haven't left the house for a year now except to shop for essentials. Now I get my shopping online so we don't go out much at all ... I do feel increasingly isolated, but we are lucky that we do get on well at home."

Blood Cancer UK found that among its members, 'people deviating from the shielding guidance were primarily doing so for unavoidable reasons or to cautiously exercise'.[35] The Arthritis Society said that almost a third of its members who were shielding had stopped early because they needed more exercise, more social contact or to get food and essentials.[36] Some were pressured to stop to maintain jobs and income. A 62-year-old said:

> "Coronavirus has caused me to shield twice ... I am worried my employer will no longer require me when shielding ends ... I continued to work through the second shielding period as I couldn't afford to shield."

A woman aged 62 working as a sheltered housing warden described the additional tasks in caring for shielders:

> "My duties have changed, I shop for people, pick up scrips [sic], I've been cooking for people without family, I've found one of my tenants passed away ... I felt vulnerable as we have no PPE, told we don't need it, I've been very tired."

There was an unprecedented burst of voluntary activity in early 2020, with the establishment of thousands of new small local mutual aid groups, and recruitment of new volunteers by existing organisations.[37] (After I realised I had antibodies to COVID, I started volunteering for a small local Somali education and employment charity, which diversified during the pandemic into delivering cooked meals to people housebound by shielding or isolation, mainly of White and Bangladeshi origin.) However, overall, it was family members who were affected by the drawn-out pressure of supporting and protecting shielders. In February/March 2021, a 19-year-old whose younger sisters had been shielding for a year said:

> "My mother mostly cannot even get out to go shopping as the single mother of disabled children. This causes me a great deal of worry daily, so I subsidise shopping delivery for my family."

In June and July 2020, schools reopened to all students, which was a concern for the 15% of CEV people with children at home. In July 2020, employers could require CEV people to return to work on site. A woman who had a child who was shielding informally said:

> "20 pupils in a classroom and only my child was wearing a mask. Yay! ... Each subject is a bubble of 20, which means at least 60 exposures per school day."

A shielder who usually worked in a school said:

> "My stress levels have gone through the roof ... people can only have one family from one other household into their house ... it seems that ... it's OK for me to be in a room with 15–30 children ... from 15–30 households."[38]

Carers UK found that 74% of its members were worried about work, and many said they would not return to work, would continue to home-school and would not invite visitors even where it was permitted by guidelines.[39]

How isolators responded to guidance and law

In February 2021, 97% of people in the UK thought isolating was an effective way to prevent COVID, 98% supported the legal requirement to isolate and 80% said it was easy to isolate.[40] However, this did not translate into perfect compliance.

Some people with COVID-19 were unaware they had the infection. Asymptomatic transmission was recognised in February 2020 (see Chapter 4), but before tests became widely available, isolation was based on people judging their own symptoms (sometimes with the aid of NHS 111). Testing was initially only available to those who had symptoms.[41] A summary of 37 DHSC surveys carried out between March 2020 and January 2021 found that only 52% of UK adults knew the three main symptoms of COVID-19. (You might want to check if you know them: cough, fever and loss of taste or smell, at least for variants up to Omicron.) A total of 57% of people in the least-deprived quarter of neighbourhoods knew the symptoms compared to 45% in the most-deprived quarter of neighbourhoods. 54% of White British people knew the symptoms, compared to 39% of Asian people and 32% of Black people.[42] The groups with the weakest knowledge of symptoms had the highest rates of infections and deaths (see Chapter 3). Poor knowledge of symptoms is an underrecognised failing in public policy and source of inequality.

The extent to which people were isolating correctly became a political issue in mid-2020. Different surveys of isolation intentions and behaviours produced varying results.[43] Fancourt et al found that in early 2020, 80% said they were 'isolating' for at least ten days when they met someone with COVID, but 50% were isolating for 21 days or more, suggesting different understandings of 'isolation', while 12% were not isolating at all and 8% were isolating for less than the required time.[44] In February 2021, the ONS found that 86% of people (including those who had not had COVID-19 or been in contact with it) said they had 'fully adhered' to the rules for isolation (without specifying the rules).[45] A summary of DHSC surveys from March to August 2020 created alarm when it found that if people were specifically asked if they had 'not left home' when they had symptoms, on average only 18% had **stayed home**.[46] It found that 79% of people said they would 'probably or definitely' would name their contacts to Test and Trace services if they were contacted themselves.[47] Meanwhile, 21% said they would not, although it is likely that many people with symptoms talked informally to their own contacts. A further summary from March 2020 to January 2021 found that on average 43% who had COVID-19 in the past week had **stayed home** as required, suggesting compliance improved over the second wave.[48]

Support for isolators

There was some evidence that practical circumstances affected the ability to isolate. The ONS found that of those who had not fully adhered to isolation rules, 27% went out to go shopping, 22% to work or school and college, 17% to go to a medical appointment and 5% to provide care.[49] Men, younger people, and people on lower incomes were least likely to isolate correctly.[50] The March–August 2020 DHSC surveys found that the main reasons to go out were to get food or medicine, because symptoms improved and for non-COVID-19 medical needs. Those most likely to go out did not know the symptoms, thought they had already had COVID, had a child or were key workers. People in deprived areas, and Black and Asian people were slightly less likely than average to say they would name contacts via NHS Test and Trace. From March 2020 to January 2021, DHSC surveys found that men, younger people, White people, households with children, people from a lower social class and people experiencing more financial hardship were less likely to stick to the rules.[51]

In February 2021, 32% of those in the UK who were working and had had to isolate said they lost income. Over the course of the pandemic, this would have meant income loss for millions. A total of 38% continued to work (many at home), 21% were not working but were on full pay, 8% were on Statutory Sick Pay (SSP, worth £95 a week) and 13% were not paid at all.[52] In June/July 2020, a 62-year-old woman working in care said:

> "Seeing staff putting their lives and their families lives at risk every day and then to tell them when they are finally tested positive that their pay will be £95 a week is heartbreaking … that is one of the factors why the virus is spreading people can't afford to be sick i.e. my rent alone is £125 a week?"

A mother of two who was a school cleaner said: "Had to self-isolate for two weeks then a further month signed off by doctor with depression. My pay went down on SSP. Still haven't recovered financially."[53] In addition, SSP was not available to people who were self-employed, on maternity leave, waiting for contracts to start and earning below the National Insurance threshold.[54] The issue was raised as early as 11 February 2020, when Matt Hancock was asked by MP Clive Efford for advice for people on zero-hours contacts.[55] In November 2020, Dominic Cummings told the House of Commons HSC/STC committee: "There wasn't any plan for financial incentives [for isolation]. There wasn't any plan for almost anything in any kind of detail."[56]

In August 2020, an isolation payment was piloted in the high-infection areas of Blackburn with Darwen, Pendle, and Oldham.[57] In September 2020, it was extended across England, with a flat figure of £500 per household, for people who had been contacted by NHS Test and Trace, who were working or self-employed, or who were unable to work at home and claiming UC or Working Tax Credit (to indicate low income).[58] By February 2021, only 2% of those who had to isolate received a Test and Trace Support payment.[59] Most applications were rejected as ineligible. The London Borough of Newham developed its own scheme, which was open to people not in work as well as those working, with household incomes up to £34,000 for claimants with dependants, and it paid up to £738.[60]

By March 2022, when the scheme ended, 541,000 households in England had received isolation payments, including 4,000 in both Blackburn and Newham, totalling £270 million.[61] Overall, inadequate support for people on low incomes to isolate has been described as being among the main flaws in the UK response.[62] Dominic Harrison, DPH for Blackburn with Darwen, said some people didn't want to give contacts as: "They do not want to cause the rest of their family … to lose their capacity to feed their family."[63] In November 2020, when looking into higher rates of infection and death among Black and minority ethnic people, SAGE recommended 'greater levels of financial payment for self-isolation'.[64] Baroness Harding, CEO of NHS Test and Trace, said:

> "It is wasteful to invest up to £37 billion of public money to detect potential virus carriers if they are not then supported to comply with an isolation request."[65]

SAGE and SPI-B advised universal support for people on low benefit incomes to improve isolation: the benefit cap should be removed at least temporarily, and the 'bedroom tax' should 'be immediately revisited'[66] (see Chapter 2). The HSC/STC said of the isolation rule and limited support, that

> "by providing a powerful disincentive to take a COVID test and to disclose all contacts, it seems likely that it will have also caused more infections and cost lives".[67]

Shielders' and isolators' households

The practicalities and social and economic consequences of shielding and isolating varied according to the person's household.[68]

Living alone

In July 2020, 26% of CEV people in England lived alone.[69] In June/July 2020, 32% of all households with self-reported shielders were one-person households and in November/December 2020, the figure was 43%.[70] Living alone had the advantage that there was no risk of transmission between household members. However, shielders and isolators living alone were dependent on assistance from outside their households. Only 9% of CEV people registered with the national helpline to get extra support, so 91% or 3.4 million relied on household members, family, private services, or local mutual aid and voluntary services.[71]

In July 2020, 14% of CEV people had received visits for care at home in the past week, whether from health or care professionals or family and friends, 4% had visits daily, 5% on some days and 5% on one day.[72] A total of 35% had social visits and deliveries from family and friends in the past week, 2% had visits daily, 14% on some days and 19% weekly.[73] In May 2020, a woman aged 62 who was shielding said "I see two members of my family once or twice a week when they drop off fresh food – but I wouldn't call it socialising". A woman aged 50 commented:

> "Previously I spent a day a week caring for my elderly parents, one of whom has mild dementia and moderate anxiety. Now I only spend a couple of hours and maintain [the] two-metre distance, in the garden only … this is an enormous emotional strain."

A woman aged 50 said "my dad is 78, lives on his own has been really hard just dropping off shopping once a week at his door and not being able to give him a hug".

Shielders living alone and following the guidelines experienced the equivalent of 'prolonged solitary confinement'. This is defined by the United Nations as being alone for 22 or more hours a day for 15 or more days.[74] Shielders living alone and following guidelines could have been alone at home 24 hours a day for a total of 129 days in 2020 before the 'pause'. The use of solitary confinement in prisons is regulated due to the proven negative effect on mental health.[75] In July 2020, 59% of CEV people said their mental health had not changed since they had been told to shield, but 37% said it was worse, 7% said it was much worse and only 4% said it was better.[76] Among women, 42% said their mental health was worse and 8% said it was much worse.

Living with others

In July 2020, 74% of CEV people in England lived with others, as did a majority of self-reported shielders and isolators. These shielders and isolators had people to socialise with and to go shopping for them, but were still cut off from most people and most opportunities. They also ran the risk of infection at home. On 26 February 2020, Conservative MP Stephen Hammond asked "what self-isolation might mean for ... a family in which one person may be symptomatic, or groups of university students?".[77] Researchers commented in May 2020:

> 'Policy advice has so far been oriented towards mitigating individual health risk, without much consideration of how old and young individuals are nested within different household[s].'[78]

While only 3% of CEV people in England were still working outside their home in July 2020, 73% were in households where someone was going out and 26% were in households where someone had gone out every day in the past week.[79] A total of 15% of CEV people lived with at least one child under 16, likely to need personal care and, from June or July 2020, to be going to school. Some 21% of these people said living with a child made it difficult to shield.[80] Family and household members of shielders took on the responsibility of trying to avoid bringing infection home, which could mean considerable constraint on activities. Isolators and their household members also had to try to avoid transmission, and not all households would be able to do so fully (see Chapter 5).

Shielders' and isolators' homes

The homes where someone had to shield or isolate were fairly typical of all UK homes (see Chapter 2). However, this meant that many were not suitable for effective shielding and isolating (see Chapter 5). In June/July 2020, 47% of multi-person households where someone had to shield did not have a spare bedroom for them, and 32% did not have anywhere they could sleep alone, while 63% lacked a bathroom for their sole use.[81]

Housing inequalities, shielding and isolating

Pre-existing inequalities in housing space (see Chapter 2) worsened during the pandemic (see Chapter 4), and became more dangerous, because they affected the risk of transmission of COVID-19 at home (see Chapters 4 and 5). There were substantial inequalities in the ability to reduce risk of infection at home by moving people between households or using spare rooms at home. It is likely that inequalities in housing space contributed to inequalities in infections and deaths (see Chapter 3).

People on low incomes were more likely to have shielders and isolators at home (and more likely to have people working outside the home; see Chapters 3 and 4), so they had more need to avoid infection at home. However, they had less capacity to do so, because they were less likely to have spare bedrooms and bathrooms (Figure 6.2).

Similarly, social renters were the most likely tenure group to have someone who had to shield or isolate, but the least likely to have a spare bedroom or bathroom (Figure 6.3). Outright owners were almost as likely to have some who had to shield or isolate as social renters, but were much more likely to be able to do so safely and effectively.

Households with a White HRP were slightly more likely than most other ethnic groups to have someone shielding or isolating, probably linked to their higher average age. However, some minority ethnic groups were much less likely than average to have the means to shield and isolate safely (Figure 6.4).

Overall, the performance of the UK housing system in providing places for effective home shielding and home isolating fits the 'inverse care law', by which people with the most health need have the least medical help or resources to deal with it.[82] These inequalities could have been mitigated to some extent through adopting some of the non-policies described above.

How UK homes served for shielding and isolating compared to those in other countries

Many people in the UK did not have the right households or homes for shielding, isolating and **staying home**. However, the UK was one of the best-housed nations in Europe for limiting risk from COVID-19 infection at home, and was better off in this respect than most other countries in the world.

In 2018, the proportion of all people in the UK living in multi-person households, and thus at risk of infection at home, was 83%, very similar to the EU average. A total of 56% of people (rather than households) in the UK were in a household with at least one spare room, which made it the fifth best-housed country in the group, after Malta, Cyprus, Ireland and Belgium, and well ahead of the EU average of 36%. The UK was also the fifth least-overcrowded country in the survey, with 5% in overcrowded households, after Cyprus, Ireland, Malta and the Netherlands, and well ahead of the EU average of 16%. In addition, in 2018, 85% of UK people lived in houses rather than flats, avoiding risks of communal spaces, the second

Figure 6.2: Percentage of households with someone shielding or isolating, and the facilities to do so safely, by income group, England, June/July 2020

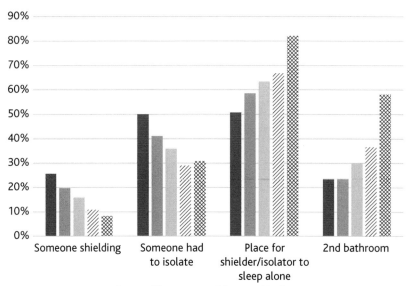

■ Lowest income quintile ■ 2nd lowest ■ Middle ⁄ 2nd highest ⊠ Highest income quintile

Source: MHCLG 2020a

Figure 6.3: Percentage of households with someone shielding or isolating, and the facilities to do so safely, by tenure, England, June/July 2020

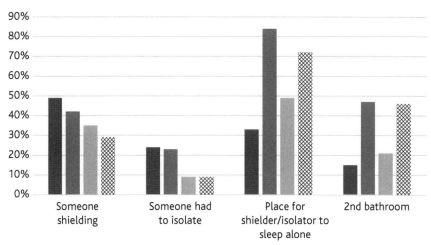

■ Social renter ■ Outright owner ■ Private renter ⊠ Mortgaged owner

Source: MHCLG 2020a, Tables T05b, T06b, T07b, T08b

Figure 6.4: Percentage of households with someone shielding or isolating, and the facilities to do so safely, by ethnic group of HRP, England, June/July 2020

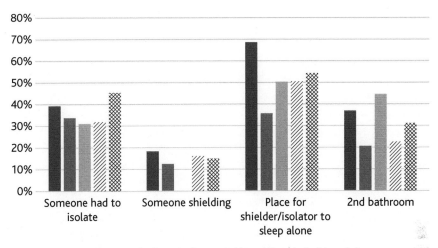

Note: Data for shielding for the Indian group not available because of small numbers
Source: MHCLG 2020a

highest proportion of houses in the EU after Ireland at 92% and well above the EU average of 57%.[83]

Avoiding other household members within the home

In February 2020, the Secretary of State for Health Matt Hancock said that in a multi-person household, isolation (or shielding) meant "trying to stay away from others living in that house. I appreciate that that is, practically, challenging and difficult".[84] In September 2020, SPI-B argued for 'clear communication' about the value of doing this, even if it seemed 'un-natural' or even 'immoral'.[85]

In February 2021, the first ONS survey of isolators who lived with others in England found that 21% could keep separate from the rest of the household all of the time, 25% could do so most of the time, 19% some of the time and 36% not at all.[86] Those with children in the household found it slightly more difficult. In May 2020, a woman aged 50 had had cancer treatment, but her husband was working, so for some weeks "I lived in one room and only came out when he was at work. This we both found very difficult". A woman aged 50 was vulnerable and her partner was working, so she had moved into the spare room:

"we do not get within two metres of each other in our own home which is difficult as our home isn't that big, we keep everything separate inc our own toilet rolls. As we don't have two bathrooms I have to clean and disinfect the one we do every time my husband uses it".

At this point, she expected that shielding would last for just 12 weeks; it only ended finally in September 2021 after 75 weeks. In February/March 2021, a shielding woman aged 62 had been was sleeping in the spare room since March 2020, trying to keep away from her husband, who was a key worker, and her adult daughter: "it has been incredibly hard".

Isolators had similar, if much briefer, experiences. In May 2020, a man aged 50 had had some symptoms, but in the absence of testing, "I was unsure I actually did have the virus but did sleep in the spare room for two weeks". In February/March 2021, a respondent who lived with their partner and both had to isolate said

"Doing ten days in isolation in a one-bedroom flat with no garden and no access to the outside at all during that time was particularly tough and put a massive strain on my relationship."

A lone parent with a son and daughter in a two-bed flat had been told to isolate: "I share a room with my daughter [in a two-bed flat] so have currently moved my bed into the living room."

Mask-wearing at home did not appear to be widely practised, although it was recommended by the later stages of the pandemic.[87] In November 2021, only 12% of those who had had visitors in their home in the past week had worn a face mask and only 5% had asked the visitor to wear one.[88]

Giving up work

Some family members gave up work and income to avoid risk to vulnerable household members. In May 2020, a woman aged 62 said her adult son was not working or volunteering, because his grandmother had moved in, and "the family feels ... he cannot risk bringing COVID-19 into our home". A woman aged 62 said "my husband is shielding so I have chosen not to work to protect him". She could not work from home and her temporary contract (with the NHS) meant she could not be furloughed. In February/ March 2021, a 19-year-old living with his parents and grandma said "I had to leave work to keep my grandma safe ... I have been using my savings to pay my phone bills and help out with rent but I am down to my last 100". A person aged 31 had rejected offers of work from their zero-hours employer, saying "I can't go to work because I live with three other people, two of whom are more or less 'elderly'". These people were providing a hidden subsidy for national pandemic policy, which cost them considerably and may have contributed to COVID-19 inequality (see Chapter 7).

Did shielding and isolation efforts work?

Shielders' and isolators' efforts cost a lot of money, effort and heartache, and are likely to have had as-yet unquantified health, personal and financial costs for them and their friends and family. The British Geriatrics Society said (albeit without quantitative substantiation): "For many older people, lockdown poses almost as much threat as contracting COVID-19."[89] Shielders and their families had strong individual incentives to make shielding work, and preventing infections in vulnerable people also had community benefits in reducing demands on the health service.

Shielding was 'impossible to implement perfectly'.[90] Vulnerability to COVID-19 risk was not always recognised, the most vulnerable people depended on at least some contact with others, and most lived with others. In addition, large numbers of people at moderate risk will always be outside any shielding strategy. However, modelling suggested that infection, illness and death rates were very sensitive to the effectiveness of shielding, so that even small changes in effectiveness could have had a marked effect on shielder deaths.[91]

Despite shielding efforts, from March to July 2020, 4% of CEV people in England had experienced COVID-19 symptoms.[92] From March to August 2020, 1% of shielders in Scotland had received a positive test, mostly in March and April and due to pre-shielding contacts. However, 0.3% died with COVID, a high infection–fatality ratio.[93] In the second wave (September 2020–July 2021), non-disabled people in England had an age-standardised positive test rate 185.5 per 100,000 person-weeks, which was higher than the rate for disabled people. The rate for those with conditions which limited them 'a little' was 164.0 and for those with conditions which limited them 'a lot' was 152.7.[94] This suggests that 'normal' disability restrictions to mobility and social contact, combined with pandemic restrictions including shielding, did reduce infection. However, this was not enough to compensate for higher vulnerability to serious disease. Despite lower infection rates, people with limiting long-term conditions had markedly higher death rates than others (see Chapter 3).

There were examples of successful shielding and isolation. For example, a man aged 50 whose wife was vulnerable got COVID-19 "and locked myself away in a bedroom for two weeks", and no one else in the house got the infection. There were also examples of tragic failures. A woman aged 50 said that her sister had heart disease and diabetes, and was shielding: "I had been shopping and cooking her meals and passing them to her through the window." Nonetheless, her sister got infected. Getting no response on one visit, "we had to break into her house not knowing how long she had been lying on the floor". She was taken to hospital, diagnosed with a COVID-related stroke and died the next day. In summary, shielding was only partly successful, despite its high personal and social costs.

Getting ill or being ill at home

Introduction

During 2020/21, millions of people were sick at home in the UK with COVID-19 symptoms, and with other conditions that would normally have resulted in hospital admission or other medical attention. Millions were providing care for household members with COVID, while trying to avoid infection, or care for pre-existing and new conditions of other kinds. Tens of thousands of people more than normal died at home.

Most people would probably prefer to be ill at home rather than in hospital, if they could be safe, comfortable and well-cared for.[95] However, the mass experience of being sick at home, including with COVID, placed extra responsibility on the sick people themselves, on their household members and other family and friends, and on homes to provide suitable places for isolation, care and convalescence. It also meant that the role of doctors, NHS 111 and 999 in triaging people into and out of professional care was all the more important.

Being sick at home with COVID-19

The WHO, PHE and the national Coronavirus Action Plan said that most patients would have mild disease, which could be managed at home.[96] By February 2021, after the second wave, over four million people, or 5.9% of the UK population, had tested positive for COVID-19. About 420,000 people had been admitted to hospital with a positive test,[97] so about 90% of those who knew they had COVID-19 were at home with the disease.

Initially there was little knowledge of how to treat COVID, even in hospitals. Early advice on home care focused on avoiding transmission from patient to carers. WHO initially recommended

> a trained [healthcare worker] should conduct an assessment to verify whether the residential setting is suitable ... [and] whether the patient and the family are capable of adhering to the precautions ... (e.g. hand hygiene, respiratory hygiene, environmental cleaning, limitations on movement around or from the house) ... a communication link with [a] healthcare provider ... should be established.[98]

From March 2020, NHS 111 recommended rest, fluids and over-the-counter painkillers for fever, avoiding lying on the back for cough, and techniques to reduce the discomfort of breathlessness. On 30 March 2020, *Private Eye*'s medical correspondent said 'we need to greatly increase community and home palliative care'.[99] In May 2020, a middle-aged woman said "I am so grateful to [my husband] and my children for looking after me when I had COVID". A woman aged 50 commented:

> "My father died of coronavirus. I caught it looking after him and felt unwell for two weeks. My brother also caught it from him and I was worried about him."

In May 2020, 28% of those aged 19, 26% of those aged 31, 41% of those aged 50 and 37% of those aged 62 said they were could not 'count on people around them for help if they were sick in bed'.[100] In November 2020, SPI-B raised the issue of what elderly couples should do when one became ill.[101]

When COVID-19 was no longer 'mild', people should seek professional medical care. In hospital, COVID-19 patients with low blood oxygen had 70% recovery rate, but 'at home they usually died.[102] In March 2020, the usual 1.5 million calls per month to NHS 111 in England rose to 3.0 million temporarily, and the number of 999 calls also increased, before falling below normal levels until April 2021.[103] Again, this was partly due to public reluctance to go to hospital,[104] but there was also hospital reluctance to accept admissions, with raised formal and informal thresholds for ambulance services and A&E admissions.[105] Calls answered between April 2020 and December 2020 were 893,000 (or 13%) below numbers for the same months in 2019, and transfers to care were 454,000 (or 11%) below. Thus, nearly half a million more people remained at home to look after their symptoms themselves, perhaps with some advice. A woman aged 62 had COVID-19 symptoms in May 2020 and said "you do feel vulnerable when your nearest hospital and surgery has become a no-go area". Most people who died of COVID-19 did so in hospital, which suggests they had been triaged and transferred in response to serious illness, although perhaps too late. In addition, some of the 3.5 million people ill at home with COVID-19 did not receive timely professional treatment. In February/March 2021, a woman aged 50 said her younger sister had died of COVID-19 in April 2020:

> "She died unexpectedly at home. The paramedics had been called out a few days earlier and she was told they would not take her to hospital and to take paracetamol … her two teenage children had been looking after her and my brother-in-law who was also poorly. I only imagine the horror they witnessed and I have never been able to talk to them about it."

Being sick at home with long COVID

Over 2020, it gradually emerged that a fraction of people who had had COVID-19 had serious symptoms that lasted for at least 12 weeks after infection. This 'long COVID' was mainly experienced at home, in some cases supported by emerging specialist clinics. In February/March 2021, a man aged 62 said he had noticed something wrong in the spring of 2020: "it seemed my lungs wouldn't expand to their usual volume … the fatigue lasted seven to eight months". A woman aged 50 said "I continued to get better and would then relapse. This carried on for months".

Continuing symptoms after COVID-19 meant that people could not do their usual paid or unpaid work. Some needed care themselves. A woman aged 50 said her husband had survived COVID, but he had had a stroke and "many long COVID-19 symptoms … we had to have our bathroom adapted before he could come home … COVID-19 has changed our lives massively". Another woman aged 50 living with her disabled son said symptoms were "impacting on how I care for him … I find it difficult to lift him and manoeuvre him". Definitions and estimates of prevalence vary, but the ONS found that by July 2021, 1% of the population, amounting to half a million people, still had symptoms that limited daily activities 12 or more weeks after infection.[106] COVID-19 appears to have created a new form of disability, which affects large numbers of people, and is the kind which employers, the benefits system, the care system and even friends and family find hardest to understand and support: medically mysterious and intermittent.

Getting sick and being sick at home

One of the key aims of UK government COVID-19 policy was to 'protect the NHS' (see Chapter 3). This was widely understood to mean ensuring that no one who would benefit from it would be denied intensive care. However, NHS intensive and emergency care was overwhelmed at certain points and in certain places.[107] For example, on 30 December 2020, my local hospital, the Royal London, wrote to staff saying that 'disaster mode' had been activated: 'We are no longer providing high-standard critical care, because we cannot.'[108] Simon Stevens, Chief Executive of NHS England, said in late 2020: "Everybody is getting intensive care and ventilators who clinicians think would benefit." However, he continued, "let's not disguise the fact that this is stretching the system in an extreme way".[109]

COVID-19 took up health system capacity, and infection control meant remaining capacity was used less efficiently. Some urgent and routine activities ceased entirely, and face-to-face attendances at doctors' surgeries and at A&E departments reduced sharply. Even including phone and video, there were 29 million fewer GP appointments from March to December 2020, compared to the same period in 2019. On 18 May 2020, a GP who had restarted home visits 'discovered many frightened people had just sat at home with serious illness – both COVID and non-COVID – and some had died'.[110] From February 2019 to January 2020, NHS England provided a total of 152.9 million outpatients appointments, daycare, admissions and emergency admissions. In 2020/21, there were 125.1 million, a reduction of 27.8 million or 18%, while 27.8 million people were **staying home** with conditions that would normally have received hospital care. In 2021/22, the number of treatments rose, but was still not back to 2019/20 levels, at 143.5 million, 9.4 million or 6% lower than pre-pandemic (Figure 6.5).

Numerous NHS targets were missed over 2020 and 2021,[111] and hospital services had not got back to pre-pandemic levels by the start of 2022.

The perceived impacts of COVID-19 on work, education, finance and relationships declined through 2020 (Figure 1.1), but perceived impacts on health and healthcare grew. In January 2021, 20% of adults in Great Britain said their health was being affected by the pandemic and 25% said their access to healthcare for non-COVID-19 issues was being affected.[112] In July 2020, 23% of CEV people said their underlying condition was worse than in March 2020, while 9% said it was better and 69% said it was the same.[113]

Figure 6.5: Estimate of hospital treatments missed, England, 2020/21 and 2021/22, millions

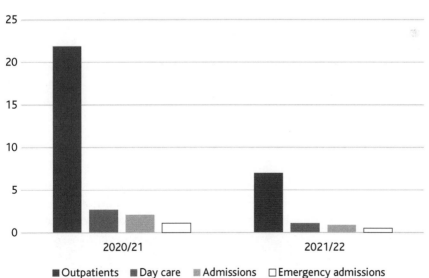

Note: Estimated missed treatments are difference between figures for February 2019–January 2020 and same periods in the following years. Figures exclude maternity admissions
Source: NHS Digital 2021a, 2022

In July 2020, 26% of adults in the UK or 14 million individuals reported that during the pandemic, they had not spoken to a GP or mental health professional when they usually would have done so. A total of 39% of adults or 21 million people reported problems getting care, while 3% of people stopped taking medication at some point because they could not gain access to it. The changes fell unequally and acted to increase health inequality. The reduction in non-COVID-19 emergency admissions was 37% higher in areas with large ethnicity minority populations,[114] and younger people, women and Black and minority ethnic people were most likely to have missed out on GP care.[115] There were also health/health trade-offs. In July 2020, 10% of CEV people, who had been told[116] to shield for the benefit of their health and whom the rest of society were trying to protect, said they were not getting any care, and 21% were missing out on some aspects of care.[117]

In May 2020, a man aged 62 said: "My wife had a significant operation cancelled and we have no idea when it will be rescheduled. It's not life-threatening but it is significant to her health." A man aged 74 noted "my treatments are currently on hold, my Cardiac nurse is currently an ICU nurse!". A woman aged 50 said her father had been given three to five years to live "but all of his hospital and medical appointments have been cancelled. I worry this will accelerate his death". Her mother was waiting for an operation on a hernia "that gives her pain on a daily basis. I have no idea when she'll get the operation now". A person aged 31 said their investigations for Crohn's disease were delayed for nine months and "by the time I received treatment in December I was bedbound". A woman aged 50 had been diagnosed with a benign brain tumour and "had been looking forward to getting my life back on track", but planned surgery had been delayed for at least four months and, due to poor balance, she had broken her foot. In February/March 2021, a person aged 62 noted that the pandemic "has resulted in my major eye condition to be undetected ... resulting in loss of vision". Some cohort members believed that changes in healthcare to manage COVID-19 risk had caused premature deaths. In February/March 2021, a woman aged 50 said her husband had had a cardiac arrest and died. The ambulance staff arrived, but

> "they took so long getting into the house as they had to put on all their PPE on ... under normal circumstances they would have come straight in and he could possibly have been saved ... we were together 32 years".

In February/March 2021 woman aged 31 said her uncle had died of cancer: "he didn't get diagnosed until late in the game because regular services were shut down, then didn't get the chemo and radiation treatment he needed".

Many preventative appointments such as smear tests, eye tests and dentists' check-ups were missed.[118] Healthcare at home, from district nurses, health visitors and GPs, was also affected by professional and patient concern about COVID-19 risk. In February/March 2021, a woman aged 62 said "I have district nurse visits for the past five years ... but won't allow them in since the virus". Access to mental healthcare also worsened. In February/March 2021, a woman aged 62 said her daughter had had a mental health crisis and "access to NHS and social care support services has been hindered/delayed." A person aged 31 with pre-existing mental health problems said "it's been hard to access help. No outreach after two hospitalisations".

In 2020 and 2021, many millions of people were at home with symptoms or conditions that at other times would have received professional treatment. At the start of 2022, NHS waiting lists were at record levels, meaning record number of people were experiencing waiting for healthcare at home, with worry, discomfort, pain and limitations. This represented a 'health/health trade-off' between COVID-19 risk and other health risks. It transferred risk between people, and over time, created new inequalities and will probably create long-term costs.[119]

Dying at home

During the pandemic, the number and proportion of all deaths occurring at home increased significantly. In 2020, 167,000 people died at home in England and Wales, an increase of 42,000 or 34% over the average for 2015–19.[120] Similarly, in Scotland from March to December 2020, 17,000 people died at home, an increase of 5,000 or 38% over the average for 2015–19.[121]

Only 8,000 or 6% of total deaths at home from March 2020 to September 2021 in England and Wales (the first and second waves) were linked to COVID-19, and only 3% of those who died from COVID-19 died at home. Instead, 70% of deaths linked to COVID-19 in England and Wales over this period took place in hospital and 22% in care homes.[122] Similarly, only 334 or 2% of total deaths at home from March 2020 to October 2021 in Scotland were linked to COVID-19, and these cases made up just 3% of Scottish COVID-19 deaths over this period. Instead, 62% of deaths linked to COVID-19 in Scotland and Wales over this period took place in hospital and 32% in care homes.[123]

Extra deaths at home during the pandemic were mainly due to other causes than COVID-19.[124] There were excess deaths among people aged 65 or more from diabetes, epilepsy and hypertensive diseases in the first wave, which the ONS reported 'could all be linked to delayed access to care'.[125] Younger people experienced excess deaths from heart conditions, which could also be linked to delayed treatment. Deaths related to dementia and Alzheimer's mainly occur away from home, in hospitals and care homes, but in 2020 the proportion at home increased sharply from 9% of the 66,000 average total over 2015–19 deaths to 14% of the higher 70,000 2020 total.[126] This suggests that some people with the conditions remained at home when they became ill, while most of the increase in deaths was accounted for by COVID-19 deaths which usually occurred in hospital. In Britain overall, the condition with the biggest increase in deaths at home in the pandemic was cancer, with 59,000 deaths at home in 2020, an increase of 17,000 or 40% compared to the 2015–19 average.[127] The total number of deaths from cancer, at 122,000, was no different to the historic average, although potentially deaths due to pandemic disruption may have occurred in 2021 or later.[128]

However, there is no clear evidence that more time at home and perhaps more exposure to the 'harms of home' named by Gurney[129] (see Chapter 3) led to more deaths. Numbers of death from causes like accidents, violence and suicide were low, and trends were mixed. Deaths at home in England and Wales as a result of accidents increased in 2020 by 19% from an average of 3,163 per year in the 2015–19 period. Deaths at home from mental and behavioural disorders other than dementia increased by 36% from an average of 368. However, deaths at home as a result of intentional self-harm and 'event of undetermined intents' (potential suicide) reduced by 3% from an average of 2,816, and deaths at home as a result of assault, injury or poisoning reduced by 20% from an average of 142.[130]

In 2020, about 47,000 or 36% more individuals and their households or groups of friends and family had to deal with final illness or sudden death at home in Great Britain in 2020 than over the 2015–19 period.[131] Pre-pandemic evidence suggested that most people would prefer to die at home if untimely death could be avoided and eventual death could be comfortable.[132] However, dying at home can be very unpleasant for the person dying and those caring for them.[133] A total of 70% of people in touch with Marie Curie who had cared for someone who died at home with COVID-19 said the dying person did not receive all the care and support they needed, and 29% said they did not have enough pain relief.[134] A carer said:

> "Because of COVID I had to [provide end of life care] virtually single-handed, I found this very stressful as I wanted to let him die at home as he wished but I felt ill equipped."[135]

Losing physical health at home

In addition to disrupting diagnosis and care, for some people, pandemic restrictions caused their own problems, and home became an actively anti-health or harmful environment during the pandemic, due to confinement, lack of social contact and worry.[136] A tour guide aged 62 said:

"When working, I crack out 20,000+ steps on an average all–day tour, but now I can't keep out of the chocolate tin and knitting just doesn't keep the weight off."

In January 2021, 34% of adults in Great Britain said their exercise routine was being affected by the pandemic.[137] By February/March 2021, the total number of smokers in Britain had not changed, but some light smokers were smoking more heavily, and roughly equal numbers were drinking more and drinking less, although heavy drinkers were drinking more.[138] Some people were doing more exercise with their extra free time (see Figure 4.4), but others became immobile. A woman aged 19 said: "Since lockdown mostly being in at home in bed watching Netflix, I feel like I've gained weight ... I feel really bad about myself for the first time ever." Working at home had negative health effects for some, including intensive computer work, as well as more eating and drinking. A man aged 31 said "working from home my back has been really bad without real comfortable chair and desk". A 50-year-old said they were "damaging eyesight working on [a] computer 8–10 hours a day".

This book explores the links between **staying home** and mental health. Readers seeking more detail on physical health-relevant behaviour will need to look elsewhere.

Worsening mental health at home

Surveys and the birth cohort studies show that many people enjoyed at least some aspects of at least the first UK lockdown. Some found that their mental health improved. In May 2020, a middle-aged man said "condolences to the dead ... however, for many I believe this has been a welcome break from the day to day rat race stress". A middle-aged woman noted "I have been enjoying this unexpected time with the children and have been taking many photographs to remember this period". A man aged 62 commented "I have actually been enjoying life under the COVID-19 restrictions more than I normally do". A woman aged 19 said that she had been on the verge of a nervous breakdown in March 2020, so "this shutdown has been an absolute blessing and I get excited when it gets extended, I cannot be more grateful". A woman aged 74 said "I feel less stressed than I have most of my life ... I cannot help [other people] in any way [now] so feel that my life is finally my own". Others at least referred to 'upsides' as well as 'downsides' of **staying home** and other restrictions. For example, in May 2020, a middle-aged lone parent who was a dentist was "extremely worried" about work, money and mortgage, but also "enjoying ... plenty of time with my lovely boys ... very relaxed".

However, on average, mental health worsened, existing mental health problems were exacerbated and new ones developed. The impact of the pandemic on mental health is of concern in its own right. It also summarises the overall multi-dimensional effects. In April 2020, 50% of adults in Great Britain said their wellbeing was being affected by the pandemic, and the figure peaked at 57% in February 2021 (see Figure 1.1).[139] A total of 37% of cohort study participants said their stress levels increased between March and May 2020.[140] Between 2019/20 and June/July 2020, the proportion of HRPs in England who were lonely 'all or most of the time' increased sharply. Anxiety increased, while life satisfaction, life being worthwhile and happiness reduced. The effects persisted until at least April/May 2021 (Figure 6.6).

One study investigating pandemic mental health using clinical measures found that the proportion of British adults with symptoms of moderate or severe depression rose from 7% before the pandemic to 19% in June 2020.[141] Another found that the proportion of UK adults with clinically significant levels of mental distress rose from 19% in 2018/19 to 27% in April 2020.[142] A third found that the average increase in mental distress was similar to the pre-pandemic difference between those in the highest and lowest income decile. In other words, the whole adult population had gone from riches to rags in terms of their mental state.[143] The authors Banks and Xu described the impact on mental health as 'one of the most important aspects of the crisis'.[144] Gurney argued that given the mental ill health associated with **staying home**, home could be seen as inducing ontological insecurity

Figure 6.6: Wellbeing, all HRPs, England, 2019/20–April/May 2021

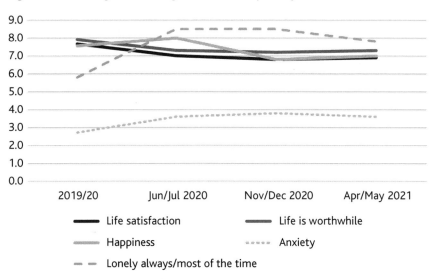

Notes: Mean scores out of ten for indicators except loneliness, which is a percentage
Sources: MHCLG 2020h, Table AT1.26; MHCLG 2020a, Tables 34Aa, Ba, Ca, Da, Ea; MHCLG 2021a, Tables 30Aa, Ba Ca, Da, Ea; DLUHC 2021a, Tables 29Aa, Ba, Ca, Da, Ea

rather than the ontological security lauded by many scholars of housing and home ownership.[145]

A man aged 62 said "at the start I was extremely worried and had two panic attacks. I was prescribed beta blockers". A 19-year-old stated "I started taking anti-depressants at the start of it all ... and have had my dose doubled since then". A person aged 50 said both their children had mental health problems which had "been worsened by COVID-19 – all the usual coping mechanisms – sport, friends, holidays events – are gone". A middle-aged woman said "my autistic younger son [aged 12)] ... is frightened of coronavirus. He started self-harming and has attempted suicide a few times". In February/March 2021, a 19-year-old said "I have found myself feeling alone, useless and even thought about suicide as I hated being confined. I need this to be over soon". A woman aged 62 said "I am usually and upbeat person who laughs a lot ... at the moment I am a nervous wreck who wakes up with a clenched jaw and panic attacks". A woman aged 50 noted "I have cried so many times and over such small things". People reported greater vigilance about their mental health and their efforts to manage it. A 19-year-old student studying at home said "I choose to soldier on. To crack on and to cling to the moments of joy to be found at the minute". A 62-year-old woman commented that she tried to be "proactive: walking, creative church work, sew, garden etc, but resilience has waned".

All three clinical studies found that young people and women were particularly affected.[146] The ONS and Pierce et al found that people in work and with dependant or primary-aged children were also particularly affected.[147] Pierce et al found that on average, men and people who were not working in March 2020 did not experience increases in mental distress.[148] In England, over 2019/20 to June/July 2020, anxiety increased most for social renters. Loneliness increased most for private renters, people on low incomes, lone parents, people who were younger, the unemployed or full-time workers (who may have been furloughed or working at home). Falls in happiness were biggest for mortgaged owners, private renters, part-time workers, younger people and people of Pakistani/Bangladeshi ethnicity.[149]

There were big pre-pandemic inequalities in wellbeing (see Chapter 2), and the pandemic generally increased them.[150] Inequality in terms of loneliness increased between income and employment groups and household types, and in terms of anxiety by tenure. Inequality between age groups increased for all measures, with the youngest being the worst-off and getting more so.[151] Some inequality in wellbeing reduced, but only through levelling down. For example, inequality in life satisfaction between tenure groups reduced because social renters' life satisfaction, which had been the lowest, changed less than that of other tenures.

Household and housing implicated in worsening mental health

Household and home were implicated in the mental health effects of the pandemic, through the effects of household size and type on **staying home**, difficulties with housing costs and concerns about the effect of the pandemic on prospects for housing careers.

Household size and type

Bear et al argued that: 'In the context of the pandemic and lockdown, "living alone" has emerged as a new discursive category of vulnerability.'[152] One-person households had relatively low wellbeing scores both before and during the pandemic. A 50-year-old woman who had previous mental health problems said "living on my own I have felt more lonely and isolated than before". In February/March 2021 a 62-year-old stated "I live alone and it has now become a bit boring". A 50-year-old said "the members of my family who live alone have really struggled". However, many other categories of people were more likely to be 'very or often' lonely and experienced bigger pandemic increases in loneliness rates than one-person households – including HRPs who were unemployed, disabled or caring, on low incomes and lone parents. Similarly, anxiety grew for many groups, but those with higher pre-pandemic anxiety generally had higher increases, so inequalities increased (Figure 6.7).

Other evidence shows little difference between people living alone and others in anxiety and depression in the period from March 2020 to April 2021, but found higher rates of anxiety for people with pre-existing mental health problems, young people, women, people with low incomes, poor physical health and minority ethnicity.[153]

A multi-person household could provide a micro-community and reduce loneliness. A 31-year-old said "renting a large old house with eight people has proved to be not so bad. Interacting with my housemates … has helped to pass the time". However, lockdown could make the well-known potential pitfalls of living with other individuals much worse, due to the time spent together, competition for space and facilities, new sources of tensions over COVID-19 risk and money, and the fact that at some points it wasn't possible to move out or get a new flatmate (see Chapter 3). A woman aged 31 said "I'm trapped in a tiny apartment with two people I thought were my friends but are not". A person aged 19 was relieved because "I now live with a close friend rather than a sharer who believed in some COVID-19 conspiracy theories". People in overcrowded homes also had worse mental health before and during the pandemic.[154]

Some moves between households during the pandemic (see Chapter 4) were associated with an above-average increase in stress, although they may have met needs in other ways. On average, 37% of cohort study participants

Figure 6.7: Anxiety, by household type, economic status and shielding, England, 2019/20–April/May 2021

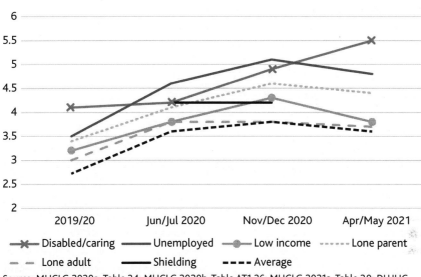

Source: MHCLG 2020a, Table 34; MHCLG 2020h, Table AT1.26; MHCLG 2021a, Table 30; DLUHC 2021a, Table 29

said their stress levels had increased since the pandemic started, compared to 42% of those who moved in with their parents, 49% of those whose children moved in, 48% of those whose children moved out and 58% of those who started cohabiting.[155]

Housing costs

Difficulties paying for housing affect mental health (see Chapter 2). In April/May 2021, renters in arrears had much higher anxiety than other tenants and they also had poor wellbeing on other measures.[156] In February/March 2021, a 50-year-old woman said her husband had lost his job and they had no savings, so they were downsizing:

> "The financial anxiety of not being able to pay the mortgage has affected my mental health ... We have decided to pay off the mortgage so we never have to go through this anxiety again."

Obstruction to housing careers

By February/March 2021, some single respondents were worried about the extended disruption to normal opportunities to meet potential partners. One person said "I am very lonely and depressed as I am unable to meet someone during lockdown and I am 30. I have put on a lot of weight'. In February/March 2021 a 31-year-old said "being single has never felt lonelier. Coronavirus has placed my whole life on hold … I may miss the window for having children". A middle-aged person said "it has become brutally impossible to carry on a relationship". The virus also interrupted transition to independent households. In May 2020, a woman aged 62 stated "my son is trying to purchase a flat and it is staking forever! Is living with us atm which is not idea for him or us as he is 35!'".

Caring and being cared for at home

Introduction

This section refers to the care of adults with additional needs or vulnerability (rather than to childcare and other intra-household care). Professional social care was an important political issue in the UK before the pandemic, and it was widely agreed that social care did not have parity of esteem or of funding with healthcare. However, the majority of social care takes place at home and, while some is provided there by paid professional domiciliary carers, the majority of care work at home is carried out unpaid by family and friends.[157]

The 2011 census found that 5.8 million people in England and Wales, or 10% of the population, provided unpaid care to family members, friends or others because of long-term physical or mental ill health or disability, or problems related to old age. One million unpaid carers provided 50 or more hours a week and 500,000 provided 20–49 hours a week.[158] In comparison, 537,000 were receiving paid care in care homes. A 2020 estimate found 9.1 million people provided unpaid care in the UK.[159] Another estimate found 11 million people provided care in the UK, five million for someone in their own households and six million for someone in another household in 2017/18.[160] In February 2020, 897,000 people on low incomes were caring for at least 35 hours a week and claiming the £67.25 a week of Carer's Allowance.[161] The ONS estimated the value of unpaid adult care at home at £69 billion (at 2020 prices),[162] alongside £443 billion of childcare (see Figure 2.5), and other estimates go up to £100 billion a year. This compares to the £39 billion spent on paid care (£23 billion on local authority care services, £12 billion on care paid for by recipients and £4 billion in the voluntary sector) (at 2020 prices).[163]

During the pandemic, residential care homes experienced very high death rates (see Chapter 5), and it was claimed their residents were initially overlooked and then too tightly restricted. However, people receiving paid care at home had similarly high death rates (see Chapter 5). During the pandemic, care at home became more important because of its role in supporting shielding, and in both creating and reducing risk of infection. However, it was again overlooked and, in addition, its tasks were increased and made more difficult.[164]

Increasing demands on care at home

Some carers said that working at home during the pandemic made their caring role easier.[165] However, overall, things became more difficult for home carers and those they cared for. The pandemic created a new category of millions of dependent people in shielders (as previously discussed). Demands on existing carers also increased because of a reduction in the use of the public and voluntary sector services, and pandemic restrictions. In April 2020, 16% of all adults in Great Britain said their caring responsibilities had increased, reduced or changed. The proportion affected fell to 7% by September 2020, before rising again over the winter of 2020 and then falling over 2021 to 5% in August 2021 (Figure 6.8).

In normal times, hours of unpaid home care can be supplemented by some hours of paid domiciliary care, day centres, respite care, and private cleaners, carers and assistants. During the pandemic, in addition to changes in the use of NHS services, the availability and use of formal care reduced, as organisations and institutions withdrew services, and clients or their relatives

Figure 6.8: Proportion of adults saying their caring responsibilities and their access to care had changed due to the pandemic, Great Britain, April 2020–August 2021

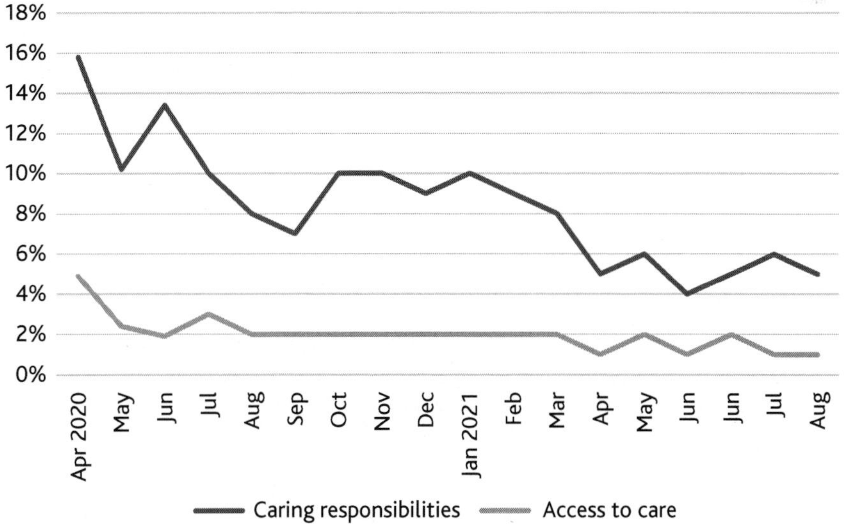

Source: ONS 2022a, Tables 8, 9, 10, 11

were reluctant to use them. Before the pandemic, 16% of those receiving care at home received some state services, but by 2021, only 6% still did so.[166] A majority of carers said domiciliary care had stopped, and a large majority said other forms of support had too. In October 2020, months after the peak of the first wave, 65% of carers reported that local charity services had not reopened, while 61% said the same for local carers' organisations, 49% for day centres and 31% for sitting services.[167]

A person aged 62 said "[I] took my son from his care home due to COVID [and] am now a 24 hour carer for him with my two other sons and some paid assistants". Rules on contact between households and fears of infection disrupted inter-household care networks and tended to concentrate work. A woman aged 62, whose mother was 95, said:

> "Having cancelled other care (cleaners, some home care provision etc) and as my other siblings are all in the vulnerable or extremely vulnerable category, it is left to me to provide care … this has left me extremely stressed at times in case I inadvertently pass it on to her."

A man aged 62 described the processes in his family:

> "[W]e might well have made moves during the past year to move my mother into residential care but we felt that the additional health risk, and the lack of visiting rule this out … access to healthcare has been made more difficult, as she does not cope well with telephone appointments. Necessary physiotherapy has been delayed a long time for the sake of shielding which has limited her mobility … My sister has been unable to travel from Italy to help … leaving my brother to cope with repeated extensions to his role as carer, which has been very detrimental to his professional life … my mother's relationship with my brother as carer broke down in December and I had to take over, currently with very little backup."

A survey in October 2020 found that 78% of carers said that the needs of the person they cared for had increased because social skills, confidence and mobility had deteriorated.[168] The pandemic and regulations also created a need for informal emotional support and checking up, as a substitute for ordinary social contact, for shielders, people with mental health problems, and the millions who were newly lonely and anxious. Phones, video calls and other technology could provide a partial substitute for social contact and checking on wellbeing. A 62-year-old living in the Netherlands spotted via Skype that his 91-year-old mother in England had had a small stroke. Shopping online for others became 'a new form of financial support or physical care'.[169]

The result was that existing networks of family and friends carers were reorganised, existing informal carers were caring more, and more people were involved in unpaid care in total. By one definition, the total number of unpaid carers increased by 4.5 million (or by 49%) from 9.1 million to 13.6 million.[170] In comparison, the well-publicised British armed forces contribution of skills and labour in the pandemic was tiny: in the first wave, about 20,000 military personnel were put on standby and about 4,000 were active daily for some months.[171] In April 2020, Carers UK found that 70% of its network of mostly full-time carers were providing more care during lockdown. For 35%, this was because of the closure of council and voluntary sector services, and for 10% it was due to reductions in services, for example when domiciliary care workers stopped doing personal care to avoid infection risk.[172] A repeat survey in October 2020 found that 81% of carers were providing more care. In October 2020, Carers UK found due to loss of respite services and help from family networks, 64% of carers had had no breaks since March.[173] Overall, women and middle-aged people took on a disproportionate share of the greater unpaid care burden.

Increases in informal care workloads represent another 'health/health' trade-off.[174] Before the pandemic, in 2016/17, a majority of unpaid carers were not satisfied with the control they had over their daily life, their social contact and the amount of support they received.[175] Unpaid carers had worse wellbeing before the pandemic, but their mental health worsened further, especially for those who had lost support due to the pandemic.[176] Blood Cancer UK found that 91% of carers felt that their mental health had been affected by the pandemic, more than the 87% of people with blood cancer themselves.[177] The Alzheimer's Society found that 91% of carers said their mental or physical health had suffered.[178] In April 2020, a survey of mostly full-time carers found that 38% surveyed were worried about their finances, and many had experienced extra costs due to limits on shopping and need for new equipment.[179] By October 2020, 31% of people who stopped work or reduced hours in order to care for people due to COVID-19 had applied for a mortgage holiday, compared to 14% overall[180] (see Chapter 7).

Thus, some of the shock of COVID-19 and measures to prevent infections in the health and care systems, was absorbed by millions of informal carers and those they cared for. Some of the risk of infection was transferred to them, part of a 'hidden cost on households and communities' of COVID-19.[181]

Support and guidance for unpaid carers

Dunn et al noted that "government ... support has not reached all parts of the social care system".[182] Carers UK told Parliament that in pandemic policy: "Carers quite often are an afterthought ... Health and care workers were clapped. Unpaid carers remained unseen."[183] Bear et al said that informal care and support was 'largely invisible in COVID-19 policy'.[184] SAGE stated in November 2020: 'There has been almost no guidance on [unpaid care] even though paid domestic workers have been given clear rules to follow.'[185] Paid domiciliary care workers were told that care involving touch required an apron, gloves, eye protection and surgical mask,[186] and some stopped doing it.

Lockdown rules which banned visits to other households had exceptions for carers, but these appeared to focus on professionals. Many unpaid carers, especially new carers and those helping less dependent people, were unsure of their status, and Carers UK said that there was 'confusion' about the rules on visiting and distancing.[187] Some carers were worrying both about infection, without much advice or equipment, and about breaking the law. A 50-year-old woman said her father had been discharged from hospital after kidney failure and could not walk or get to the toilet, and her 72-year-old mother could not cope: "He has fallen and there have been times when we HAD to go and help mum." A 50-year-old woman who had visited her mother twice a day before lockdown commented that "unfortunately I had no choice but to break the rules after a week, with no help from council services". A 50-year-old woman who visited and care for her mother other every other day said she was: "Trying to keep social distance and wearing a mask but that is hard when comes to giving a bath or shower."

Government support to unpaid carers was modest. From 30 March 2020, Carer's Allowance would continue to be paid if carers had to stop caring due to having COVID-19, and hours providing 'emotional support' could count towards the minimum 35 hours of care required. On 8 April 2020, the government published guidance for unpaid carers, but it mainly repeated other guidance and urged unpaid carers to take on another task – to plan cover in case they became ill. In April, local authorities and the NHS were asked to provide unpaid carers with letters in order to give them access to priority in shops. In May 2020, unpaid carers were added to the priority list for testing, but the people they cared for were not.[188] In September 2020, DHSC guidance clarified that disabled people could use support from outside their household to get around outside their homes, employers had to furlough informal carers of shielders in the same way as shielders, and carers were exempt from restrictions on travel and visiting other homes.[189] On the other hand, the Coronavirus Act allowed local authorities to apply to lift statutory requirements for assessing needs for social care, including domiciliary care.

As in pre-pandemic times, there were numerous non-policies on support for carers. SPI-B suggested that 'paid emergency care workers' (or additions to the domiciliary care workforce) should support households with several sick or isolating residents or where unpaid carers were sick or isolating.[190] Carers UK wanted more guidance, better access to testing, access to PPE, monitoring service gaps and support for the wellbeing of carers. It also wanted an increase in Carers Allowance.[191] LSE researchers argued there should be 'a care supplement similar to a Child Benefit' to support unpaid carers at least during the pandemic.[192]

7

The impact of COVID-19 and COVID-19 policy on incomes, housing costs and housing security

The impact of the pandemic on work, income and living standards

Introduction

As an economic crisis, the COVID-19 pandemic acted mainly through the labour market. In 2020, more people were in work than had ever been recorded before (see Chapter 2). A total of 62% of HRPs in England were in work in 2019/20, and thus at least this many households were exposed to the effects of the pandemic on work and work incomes.

Changes in employment income through furlough, redundancy and short hours were the culprit in 83% of cases of income loss in England November/December 2020 to April/May 2021.[1] Pandemic work income loss was concentrated among those in the worst-hit sectors, in roles that could not be done at home, and in the places where these jobs were concentrated.

Across the world, countries like the UK with high incomes and good credit were able to make dramatic responses.[2] Tooze argued that policymakers 'drew directly on the lessons of 2008'[3] (Chapter 1). In March 2020, the UK government invented whole new jobs support and benefits policies. Hale et al's index rated the UK's economic support policies as the fourth most generous in the EU plus the UK, after Cyprus, Ireland and Austria, over January 2020 to November 2021.[4] While they operated, these policies compensated for weaknesses in the normal welfare safety net (see Chapter 2) and effectively increased its generosity slightly.

By May 2020, 45% of UK individuals were in households that had lost at least a tenth of their income.[5] In response, 26% of all individuals used their own savings and 12% received help from friends and family, demonstrating the significance of family in emergency welfare (see Chapter 2). In pre-pandemic times, research found that claimants said that claiming was a last resort due to the difficult and unpleasant process.[6] During the pandemic, only a minority used emergency policy supports: 8% applied for UC and 8% for the Self-Employed Support Scheme (SEISS), 8% applied for a mortgage holiday and 8% borrowed, while 2% used a food bank.[7] A small group cut housing costs by moving in with others (see Chapter 4). Some had reduced costs from commuting and travel (Figure 4.4).

Income loss

'Furlough' or the Coronavirus Job Retention Scheme

To forestall mass redundancies when employers were asked to close businesses on 20 March 2020, the Treasury had developed 'furlough' or the Coronavirus Job Retention Scheme. This allowed employers to nominate employees whose labour they could not use, who would remain employed, and would receive 80% of their wages up to a cap of £2,500 a month from the government. Employers had to continue making National Insurance payments. This scheme ran from March 2020 to September 2021 via the Treasury. A total of 3.8 million claims were made in the first three days and 6.3 million in the first two weeks (see Figure 7.1).[8] As restrictions eased, and then retightened, workers went off and on furlough. From 1 July, workers could work part-time and be furloughed part-time. From September 2020, government reduced its support to 70% of wages, with employers being required to make up the remaining 10%, and in October government support stepped down again to 60%, before going back to 80% in November to reflect the second English and Welsh lockdowns (Table 3.2). The scheme was extended in November 2020, and in December 2020 the total live claims peaked at 9.9 million.[9] By April/May 2021, 19% of working HRPs in England had been furloughed (in many cases alongside other household members).[10] When it ended, the scheme has supported 11.7 million individuals in the UK and cost £70 billion.[11]

Working HRPs in England who were most likely to have been furloughed by April/May 2021 included those in lower supervisory and technical jobs and routine jobs, lone parents, people with lowest quintile incomes, part-time and semi-routine workers, people in the West Midlands and private renters. A total of 29% of households with a HRP furloughed by April/May 2021 were in the lowest quintile of income.[12] People could be furloughed multiple times from the same or different jobs, and furlough could end in job loss. In February/March 2021, a 62-year-old woman said "my two daughters have suffered, one being furloughed three times now and the other furloughed then made redundant".

The decision to set furlough at 80% of income was significant. A woman aged 62 said "for three months our boss topped up our furlough pay which was very kind", but he then stopped. However, throughout 2020, 95% of furloughed HRPs in England had lost pay.[13] While 80% of income was well above UC levels in most cases and most households had more than one earner, for many a 20% income cut was difficult. A parent of a 19-year-old said "reduced pay [furlough] has put a big strain on our finances". A man

Figure 7.1: Number of employed people furloughed (first and second waves), Great Britain, March 2020–September 2021

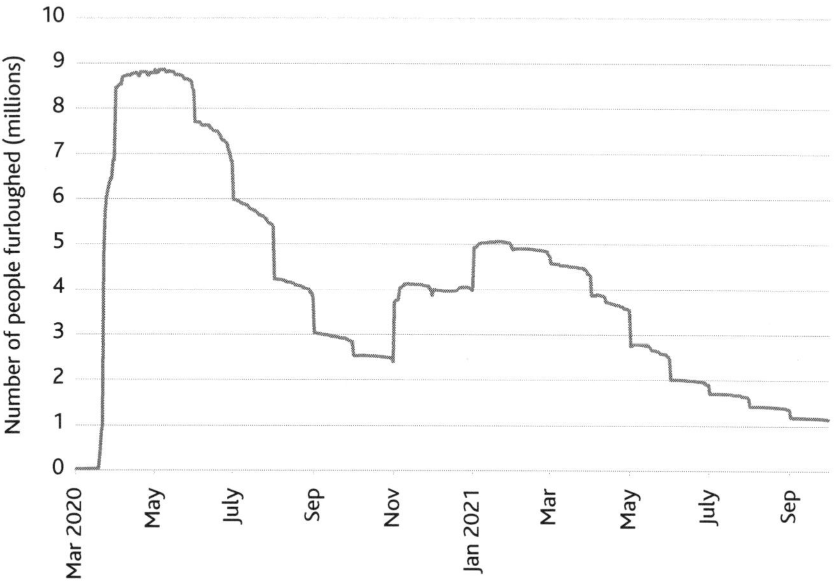

Note: The scheme launched on 20 April 2020, but claims could be backdated to March
Source: HMRC 2021a

aged 31 stated "we can keep up with rent and bills, however we are currently having to be extremely careful with our money". Self-employed people were not legible for furlough, but the existence of the scheme prompted some clients to follow its principle. A woman aged 62 said "I miss my cleaner coming, although [I am] continuing to pay her".

Increases in unemployment and economic inactivity

Some people were made redundant in shutdown industries and others in order to avoid furlough costs, because of medium-term uncertainty or for other reasons. Some people left the labour market and became inactive because they were unemployed and had little immediate prospect of finding a new job, they had been refused furlough, wanted to shield or as a form of early retirement. The millions of furloughed staff remained 'employed' in statistical terms. In 2019, 3.9% of economically active people aged 16 or over were unemployed. During the pandemic, unemployment only rose slightly from June 2020 when furlough numbers started to fall, and by October reached 5.0%, while economic inactivity increased. However, these changes were small compared to previous recessions, and unemployment reduced again from late 2020.[14] The OBR estimated that without furlough, UK 2020 unemployment would have peaked at 10% rather than 5%, and these unemployed people would probably have made millions of additional UC claims.[15] Jobs most likely to be lost were in hospitality, non-essential retail, travel and business services, and part-time jobs. The first wave had a bigger impact on the employment of young people, ethnic minorities, people with low qualifications, tourist areas and big cities, especially London.[16] For example, many students had lost part-time jobs, often in hospitality. A 19-year-old student said "this has caused me a *lot* of stress". However, these inequalities had largely faded by March 2021.[17]

As after the GFC, people who had not been furloughed or unemployed could also lose income. For example, in February/March 2021, a 31-year-old said "my contract has been reduced from 43 hours plus generous overtime to 37 hours [sic] flat week, although I am working an average of 57 hours a week'.

New Universal Credit claims

People who had been made redundant or lost hours in the pandemic could make a UC claim if they had low or no income and savings or capital less than £16,000. Tenants – but not owners – could also claim for money to pay all or part of their rent.

The number of UC claims had been rising gradually from 2012 to March 2020, as new claims were put on to UC rather than the older 'legacy' benefits it was replacing (see Chapter 2). However, there was a dramatic break in the trend in March 2020. Between March and April 2020, the total number of households claiming UC rose from 2.7 million households to 3.8 million, or by 39%. These claims included many first-time applicants. One housing association found that the number of its tenants claiming UC rose from 4,000 to 8,000, and devoted staff time to help to make claims and challenge incorrect awards. The association said

> some of them had never had to claim benefits before, found the process quite complex and were shocked at the amount they were entitled to.[18]

UC claims then continued to grow, but largely in line with the pre-March 2020 trend, before starting to fall for renters in March 2021. There was a marked increase in UC claims by renters, and a dramatic and increase in UC claims by home owners, which only began to reduce a year later in March 2021 (Figure 7.2).

In March 2020, UK government announced an emergency increase of £20 a week in UC for working and non-working households. Claimants on 'legacy' benefits (whose claims had started before UC was introduced in their area) and on non-means-tested benefits such as disability benefits were not included.

Figure 7.2: Number of Universal Credit claims, by tenure of claimant, Great Britain, August 2019–August 2021

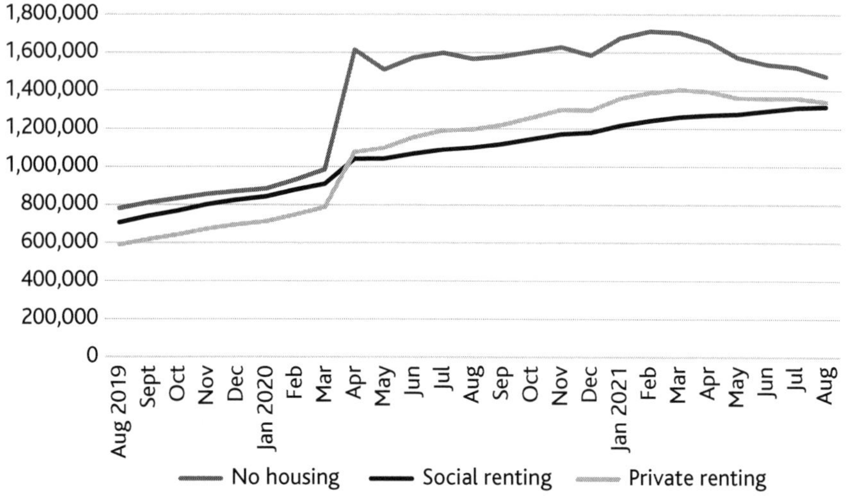

Source: DWP 2021c

Chancellor Rishi Sunak explicitly said that this was intended to 'strengthen the safety net'[19] (see Chapter 2). For people claiming over the whole March 2020–October 2021 period, the increase amounted to an additional £1,700, and the total cost was approximately £5 billion.[20] Of course, the proportionate gain was largest for households with the smallest claims, for example, amounting to a 37% increase for a single person over 25 not claiming for rent. The uplift due to expire in April 2021, but was extended. It finally ended in October 2021, when a small reduction in the taper rate was introduced.

LHA is the maximum amount of rent that UC will pay for low-income renters and had been frozen to the 2016 absolute value of the lowest 30th percentile of local private rent (see Chapter 2). In March 2020, LHA also received an uplift, being increased to the 2020/21 30th percentile, meaning an increase in support for paying rent to most private renters on UC.

Including the 'uplift', over the year 2020/21 a single person over 25 received £323 a month, a couple £507 and a couple with two children £979 to £1,071 depending on the age of the children.[21] Even with the uplift, these incomes remained well below average incomes and were close to the poverty line (60% of median equivalised income). This is why the UK welfare state has been described as 'ungenerous' (see Chapter 2). However, the overall effect was an increase in incomes for many households on benefits, and benefit levels temporarily came slightly closer to the Minimum Income Standard. This is the income needed to meet the minimum standard required for participation in society, as defined by members of the public[22] (Table 7.1).

Table 7.1: Value of benefits as a proportion of minimum acceptable incomes (according to the Minimum Income Standard), UK, before and after pandemic policy changes

	Single person of working age	Couple with children aged 4 and 7	Lone parent with children aged 4 and 7	Pensioner couple
2019	32%	56%	58%	90%
2020 UC	43%	61%	65%	92%
2020 legacy benefits	34%	57%	60%	92%

Source: Hirsch 2019, Table 4; Davis et al 2020, Table 4

Most of those who moved from work on to UC experienced greater income drops than the 20% drop for those who were furloughed. In addition, a majority of new claimants did not receive the full UC amount. In August 2020, 41% of all UC claimants, and 60% who had started a claim in April–August 2020, were making repayments of debts to the DWP itself, of about 10% of the amount on average.[23] Because of the low level of the LHA (see Chapter 2), 25% of private renters claiming UC before the crisis were unable to fully cover their housing costs, but for those who made claims during the crisis, who may have chosen their home without considering the level of the LHA, the figure was 42%.[24] Some new social renting claimants were affected by the 'bedroom tax' (see Chapter 2). Those already affected by the benefit cap (mainly larger households in London) received no uplift and the proportion of total claims capped increased from 2% to 3% between February and August 2020.[25]

A man who had been made redundant from university catering said "my income dropped from £130 per day to £12 a day". A pregnant woman aged 31 had been made redundant: "I have been left with no income for 2 months. I also lost my maternity package … I am about £700 a month worse off than before." A shielder aged 62 who had stopped work when new variants arrived said in that UC "doesn't give us enough money for bills and food so we have a shortfall and are using credit card to get by". A 62-year-old said that her daughter had graduated in 2020 and hadn't been able to get work: "UC … doesn't even cover her rent so she lives off mainly potatoes".

The Self-Employed Income Support Scheme

The SEISS was available from March 2020 to June 2021 to those who had made at least 50% of their income from self-employment in 2019/20. It paid 80% of estimated lost income, with no maximum. By June 2021, a total of 2.9 million self-employed people had made claims. Another 1.0 million made claims which were rejected. Successful SEISS claimants received on average £8,800 in total, much less than furlough. The total cost of the SEISS was £25.2 billion.[26]

The 'missing millions' not supported by government schemes

Furlough was provided at employer discretion. About 1.4 million self-employed people did not qualify for the SEISS because less than half of their income should be from self-employment.[27] Another 225,000 self-employed people were excluded because they earned over £50,000, as were 200,000 who were newly-self-employed.[28] A total of 400,000 contract workers were excluded from support because they were between jobs,[29] while 710,000 company directors who paid themselves through dividends were excluded. A lobby group was established to campaign for the 'three million' who were unsupported.[30] In May 2020, a 31-year-old who had recently started as a pub landlady said "my weekly income dropped from approximately £2,000 to £0". Although her partner was furloughed, continuing rent and bills meant "the adults in the household eat one meal a day to ensure there is enough food for the children". A woman aged 50 said "company directors, the employers and business owners of the country, have been totally overlooked". Some of these people were not eligible for UC. In addition, people working in the grey and black economy were obviously not eligible, although they may have lost income.

Change in income from rent and investments

In 2019/20, 5% of UK household income was derived from investments, including rental housing.[31] In 2018, the average landlord received £15,000 a year before tax.[32]

During the pandemic, rental income could supplement lost work income employment and fill in gaps in support. A writer and performer aged 31 thought that she was not eligible for the SEISS, but "I have savings and rental income that luckily I could fall back on". This is an example of 'asset-based emergency welfare' in action. However, rental income was also put at risk by the pandemic, an example of the redistribution of financial risk though the financialisation of housing (see Chapter 2). In England, landlords could not relet homes from 23 March to 13 May 2020 (see Chapter 8). Existing possession cases, including those for arrears, stopped, and no new ones started. From the first national lockdown to 17 May 2021, overnight stays, including in holiday accommodation, were prohibited for a total of over 35 weeks. In total, 2% of the households in England that lost income during the pandemic had lost rental or investment income.[33] A survey of Scottish landlords found that, while 55% thought the moratorium was necessary, there was a deep sense among some landlords that the temporary legislation, and more generally the Scottish Government, was biased against them.[34]

A 62-year-old said "we have rental properties including a holiday let and have lost up to £2,000 most months". Another had lost income due to "my tenants not being able to keep up rent payments and my inability to offer B&B". A 50-year-old noted that "a tenant has vacated my property and is not yet replaced. If not for financial help from my partner I would be in financial difficulty".

Overall changes in income and the impact on income inequality

Income change was a mass, possibly majority, experience in the pandemic period. A total of 42% of households in England said their income changed in some way between March and June/July 2020,[35] and between June/July and November/December 2020, the figure was 39%.[36] Similarly, 49% of UK working-age adults experienced income change over the seven months from February to September 2020.[37] In January 2021, 18% said their household finances were being affected.[38] However, income change is a mass experience in normal times. Over the year 2017/18–2018/19, 46% of UK adults experienced an income change big enough to move them between income quintiles.[39] Although many individuals and households experienced income loss in the pandemic, people on higher incomes as well as lower incomes were affected, and income inequality as measured by the Gini coefficient was slightly lower in 2020/21 than before the pandemic in 2019/20.[40]

From February to May 2020, 45% of UK adults were in a household that had lost a tenth or more of its income. This included more than half of households with self-employed people, those with employer-set hours, those in the lowest income quintile and those aged 60–65.[41] By October 2020, 38% of adults felt that their broad 'financial situation' got worse due to COVID-19, while only 14% saw things improve.[42] The number of people with 'low financial resilience' increased from 10.7 million to 14.2 million, or by 33%, from March to October 2020.[43] Among people living 'comfortably' before the pandemic, 21% said things had got worse between March and July 2020 and 20% said they had got worse between July and December 2020. Among people finding things 'very difficult' before the pandemic, 57% said things were worse between March and July, and 70% said things were worse between July and November 2020.[44] However, as the pandemic progressed, more people said they were living comfortably and fewer found things difficult, including those in the lowest income quintile.[45]

By March 2021, the Institute of Fiscal Studies (IFS) described the cumulative effect of changes in work, income and savings as 'nuanced and sometimes surprising'.[46] Overall, both relative and absolute poverty were

Figure 7.3: Percentage of people in relative poverty (below 60% median equivalised income after housing costs), by age group, UK, 2002/03–2020/21

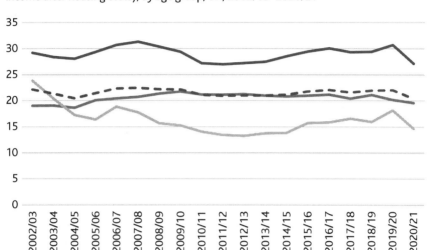

Sources: ONS 2022d, Tables 1.4a, 1.5a, 1.6a

lower in 2020/21 than in 2019/20. The proportion of people in the UK in relative poverty (with incomes below 60% of the median) after housing costs (AHC) fell from 22.0% in 2019/20 to 20.3% in 2020/21. The total numbers in relative poverty AHC fell from 14.5 million to 13.4 million. Relative poverty rates fell further for children (by 3.6%) and for pensioners (by 3.5%). This was a contrast to a trend of rising poverty for children and pensioners since 2010/11 (Figure 7.3).

The proportion of UK residents in severe poverty (below 50% of the median income) also reduced, from 11.0% in 2019/20 to 9.5% in 2020/21 before housing costs (BHC) and from 15.1% to 14.1% AHC.[47]

The slight reduction in relative poverty, measured in relation to median incomes, was partly due to the fact that median incomes fell slightly. Between 2019/20 and 2020/21, the median income dropped slightly in nominal (and real) terms from £547 to £539 per week BHC and from £476 to £472 per week AHC.[48] Some people on average and above-average incomes lost out in absolute terms, while some of those on very low incomes, including many children and pensioners, received a boost in relative terms as the median income fell and in absolute terms from the UC uplift. There was a slight reduction in overall income inequality as measured by the Gini coefficient, which fell from 35 to 34 for income BHC and from 39 to 38 for income AHC.[49] However, there was also a reduction in absolute poverty. The percentage of those poor relative to the money value of the relative poverty line from 2010/11 reduced from 14.0% to 13.3% BHC and from 17.9% to 16.8% AHC.[50]

Some caution is needed in interpreting these small changes, given the smaller sample size achieved in the underlying Labour Force Survey during the pandemic. However, the IFS said that the UC uplift tended 'to actively equalise incomes rather than simply mitigate the effects of the crisis'.[51] Citizens Advice described the uplift as 'one of the government's most successful pandemic policies'.[52] Davis et al said that the UC and LHA uplifts provided a 'demonstration of what more adequate support looks like'.[53]

Nonetheless, many hundreds of thousands of people experienced increased hardship, at least temporarily. Expenditure reduced for some households, especially those on higher incomes, due to fewer opportunities for discretionary spending on travel and leisure and caution about the future.[54] Others, especially those on lower incomes, experienced a rise in costs due to the cost of **staying home**, disruption to shopping patterns and rising costs, including for food, petrol and gas.[55] Cleaning costs increased,[56] and changes in schooling made it more difficult to budget for new uniforms and food at home.[57] The cost of the minimum income standard increased by 2.5% in 2021. A person aged 62 said in February/March 2021 "financially things have not changed much as benefit stays the same but it has been more difficult as food and shopping has increased". The Financial Conduct Authority (FCA) found that between February and October 2020, 37% of households decreased their spending, while 19% increased it.[58] On a larger scale, stopping and starting demand caused worldwide cost and price increases.

Estimates suggested the number of people who were 'destitute' (being unable to afford two or more of six essentials or on 'very low' income) would have increased by 50% between 2017 and 2020 without COVID-19. However, the number of destitute people more than doubled in this period with COVID-19.[59] One estimate suggested that COVID-19 had the biggest effects on destitution in the East and West Midlands, followed by the South East, for people of working age and families with children.[60] Figures from the Labour Force Survey suggest that between 2019/20 and 2020/21, the proportion of the population who were 'food insecure' reduced in line with poverty, from 7.8% to 6.4%.[61] However, the Trussell Trust, the UK's biggest group of food banks, provided 2.5 million food parcels across the UK in 2020/21, an 'unprecedented' annual increase of 600,000 or 33%.[62] In October/November 2020, 1.8% of adults aged 16–75, or 800,000 people, in England, Wales and Northern Ireland received food from a food charity because they lacked the money to buy their own.[63] Food insecurity was highest for young people, families with children, people of Black ethnicity, people in poor health or with disabilities, and in the North East and North West of England.[64] A teacher aged 31 said "many of my students at school have been forced to use foodbanks due to parents being furloughed or not being able to work". On the basis of evidence available at the start of 2022, the IFS said 'it seems likely that material deprivation worsened along several margins in the immediate wake of the crisis. It is less clear whether, or how much, it has recovered since'.[65]

During the pandemic, access to many of the items used to define material deprivation was restricted by law, regulations or fear of infection, as well as or instead of by a lack of money. Material deprivation due to lack of money for items not affected by the pandemic changed little for pensioners and children. While the data for 2020/21 are not a good indicator of deprivation due to poverty, they do reflect deprivation of important consumption or experiences, such as going out socially at least once a month or taking part in school trips, including for those who could usually afford them.[66]

In early 2022, the IFS warned that in terms of poverty and inequality, the pandemic may have been the calm before the storm rather than the storm itself. New late-pandemic policies, including the removal of the UC uplift and the refreeze of the LHA, will increase poverty and inequality, as will new late-pandemic economic trends including rising gas prices, general inflation, low growth and potential renewed austerity (see Chapter 2).

Changes in savings and borrowing

In the early phases of the pandemic, more households were spending savings and borrowing than building savings and paying off loans. The FCA found that 36% of adults in the UK had fewer savings in October 2020 than in February 2020, and 14% had taken out or extended unsecured loans.[67] In May 2020, a 50-year-old woman said her husband had lost his job and they were using his redundancy payment and savings to pay the mortgage: "this is worrying". In February/March 2021, a man aged 62 said "all our savings are depleted, years of work gone". A woman aged 62 said her daughter had been furloughed, then made redundant, then got a part-time job, but "has to dip into her savings each month to pay the rent". In addition, it was households without savings in 2019–20 that were most likely to be furloughed or unemployed.[68]

On the other hand, from February to October 2020, 26% of UK adults had increased their in-cash savings and 19% had reduced their unsecured loans.[69] The savings rate reached a historic peak at 29% in July–September 2020[70]. In February/March 2021 a middle-aged woman said "I have saved a shedload of money". A 31-year-old said "I made some good investment decisions when the stock market dropped and … paid off more of my mortgage". Bank of England research found that among households with moderate savings before the pandemic, mortgage holidays led to further saving.[71]

Over the pandemic period, 12% of households were able to save for the first time. In 2019/20, 45% of households in England had no savings at all.[72] In June/July 2020, the figure had not changed, in November/December 2020, it was 33%,[73] and by April/May 2021, it was 26%.[74] The position changed over the course of the pandemic. In April/May 2021, 23% of HRPs in England had spent savings since November/December 2020 and 22% had built them.[75] However, overall inequalities in savings and debt increased.[76] Individual and family savings had consequences, including for housing careers (see Chapter 8). A 31-year-old said "we're in a privileged position where our jobs haven't been at risk and we've been able to save for a deposit!". A CEV 31-year-old had been "shielding for months which is difficult. I have been able to save money, and get onto the property ladder ... unobtainable 18 months ago". Another 31-year-old commented "I work in finance, the reality of COVID-19 as something to make the rich richer is obvious to me".

Familial support

After their own savings, the most frequent resort for those who had lost income was family and friends. In February/March 2021 a 62-year-old said that their children and grandchildren "are stretched or have raided savings. We've helped where we can". Another 62-year-old stated that "my son is self-employed so we are helping him out financially as he has three children under eight". A furloughed 50-year-old said "I privately rent my house but after the pay cut it had become impossible to balance all the bills. I've had to rely on a relative to buy food". A 19-year-old student noted in February/March 2021:

> "I have had to provide a considerable amount of financial support to my family ... totalling up to nearly £5,000 ... due to unemployment and housing issues. This money came from my house deposit savings account."

The impact of the pandemic on incomes, savings and affordability by housing tenure

The proportion of HRPs in England in work in reduced over the pandemic in all tenures. However, the rate of employment reduced more for private renters, social renters and outright owners, who had lower proportions of employed HRPs before the pandemic (Figure 7.4). Thus employment inequality between tenures increased. Among private renters, the total proportion in work fell, but the proportion in part-time work increased, due to people returning part-time from furlough or switching from full-time to part-time jobs. The proportion of HRPs unemployed was unchanged for outright owners, and increased from 1% to 2% for mortgaged owners, but there were significant changes for renters. For private renters, unemployment increased from 3% to 7% for HRPs and from 6% to 11% for social renters. The proportion of economically inactive HRPs, due to being retired, studying or for other reasons such as caring or disability, increased slightly in all tenures.

Figure 7.4: Proportion of HRPs in employment, England, 2019/20 and 2020/21

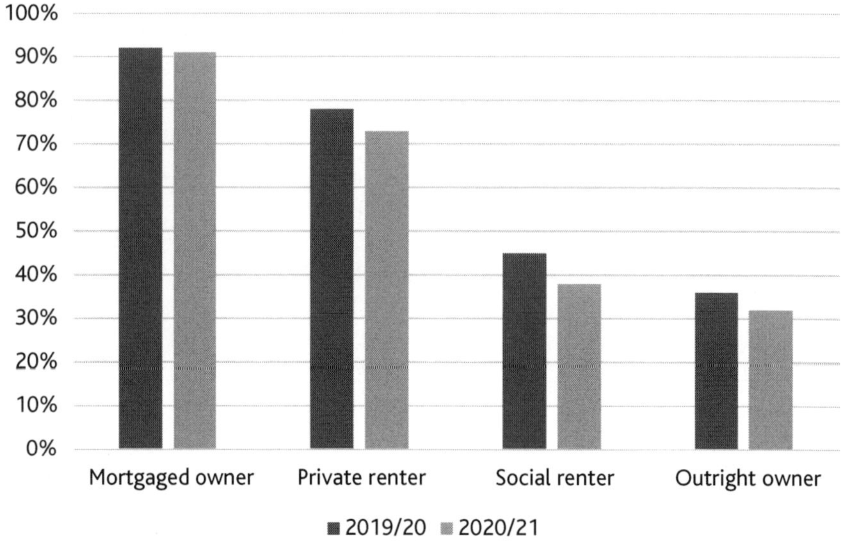

Source: DLUHC 2021d, Figure 1.4

Households where HRPs lost work or hours would have lost income, unless other household members could make it up. Over the pandemic, renters lost out slightly on income relative to owners. In 2019/20, 5% of mortgaged owners were in the lowest income quintile, roughly equivalent to being in poverty, compared to 20% of outright owners and private renters, and 47% of social renters. In 2020/21, 4% of mortgaged owners, 18% of outright owners, 22% of private renters and 50% of social renters were in the lowest quintile.[77] Thus, income inequality between tenures increased. This was in contrast to the overall reduction in income inequality and reversed the trend of growing convergence in incomes between tenures.[78]

Any loss of income made existing housing costs loom larger. Average housing affordability worsened slightly in each tenure in England over the pandemic between 2019/20 and April/May 2021. By June/July 2020, the median social tenant as well as the median private tenant paid more than 30% of household income on their housing, so all renting had become 'unaffordable' on average, and this was still true in April/May 2021.[79] The proportion of private renters and owner occupiers finding it 'difficult' to meet housing costs also increased.

Mortgaged owners

Mortgaged owners need income to access and pay a mortgage. In 2019/20, 92% of mortgaged owner HRPs in England were working, making them the most exposed to loss of income from work. They were the least likely to be unable to work during the pandemic due to their role or childcare, but still 50% were unable to so.[80] By June/July 2020, 22% of mortgaged owners had been furloughed.[81] However, on average, mortgaged owners had the highest incomes before the pandemic, the lowest risk of unaffordable housing after outright owners, and in March 2020 67% had savings. Among those who did, 20% used them to pay housing costs by November/December 2020 and 23% had used them to pay household bills.[82]

The average proportion of income spent on mortgage costs rose from 14% in 2019/20 to 15% in April/May 2021, so remained affordable.[83] However, a minority of these owners had serious problems. Mortgaged owners had the lowest pre-pandemic rates of UC claims, but in March–April 2020, the number of households receiving UC with no housing entitlement (usually mortgaged owners)[84] increased from 1.0 million to 1.6 million, or by 60% (Figure 7.2). Some owners realised just at the wrong time that they could not get UC to help pay housing costs or at all. A middle-aged woman said: "I felt I was being penalised for working and having a mortgage. They failed me the one and only time I ever needed them". A woman aged 50 commented "I cannot get UC because I have capital in a buy-to-let flat … I cannot sell the flat".

The proportion of mortgagors in England with difficulties paying the mortgage more than doubled, from 5% in 2019/20 to 11% in April/May 2021. The reasons were more directly linked to the pandemic than for those in other tenures: being furloughed, working fewer hours or less overtime and unemployment.[85] Mortgagors most likely to experience difficulties in June/July 2020 included households with an HRP who was of Pakistani or Bangladeshi origin, who were unemployed, furloughed, lone parents and with lowest quintile incomes. A newly unemployed 62-year-old whose mortgage had eight years to run said: "The mortgage company are pressing me to resolve the arrears which means I will either have to sell the house or consider equity release."

FCA data show that the proportion of mortgages in arrears of at least 1.5% of the loan balance fell steadily from 2.4% in 2009, including through the pandemic, to 1.3% in January 2021.[86] The number of mortgages in arrears remained close to 40,000 before and throughout the pandemic. This was very different from what happened after the GFC (Figure 7.5).

DLUHC data show that the proportion of households in England with at least some rent and mortgage arrears rose during the pandemic (Figure 7.6).

Private renters

In 2019/20, 77% of private renting HRPs in England were working. They had intermediate incomes compared to other tenures, but the highest risk of unaffordable housing, and only half had savings.[87]

Figure 7.5: Number of mortgages in arrears, UK, 2007–21

Source: Bank of England/FCA 2022

Figure 7.6: Proportion of households in rent and mortgage arrears, England, 2019/20–April/May 2021

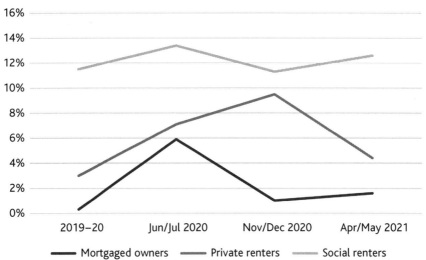

Source: MHCLG 2020h, Tables AT 1.13, 1.14; MHCLG 2021a, Figure 2.3, DLUHC 2021a, Tables T08, T15

By June/July 2020, 24% of private renting working HRPs had been furloughed.[88] If all earners were furloughed, a typical renting household would lose 35% of their disposable income after housing costs.[89] By November/December 2020, among the half of private renters who had savings, 32% had used them to pay housing costs and 30% had used them to pay household bills.[90] Before the pandemic, private renters had an intermediate rate of UC claim, but in March–April 2020, the number of private renting households receiving UC to help pay rent increased from 0.8 million to 1.1 million, or by 36% (Figure 7.2). If they experienced a big drop in income, they could apply for UC, but despite the uplift in UC and the LHA, due to changes in the 'housing safety net' (see Chapter 2), for many UC would not cover all their rent.

The median private rent was already unaffordable before the pandemic and affordability only worsened during it.[91] Combined data on all renters showed that households mostly likely to have difficulties paying rent by June/July 2020 had a HRP who was Black, self-employed or who had been furloughed. A 50-year-old said her children "lost jobs/have rent but no income". A 31-year-old tenant on UC commented "we've built up a considerable amount of debt with our landlord ... [this] is hanging over us to pay later". A 19-year-old living with his parents, a sibling and his grandmother had stopped work to protect her, but said "we might have to move to a smaller house because the five of us living here can't bring up enough money to pay the bills".

The proportion of private renters with arrears grew over the pandemic. By November/December 2020, it was close to that for social renters (Figure 7.6), but then dropped sharply, probably reflecting better work opportunities. In January 2021, Citizens Advice estimated that the average UK private renter in arrears owed a relatively modest £730 and the total national debt was £360 million, or about twice the annual budget for Discretionary Housing Payments (DHPs) and modest compared to many pandemic costs.[92] However, given affected tenants' tight budgets, the arrears would take an average of seven years to repay using Citizens Advice affordable repayment plans.

Many student renters were in a special position, facing paying rent for homes they couldn't occupy or didn't need for large parts of the 2019/20 and 2020/21 academic years. Some students, particularly those in university halls, were able to get rent cancelled. A 19-year-old said "I used the money saved on uni rent to build my very first PC". However, most private halls and private landlords continued to charge. A parent of a 19-year-old commented in February/March 2021 "one year of unnecessary rent at almost [£]600 per month". A 50-year-old with a student daughter said "the money we are paying out in rent for a house she is not allowed to live in is criminal". Many were unable to get their usual part-time jobs, which added to the pressure for some. A woman aged 50 with two student children stated "this has placed strain on them and me as their guarantor. I am a single parent so the burden is all mine".

In April/May 2021, only 63% of private renters in England thought eviction by the autumn was very unlikely.[93] HRPs in both rented tenures who were most worried included those of Black or Other ethnicity, lone parents, unemployed, furloughed or in the lowest income quintile.[94]

Social renters

In March 2020, social renters in England had the lowest average incomes of the tenures, were the most financially vulnerable and were the most likely to have 'unaffordable' housing. A total of 57% were claiming UC (or its predecessor, Housing Benefit) to help pay housing costs, they were the tenure the most likely to be in arrears[95] and only 30% had savings. Access to social renting prioritises those in housing need, who are likely to have low incomes, and in 2019/20 23% of social renting HRPs were disabled or caring, 25% were retired and 6% were unemployed. However, rates of employment rose after lows in the 1980s and 1990s,[96] and in 2019/20, 45% of social renting HRPs were working and exposed to the work income effects of the pandemic.

Those in work were very unlikely to be unable to work during lockdown due to their roles or need for childcare (79%).[97] By June/July 2020, 19% of social renting working HRPs had been furloughed.[98] Social renters had the highest pre-pandemic rates of UC claims, but experienced the least change. Their claims increased from 0.9 million to 1.0 million, or by 15% (Figure 7.2). The proportion of social renters finding it difficult to meet housing costs actually reduced over the pandemic, probably due to the UC uplift. By June/July 2020, the median social tenant as well as the median private tenant paid more than 30% of household income on their housing, so all renting had become 'unaffordable' on average, and this was still true in April/May 2021.[99] By November/December 2020, of those who had savings, 32% had used them to pay housing costs and 43% of had used them to pay household bills.[100]

Social tenants in England already had relatively high rates of rent arrears before the pandemic (Figure 7.6), but after an initial increase, the proportion in arrears were back to pre-pandemic levels by November/December 2021. Data from social landlords show that UK social tenant current rent arrears rose from 3.0% (as a percentage of expected income) in March 2020 to 3.7% in December 2020, and then reduced to 3.5% in March 2021.[101] Overall, half of social landlords ended 2020/21 with higher arrears and half with lower arrears. Landlords with fewer tenants working in March 2020 had lower arrears, and arrears were higher at the times and in the places with higher pandemic restrictions, which affected working tenants' incomes.[102] In April/May 2021, only 76% of social renters in England thought eviction by the autumn was very unlikely.[103]

Outright owners

Most outright owners achieve this status over time, after paying off a 25- or 30-year mortgage, and in 2019/20, 61% of outright-owner HRPs were retired. Outright owners were the least exposed of the tenure groups to income loss (although, with the highest average age, they were at most risk from COVID-19 infection; see Chapter 3). A total of 36% of HRPs were working in 2019, and by June/July 2020, 21% of working outright owners had been furloughed.[104] However, although they had to meet repairs and other household costs, their housing was generally affordable and 87% had savings. By November/December 2020, 22% of outright owners with savings had used them to pay household bills, a lower proportion than other tenures.[105] Many outright owners felt they were 'lucky' in normal times and especially in the pandemic. In May 2020, a middle-aged man said "we have few worries that might surface ... a reasonable, guaranteed income and no outstanding mortgage". Another woman aged 50, whose husband was facing redundancy, commented "we don't have a mortgage ... which we are incredibly grateful for in this situation".

Policies to protect work, income, housing security and the housing system

Introduction

In mid-March 2020, the UK government simply appealed to landlords to exercise compassion if tenants were having difficulties paying rent.[106] The emergency Coronavirus Bill did not initially address housing. However, some important housing provisions were hurriedly included to it, and other policy developed. On 26 March 2020, the UK Secretary of State Robert Jenrick tweeted in response to the housing NGO Shelter that 'no one should lose their home as a result of the Covid epidemic'.[107] The *Homelessness Monitor* said this promise was 'without precedent in the UK'.[108] However, it was soon clear that the UK government was not planning to provide borrowers or tenants with help to meet housing costs, with the exception of the LHA uplift for private renters on UC and general emergency funding to local authorities. It was not planning to compensate lenders or landlords for unrecoverable arrears that might develop. Instead, the government regulated how and when housing debts accruing during the pandemic would be dealt with.

Mortgage 'holidays'

On 17 March 2020, before lockdown, the FCA said that pandemic uncertainty had already created 'exceptional circumstances outside of the customer's control'. In a novel move, it told lenders it must offer mortgage payment deferrals (widely but somewhat misleadingly known as 'holidays') to those who were having difficulties due to loss of income due to COVID, and holidays must not count as missed payments in credit scoring.[109] These holidays would help mortgagors, but also, and perhaps more importantly, mortgage providers and the market as a whole. This built on international experience from the 1991 and 2008 recessions. As a German commentator noted: 'Without government intervention ... homes would be sold in an emergency frenzy, causing the market to crash.'[110] The closing date of the scheme was extended to 31 October 2020 and then to 31 March 2021, with the last holidays ending in July 2021. In addition, in September 2020, lenders were required to offer extra 'tailored support' where needed, although this would affect credit scores. The FCA warned borrowers that interest would still accrue, monthly and total payments would be higher after holidays, and that holidays could affect credit scoring.[111] In May 2020, a man aged 50 had been furloughed, but said:

> "A mortgage holiday didn't appeal to me because it just increases your payments after the holiday period rather than increasing the term of the mortgage. I've cut my living costs down ... but my bank balance is low and concerning."

Overall, mortgage holidays were a mass if not majority experience for homebuyers. A total of 23% of mortgage holders in the UK, or 2.6 million households, had made use of holidays at some point between March and November 2020.[112] In January 2021, FCA data showed that there had been a total of 1.9 million mortgage holidays, of which 94% had ended, and 120,000 were outstanding.[113] International data on the take-up of mortgage policies are patchy, but the take-up in the UK appears to be relatively high.

The HRPs in England most likely to have a holiday in June/July 2020 were unemployed, self-employed, economically inactive, furloughed, in the lowest quintile of incomes and shielding,[114] with pre-existing debts, income loss, or with two mortgages.[115] FCA data showed that UK households most likely to have a holiday by October 2020 were those for whom bills were a heavy burden or who were already behind when the pandemic began, who lost their jobs due to COVID, who stopped work or reduced hours to provide care due to COVID, those on fixed-term, temporary, zero-hours or agency contracts, and those who had been furloughed.[116]

In May 2020, a middle-aged woman said that her household took a mortgage holiday after she was furloughed. A man aged 50 said he and his wife took out a holiday after her travel business was devastated. A woman aged 50, whose income from childminding dropped dramatically as parents withdrew their children, had also taken a holiday. A woman aged 50 noted that although she was receiving maximum furlough pay and a top-up from her employer, her husband had lost all his income and "money is tight now so we have had to take a mortgage holiday". For some already in difficulties, the pandemic policy came as a stroke of luck. A middle-aged man had been in arrears before COVID-19 and his request to extend the term had been refused at that time, but then

> "due to the outbreak, not only have they deferred the arrears they have also given me a mortgage holiday of three months, so I've gone from feeling like I was going to lose my home every day to getting some respite and an opportunity to get on top of things".

The FCA found that 5% of people who took the holiday didn't need it, and 27% took it as a precaution, but 71% would have struggled without it and 40% would have struggled 'a lot'. This suggests that 1.4 million households were protected from struggle by the scheme by January 2021.[117] Most households that took holidays were able to resume payments on time. A woman aged 31 said that when her husband was unable to work during lockdown, they had taken a mortgage holiday, a loan payment holiday, UC and a job in a supermarket. By February/March 2021, they both had work and "we spend much more cautiously now and have vowed to get some savings behind us". A 62-year-old business owner said he and his wife "had survived financially due to government support and a mortgage holiday". For some, holidays provided relief, but did not end financial and housing worry. The Bank of England found that households with low savings who took mortgage holidays for the full six months reduced consumption when these holidays ended,[118] and of the 1.3 million households taking holidays from the top six mortgage providers, 19% needed further 'tailored support' after the holiday.[119]

Moratorium on repossessions for mortgaged owners and tenants

In 2019, 2,182 mortgaged owners in England and Wales had their homes repossessed after failing to keep up with mortgage payments,[120] and more came to 'voluntary agreements' with their lenders resulting in loss of ownership. A total of 20,647 tenants, both social and private tenants, had their homes repossessed for rent arrears or other issues.[121] In England, private renters could be asked to leave after 6 or 12 months even in the absence of rent arrears or any tenancy infraction (see Chapter 2).

On 20 March 2020, the FCA told UK lenders that they 'should not commence or continue repossession proceedings against customers at this time, given the unprecedented uncertainty and upheaval they face'.[122] Similarly, the Coronavirus Act for England and Wales extended the notice period private and social landlords had to give before seeking possession from two months to three months. The next day, supplementary regulations ordered a pause on all eviction and repossession cases in England and Wales, initially for three months to June 2020 and later extended to six months to September 2020.[123] Similar measures were introduced in the other nations.[124] In Scotland, the notice period was extended from 28 days to six months, and landlords were required to apply a 'pre-action plan', to negotiate with tenants before starting possession proceedings, initially until September 2020 and then to August 2021.[125]

From November 2020 to January 2021, a ban on the use of bailiffs to enforce repossessions was introduced in England, which was later extended to February and then to the end of May 2021.[126] This meant lenders and landlords could get a suspended legal permission to repossess, but could not exercise it. Unlike in many cities and states in the USA, in the UK these measures were not challenged in court by landlords or others.[127] While landlords and tenants benefited from policies which supported tenant incomes, in effect the moratorium 'transferred some of the costs of the pandemic from individuals and public bodies onto private landlords'.[128]

Mortgaged owners had a formal, structured, regulated means to repay the 'holiday' over the life of the mortgage, with regulators overseeing the process. Tenants and landlords were left with uncertainty about how accruing arrears would be managed and repaid, although it was unlikely that the sum could be spread out over years, as it could for buyers.[129] A woman aged 31 said future repayments would be difficult: "most people rent because they can't afford to get a deposit together for a mortgage and could not afford to increase their rent at a later date".

Another tenant aged 31 who faced double rent after her flatmate moved out said:

> "I think the differential treatment of home owners (with the guaranteed mortgage holiday) and tenants (where everything is left up to the landlord's discretion) amounts to indirect discrimination as its younger people, women and other minorities who are more likely to be in rented accommodation."

Bank of England research showed that among households with limited savings before the pandemic, spending during the pandemic was higher for mortgaged owners with holidays than for renters and outright owners.[130]

Discretionary housing payments for tenants

In 2012, when the benefit cap, the bedroom tax and reductions in the LHA were first introduced (see Chapter 2), the UK government introduced a new fund for local authorities to distribute as 'discretionary housing payments' (DHPs) to tenants in difficulty due to the reforms. This was in effect a patch over the holes in the safety net due to reforms, but the size of the DHP funds amounted to only a fraction of the eligibility removed, at just £60 million across Great Britain in 2012/13, and had fixed annual budgets, regardless of need. During the pandemic, the budget for DHPs in England and Wales increased from £140 million in 2019/20 to £180 million in 2020/21, or by 29%. The extra pandemic funds were entirely envisaged for use by private renters with shortfalls due to the LHA (see Chapter 2). The number of tenants receiving payments was 250,000 in 2019/20 and did not change in 2020/21, although the average payment rose from £527 to £679. The DHP budget reduced to £140 million again in 2021/22, a real-terms cut on the amount of two years before.[131]

The impact on housing security, evictions and repossessions

Introduction

Despite Secretary of State Robert Jenrick's promise, there is evidence that thousands of people did lose their homes because of the COVID-19 epidemic.[132] However, like unemployment, poverty and arrears, homelessness remained relatively stable despite the COVID-19 shock.

There were marked inequalities in vulnerability to income loss, falling behind with costs, perceptions of security of housing and actual repossessions.

Lenders, mortgagors, landlords and tenants' responses to arrears

Large minorities of mortgaged owners and tenants approached their lenders and landlords because of difficulties meeting housing costs. Mortgage holidays were mandated, institutionalised and regulated forms of remortgaging. In contrast, landlords and tenants were told by government to put their heads together: 'in this unique context we would encourage tenants and landlords to work together to put in place a rent payment scheme'.[133] Mortgaged owners, with the best affordability and the least difficulties with housing costs, were the most likely to get help, mainly through mortgage holidays. Private tenants, who had the most difficulties, were the most likely to seek help, but also had the highest chance of being refused.

Private landlord and tenant responses

By May 2020, 10% of private renters in Britain had tried to negotiate with landlords, and 3% received a rent reduction and 2% a rent holiday.[134] A woman aged 31 said she had to move back into her parents' home because her flatmate had lost income and the landlord would not offer them a rent holiday, even though he received a mortgage holiday himself. By April/

May 2021, probably more than half of all private tenants had negotiated with landlords over the pandemic (although some may have done so more than once).[135]

Some private landlords said that tenants had been paying as normal, but many described negotiations and concessions. A woman aged 62 her tenant had got behind, but "we have agreed ... this outstanding rent will be paid at a later date when the tenant receives a business grant". Another woman aged 62 noted that "my tenants are struggling to pay rent, so I am reducing it for those out of work for a period of time". There appeared to be fewer examples of forbearance in February/March 2021 than in May 2020.

Social landlord and tenant responses

Social landlords were very concerned about arrears because of the effect of income losses on their business plans, and their ability to borrow and to build new homes. Arrears were among the main topics discussed in a WhatsApp group set up for 200 housing associations CEOs in March 2020, as well as greater tenant deprivation.[136] In practice, social landlords faced modest additional pandemic arrears (Figure 7.6). By April/May 2021, up to 45% of all social tenants had negotiated over the pandemic (although again some may have done so more than once).[137] However, only a few percent had agreed a payment holiday, compared to 23% of mortgaged owners, and the FCA commented on the contrast.[138] However, social landlords used 'very active outreach'[139] to help tenants improve their incomes. There was also forbearance. On 24 March 2020, the housing association CEOs in the WhatsApp were saying that they were 'not publicising [it] but not evicting for Covid arrears'.[140]

However, the focus on arrears had knock-on effects.[141] In August 2021, L&Q, one of the largest social landlords in the UK with 107,000 homes, reported better-than-expected financial results over 2020/21 because rent collection and sales of market-price and affordable homes were above targets. However, L&Q had reduced repairs and improvement work, only 68% of residents said they found their landlord 'easy to deal with' against a 90% target, and it was taking 170 days to relet homes with minor repairs needs against a 22-day target.[142] In its annual report, the landlord said:

> There have unfortunately been times in the past year when we have badly let our customers down with poor service and poor standards that cannot be blamed on the pandemic ... we must do better.[143]

Repossessions from home owners and renters

Many commentators, resident advocates and residents themselves spent much of 2020 and 2021 concerned about a potential 'tsunami' of unemployment, housing arrears, evictions, repossessions and resulting homelessness.[144] Some felt that emergency policy was only delaying the flood, which would appear as soon as furlough or the moratorium on evictions ended. By the start of 2022, it appeared that thousands of people had lost their homes as a result of COVID-19.[145] However, the tsunami of arrears, evictions and repossessions and resulting homelessness did not appear.

The repossession moratorium had a dramatic impact. Repossession claims against renters and owners dropped to a tenth of the average 2015–19 levels, and the number of warrants and repossessions dropped even further. The moratorium first ended at the end of May 2020. Claims rose slowly. There was a small peak in landlord claims in October–December 2020, before the November–December 2020 ban on the use of bailiffs had its effect, and by October–December 2021, figures had reached 14,000, about half of the pre-pandemic level (Figure 7.7).

Actual landlord repossessions in England and Wales dropped to a few hundred per quarter, and lender repossessions dropped to double figures over January–March 2020, and had not increased by April–June 2021 (Figure 7.8).

In combination, mortgage holidays, informal landlord forbearance and moratoria provided lengthy reprieves for those who fell into arrears during the pandemic, and for those who were already behind (Figure 7.6). From March to December 2020, there were 4,000 fewer repossessions by lenders, 13,000 fewer by social landlords and 15,000 fewer by private landlords than in the same months in 2019. Thus, a total of 32,000 households had their home repossession at least significantly delayed by the moratoria.[146] Backlogs

Figure 7.7: Quarterly mortgage landlord and lender repossession claims, England and Wales, January–March 2019 to October–December 2021

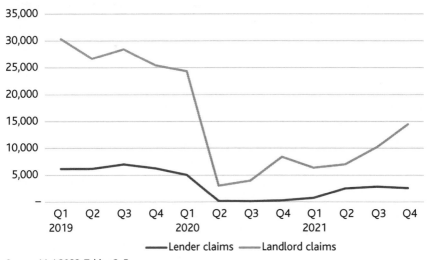

Source: MoJ 2022, Tables 2, 5

Figure 7.8: Quarterly landlord and lender repossessions, England and Wales, January–May 2019 to October–December 2021

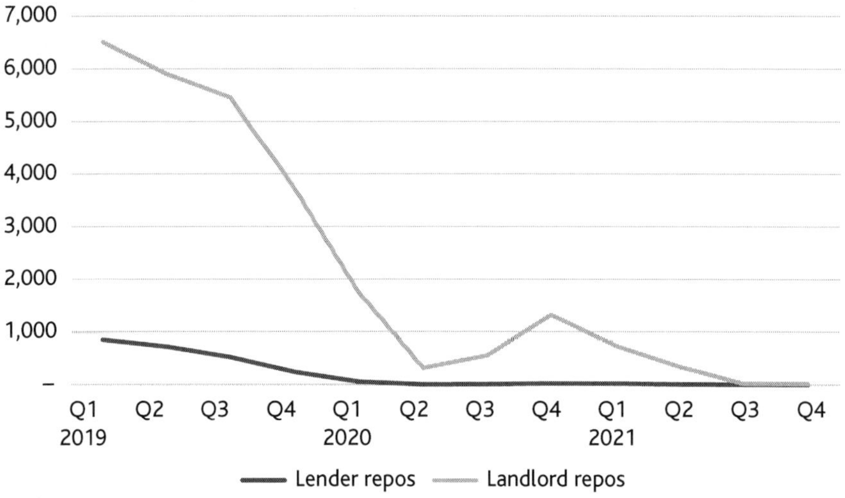

Lender repos — Landlord repos

Source: MoJ 2022, Tables 2, 5

of cases will create additional delays. In February/March 2021, a person aged 62 who worked for the Court Service said "all the extra work created by COVID restrictions means huge amounts of backlog and raised stress levels every day! I and most others in the court frequently cry".

While the prolonged period of uncertainty would have been very unpleasant, some households were able to use this extra time to improve their finances or to negotiate with landlords and lenders. Postponing evictions may have benefits that go beyond housing and the household concerned. US modelling suggests that ending state and city eviction moratoria was associated with 2.1 times more COVID-19 cases and 5.4 times more COVID-19 deaths after 16 weeks, after controls for other control measures, population characteristics and epidemic phase, because it increased overcrowding.[147] Thus, 'policies to stem evictions are a warranted and important component of COVID-19 control'.[148]

By the start of 2022, there had been no evictions tsumami. Resilience had been provided through the policies to support resident incomes, low unemployment, lender and landlord support, and forbearance and losses. It had also been provided by residents using savings, help from family and friends, and moving in with family and friends, including into overcrowded circumstances, which are potentially problematic for individuals and society overall. In addition, the Ministry of Justice figures (Figures 7.7 and 7.8) do not include cases where home owners 'voluntarily' returned unaffordable homes to lenders, and where tenants were asked or pressured to leave (potentially illegally) without a possession order. A total of 340 households in England were recorded as becoming homeless in 2020/21 due to illegal eviction, undoubtedly an underestimate, but the same as the year before.[149] Other sources record at least some forced moves during the pandemic and it is likely that there were more than in normal times.[150] A 31-year-old had been forced out "as the landlord would not take a moderate rent reduction, threatened with violence to force eviction. Had to leave London as could no longer afford the rent". In addition, some formal cases were ongoing, but were subject to court delays.

At the start of 2022, it was not clear if repossessions would rise in the year, even back to 2019 levels. Court capacity was still restricted. In addition, as time passed, it was likely that some serious arrears would be dealt with by residents increasing incomes, borrowing, moving out or landlords absorbing bad debts – as Burchardt noted, 'a crisis which will wash away'[151] (see Chapter 1) or turn into a continuing stream rather than a tsunami. However, planned rises in social rents and the cost of living will create new problems, and it is likely that 'the arrears crisis will have a long tail'.[152]

The impact on homelessness

Introduction

The pandemic created multiple additional potential causes of homelessness, from arrears to fear of infection and family conflict. It showed what happens when family emergency housing is put under strain (see Chapter 2). It had a major impact on the numbers and types of households applying to local authorities for help because they were homeless or were threatened with homelessness, and assessed as owed help from a local authority (whether prevention, relief or a 'main duty'). It also created new reasons to prevent or end homelessness, due to fear of infections.

Statutory homelessness

Statutory protection for homeless households is a key element of the UK 'housing safety net' (see Chapter 2). In England, this applied to unintentionally homeless households in priority need. Since the implementation of the Homelessness Reduction Act in 2018, local authorities could assess an applicant as not owed help, owed help to prevent homelessness, owed relief of homelessness, or owed a 'main duty', so that the local authority had to secure housing for them (see Chapter 2).

In May 2020, a woman aged 31 said "soon to be homeless. Uncertainty. Uncertain. Trapped. Inflation". However, in 2020, mortgage holidays, the freeze on repossessions and 'Everyone In' contributed to a decline in approaches to local authorities in England by home owners, tenants and rough sleepers.[153] In addition, 80% of local authority respondents interviewed by the *Homelessness Monitor* in the summer of 2020 said the furlough system had made an important contribution to preventing homelessness.[154]

There was a marked reduction in the months in numbers of households approaching local authorities after the first national lockdown, but the numbers increased again from July to September 2020. Over 2020/21, 39,210 households in England approached councils and were assessed as owed a main homelessness duty, a 3% decrease from 2019–20. A total of 149,160 households were owed a relief duty, a 6% increase on 2019–20, and 119,400 households in England were owed a prevention duty, a 20% reduction on 2019/20.[155]

Nonetheless, there is strong circumstantial evidence that thousands of people did lose their homes due to COVID-19.[156] Despite the overall fall in numbers of households provided with prevention and relief, the number helped who were homeless because family and friends were no longer able to house them rose, from 74,000 to 87,000 or by 17%. A local authority worker said:

> Many people who would ordinarily sofa surf, were finding those that were allowing them to stay with them, were asking them to leave due to fear of transmission of COVID.[157]

The number of households homeless because of domestic abuse rose from 27,000 to 31,000 or by 17%, and the number of households homeless due to non-violent relationship breakdown also rose slightly from 23,000 to 24,000, or by 7%.

All other causes of homelessness fell. There were particularly big falls in private renters homeless because the landlord wanted to sell or relet the house, from 27,000 to 16,000 or by 42%, due to the moratorium. There were also big falls in the number of households made homeless due to rent arrears. Numbers of private renting households homeless due to arrears fell from 12,000 to 6,000, or by 49%, and for social tenants fell from 11,000 to 4,000, or by 62%.[158] However, it seems very unlikely that COVID-19 played no role at all in these arrears.

In March 2020, 92,000 households in England were in temporary accommodation arranged by local authorities under homelessness legislation, ranging from bed and breakfasts to private rented houses leased by local authorities (see Chapter 2). By March 2021, the number was 95,000, a 4% increase, but this was less than the average annual increase over the 2010-19 period. Households with children make up the majority of those in temporary accommodation, but over 2020–21, the number of households with children fell by 6%, and the number of single people increased from 23,000 to 29,000, or by 25%.[159] This partly reflects attempts to house homeless single people through 'Everyone In'.

Rough sleeping

Many commentators have seen 'Everyone In' as one of the strongest features of the UK government's COVID-19 response in England[160] (see Chapter 4). The policy appeared to have successfully suppressed infection among rough sleepers and hostel residents in England. In May 2020, an NGO staff member said there had been 'disproportionately low levels of symptomatic people who have come from rough sleeping in the streets'.[161] Research published in *The Lancet Respiratory* found that from February to May 2020, 'Everyone In' prevented an estimated 266 COVID-19 deaths, 338 intensive care admissions, 1,164 hospital admissions and 1,092 infections in England.[162] The similar policies adopted in Wales resulted in COVID-19 infection rates for people who had been sleeping rough or in hostels or temporary accommodation before the pandemic lower than the Welsh average.[163] Men and women identified in GP records as homeless, a larger group than those targeted by 'Everyone In', had a higher risk of hospitalisation and death with COVID-19 by August 2020 than average, but a lower risk than for people living in care homes.[164] An estimated 12 homeless people died of COVID-19 in 2020, making up 1.9% of all deaths of homeless people. There was no statistically significant difference in the number of deaths from all causes of homeless people in England and Wales between 2019 and 2020.[165] If more attention had been paid to risks of COVID-19 at home in private households, the health benefits of 'Everyone In' could have been achieved on a much wider scale.

However, success in helping people off the streets was not complete or sustained. It was not matched by success in preventing new people becoming homeless. Single people, like families, did lose their homes because of the pandemic. A local authority worker said "there was probably about six seconds in London where you [literally] had almost everybody in".[166] The snapshot survey found 2,688 people sleeping rough in England in the autumn of 2020.[167] These people remained at higher risk from COVID, and while this was a considerable reduction on the 4,266 figure in 2019, clearly not everyone was 'in', the number remained higher than it had been in the 2010s and the government target of ending homeless by 2025 was becoming unachievable (see Chapter 2).

The effectiveness of schemes varied between places[168] due to variation in pre-existing council-NGO-landlord networks, as well as problems in the availability of hotels and other housing, such as in rural areas. There is particularly detailed information for London, where outreach workers count and categorise all the individuals they come across sleeping rough. Many established rough sleepers successfully left the streets during the pandemic through moves into accommodation. Before the pandemic, outreach workers found 377 individuals 'living on the streets' (seen at least five times over at least three weeks) over the January–March 2020 period. Over the April–June 2020

Figure 7.9: Numbers of individual rough sleepers encountered in London, October–December 2018 to October–December 2021

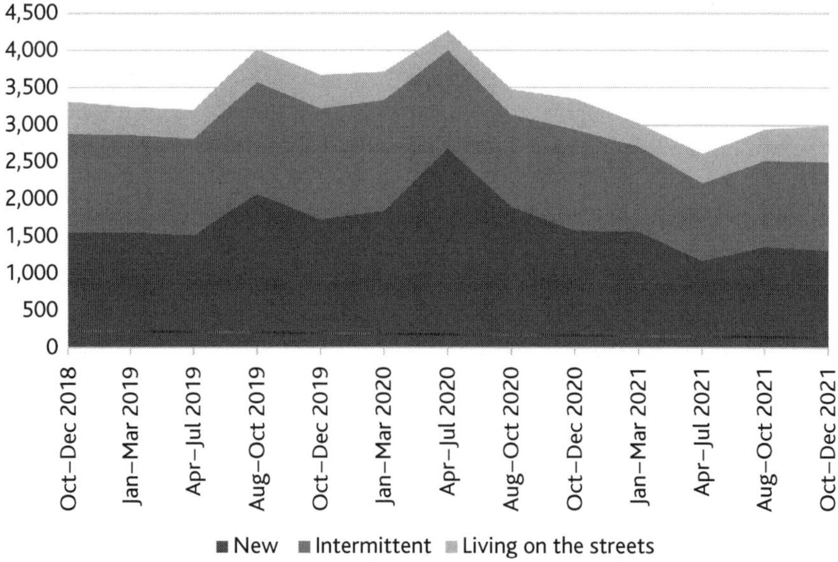

Source: Greater London CHAIN reports, https://data.london.gov.uk/dataset/chain-reports

period, this had reduced by 113 (or 30%) to 264 people. However, already in July–September 2020, the numbers living on the streets started creeping up, in October–December 2020, they were higher than before the pandemic, and in July–September 2021, 425 were living on the streets in London.[169]

The total number of people identified sleeping rough at least once in the capital actually rose, from 3,713 different individuals in January–March 2020 before the pandemic to 4,266 in April–June in the first lockdown. From this peak, the number came back down again to close to pre-pandemic levels at 3,476 in July–September 2020, and by October–December 2021 was below the immediate pre-pandemic level at 2,989 (Figure 7.9).

In January–March 2020, London rough sleepers included 1,493 UK citizens, and the number was almost exactly the same in October–December 2021. The modest reduction in numbers in 2020 and 2021 was due to a reduction in non-UK rough sleepers, and is likely to have been due to Brexit more than to the pandemic or 'Everyone In'.

Overall, 'Everyone In' was successful in reducing infections and deaths for some homeless people and showed that the target of ending homelessness was realistic. However, it had a limited effect on the total numbers sleeping rough in London and elsewhere. Firstly, it did not address the usual underlying causes of homelessness, and pandemic measures generated more homelessness. In London, outreach workers found 1,841 people new to the streets (seen just once) in January–March 2020, but 2,680 in April–June 2020 during the first lockdown, a 46% increase. In July–September 2020, as the first lockdown eased, the number of new rough sleepers declined to 1,901 people, close to the pre-pandemic normal, and by July–September 2021 was below the pre-pandemic level at 1,157. Secondly, the people targeted for safe, self-contained emergency accommodation included not only rough sleepers, but also a larger number in shared accommodation such as night shelters and homeless hostels.

There were some new aspects to homeless support during the pandemic. For example, with the huge decline in activity in city centres and the suspension of NRPF regulations, charities came into contact with more people who were willing and able to accept help.[170] However, the *Homelessness Monitor* argued that the COVID-19 experience generally 'illuminated and reinforced' what was already known about what was need to reduce homelessness:

> firm leadership by central government; appropriate levels of funding and guidance to local government, health and third sector partners to enable effective implementation; an adequate welfare safety net; and a decent and affordable offer of accommodation.[171]

UK emergency housing policies compared to those in other countries

During the pandemic, 21 of the 27 EU Member States and the UK introduced some kind of emergency housing policy (Table 7.2). Six EU nations – Bulgaria, Estonia, Finland, Latvia, Lithuania and Romania – did not. The clear majority of emergency policies were introduced in March and April 2020. Measures to help tenants were generally introduced earlier than those for owners.[172]

However, the UK stood out compared to most of the 27 EU nations and 8 others included in the study because of the range of its policies and the range of residents they were aimed at. Just three countries – the UK, Belgium and France – provided support for mortgage holders, and tenants and homeless people. The UK was the only country where the prohibition on repossessions applied to all tenants rather than just those vulnerable in some way. Apart from Spain, which has a history of large-scale and high-profile campaigns against mortgage repossession since the GFC, it was the only one where the prohibition on repossessions applied to home owners too. In addition, for example, mortgage holidays in the UK were unusual as they covered both interest and principal payments.[173]

Like the UK, other countries in Europe also introduced policies to replace income lost due to the pandemic, which acted as a complement or alternative to emergency housing policies to prevent extra risk of loss of housing in the pandemic.

Table 7.2: Types of emergency housing policy adopted in EU nations

	UK and EU countries	Countries
Some emergency housing policy	22	UK, AT, BE, CY, CZ, DK, GE, GR, SP, FR, IT, PT, IR, LU, MA, PL, NL, HU, RO, SK, SV, SW
Support for both tenants and owners	11	UK, AT, BE, CY, CZ, GE, GR, SP, FR, IT, PT
Support for tenants only	4	IR, LU, PL, SK
Support for owners only	5	NL, HU, RO, SW, SV
Support for homeless people	8	UK, BE, DK, HU, FR, LU, PL, SK
Policies adopted by the UK		
Mortgage holidays	11	UK, AT, BE, CZ, HU, IT, NL, PT, RO, SW, SV
Prohibition on eviction of tenants	12	UK, AT, BE, CY, GE, SP, FR, IR, IT, LU, PL, PT
Other help for tenants	9	UK, BE, FR, GR, IT, IR, LU, MA, PL
Increase in/extension of eligibility for housing allowances	7	UK, BE, FR, SP, IT, IR, LU, MA, PL
Prohibition on repossession of mortgaged owners	2	UK, SP
Policies not adopted by the UK		
Rent freeze/reduction	6	BE, CZ, GR, CY, IR, LU
Rent payment deferral	2	SP, PT
Extension of tenancy length	3	GE, PT, SK

Note: EU members: AT = Austria, BE = Belgium, CY = Cyprus, CZ = Czechia, DK = Denmark, FR = France, GE = Germany, GR = Greece, HU = Hungary, IE = Ireland, IT= Italy, LU = Luxembourg, MA= Malta, NL = the Netherlands, PL = Poland, PT = Portugal, RO = Romania, SW = Sweden, SV = Slovenia, SK = Slovakia, SP = Spain

Source: Adapted from Baptista et al 2021

Non-policies on the impact of restrictions on housing security

Rent holidays were introduced by two EU countries with an established history of rent strikes and resistance to eviction after the GFC: Spain and Portugal.[174] Introducing and enforcing rent holidays on private landlords in the UK would have been more difficult than for mortgage lenders, due to the less established state of regulation, registration and representation of landlords. In addition, in contrast to mortgage holders, given high poverty rates in the tenure (see Chapter 2), many renters would struggle to pay back debt accumulated over a holiday, even if short- and medium-term loan products to enable them to do so had been available. In Wales, the government introduced a Tenancy Hardship Loan to help private tenants in trouble from December 2020.[175] In June 2021, when the evictions ban ended, it introduced a £10 million Tenancy Hardship Grant to help renters with significant arrears incurred between March 2020 and June 2021 to avoid evictions,[176] and existing loans were changed to grants.[177]

Rent freezes were introduced by six EU countries.[178] Most mechanisms to limit rent increases or make them conditional were removed in the UK in 1988. However, renewed measures became part of English housing policy discussions in the 2010s, and in their 2017 general election manifesto, Liberal Democrats promised to limit rent increases to local rent inflation. They and Labour wanted to reinstate LHA to its 2016, pre-freeze level[179] (see Chapter 2). In Scotland, rent limits have been implemented in high-price areas. However, the pandemic did not persuade any UK nations to introduce any form of emergency rent control.

Tenancy extensions were introduced in Greece and Portugal, to protect tenants including those in arrears.[180] In their 2017 manifestos, Labour and the Liberal Democrat promised to extend the standard English private rented sector tenancy to three years.[181] The moratorium on repossessions in effect extended many tenancies in the private rented sector by more than a year.

The impact of COVID-19 and COVID-19 policy on the housing market

Introduction

This chapter describes UK and national government policies to mitigate the impact of pandemic restrictions on the housing market, and how they worked. Policy was driven by the idea that the housing market could be used to combat pandemic unemployment and recession. In contrast to other aspects of the housing system and the economy, the housing market appeared relatively untroubled by the pandemic shock, and even flourished. This was opposite to predictions, and has been described as 'uncanny'[1] and 'unprecedented'.[2] Housebuilding and home letting and sales had particularly short shutdowns, and returned to normal levels of activity before the end of 2020. However, in another interpretation, policy and market reactions in the pandemic were only a 'solidification' of pre-pandemic policies and markets: low interest rates, high demand for housing and rising prices, in the UK and across Europe.[3] The housing market was able to help and benefit those who did well despite the pandemic: with stable incomes, and growing savings and equity, but overall the pandemic housing market increased inequality in wealth.

Supply

A small decline in construction of new homes

Construction work ceased in the UK on 23 March 2020 at the start of the first lockdown, but in England, it restarted from 13 May 2020, after just seven weeks, as long as sites could be 'Covid-secure'.[4] It emerged that housebuilding posed less risk of transmission than many other occupations (see Table 3.1), but nonetheless its early reopening demonstrates the salience of housebuilding to the UK government. Many companies started work, with some adaptation to distancing guidelines. Total investment in construction and repair rebounded in mid-2000 and remained 'strong' in 2021.[5]

Housing starts and competitions in England fell January–March 2020 and dropped dramatically April–June 2020, but by July–September 2020, both starts and completions were slightly above pre-COVID-19 levels. Construction work continued during the second and third lockdowns. In 2019/20, 243,000 net additional homes were built or converted in

England,[6] but over 2020/21, the first year of the pandemic, the number of net additional homes built or converted in England reduced from 243,000 to 217,000, or by 11%. This was markedly larger than fall in UK GDP over the same period, reflecting the fortunes of the whole economy, of 4.8%.[7] The government's 2019 manifesto target of 300,000 net additional homes per year target for England was further out of reach than it had been before the pandemic.[8] There were biggest reductions in regions which had lower prices before the pandemic: Yorkshire and Humberside (21%), the West Midlands (20%) and the North East (19%).[9]

Despite its early reopening, the construction industry also made substantial use of the furlough scheme and received £5.5 billion, or 8% of the total[10] (see Chapter 7). In addition, it benefited disproportionately from the SEISS, receiving six times as much as the next most-supported sector. A total of 970,000 self-employed people working in construction received SEISS payments. £10.4 billion or 41% of the total paid out went to self-employed people in the construction industry[11] (see Chapter 7). These payments represent a substantial government contribution not only to incomes and housing security of workers, but also to maintaining capacity in this specific industry.

Demand

Temporary stamp duty 'holidays'

Stamp duty is a tax that buyers of homes worth £125,000 or more pay on the value of their home at the point of purchase. Stamp duty is a wealth tax, but is not progressive and acts as a deterrent to moving. Among researchers, there is 'a near-universal consensus that stamp duty is a bad tax'.[12] Temporary reductions in stamp duty were used from 2008 to 2012 to stimulate the economy after the GFC. From 2017, first-time buyers of homes worth up to £300,000 in England stopped paying the tax. These concessions had a marked, but temporary effect on transactions, and about half of the value of the tax holidays fed through to higher prices.[13]

When transactions and lending had dropped (Figure 8.1), but already passed their nadir, the UK government increased the price at which stamp duty started in England and Northern Ireland to £500,000, from July 2020 to the end of March 2021.[14] From April to September 2021, the holiday was extended at a starting point of £250,000. The stated aims were to help buyers who had lost income since March 2020 (Chapter 7), and to provide a general stimulant to the economy. The holiday cost £4.7 billion in England and Northern Ireland alone. Stamp duty policy had been devolved to the Scottish government in 2015 and to the Welsh government in 2018. These governments started holidays at the same time as the rest of the UK, lasting until 31 March and 30 June respectively,[15] although Welsh housing professionals felt the policy was not suited to their (low-priced) nation.[16]

The cuts were of most absolute benefit to existing owners buying the most expensive homes, and of most proportionate benefit to those buying homes worth £500,000, well above the average cost.[17] A 62-year-old decided to retire after redundancy and move from London to the south coast "taking advantage of the stamp duty and the increase in property available as a result". A 31-year-old had saved £15,000 in duty and another 31-year-old had used the holiday to buy two homes, including one to rent out: "overall we're doing well". A 62-year-old noted that the policy "has kickstarted the housing market, with the side effect that it is almost impossible to employ a builder". By February/March 2021, a 31-year-old said the cut "has priced me out of the market as a first-time buyer as everyone has bought second homes". Evidence suggests that while the holidays may have contributed to price rises, prices rose fastest in high-price areas where the holiday made least proportionate difference to the cost. Judge et al said holidays 'have been problematic less because they were inflationary, and more because they have been wasteful'.[18]

Activities related to letting and selling homes for rent and sale and house moving also ceased at the start of the first lockdown. By the start of April, almost no new homes were being put on the market.[19] In May 2020, a man aged 50 said "we were halfway through moving when lockdown began. Myself and my wife had to move everything ourselves". The number of purchases dropped faster in March and April 2020 than in the GFC, and reached a lower nadir.[20] In May 2020, a woman aged 19 said she had lost her job in mortgages, "which is what I really wanted to do".

However, the market opened again in May, after just seven weeks. By June 2020, the number of homes on the market was close to pre-pandemic levels.[21] However, even in February/March 2021, a woman aged 62 who was viewing homes with her son said "we were constantly aware of the possibility of encountering the virus in houses we visited" and a 31-year-old noted that "our offer for a mortgage/flat nearly fell through because of COVID delays". Nonetheless, by October 2020, transactions had returned to average 2019 monthly figures. Transactions then rose to a peak of 200,000 in June 2021, well above the 2007 peak[22] (Figure 8.1).

Comparing total transactions from March 2020 to October 2021 with the same months before the pandemic, there was very little difference in the total number of sales, but over 2020 at least, flats made up a reduced proportion of all transactions.[23]

Social landlords also responded immediately to lockdown in March 2020. UK social lettings dropped from 27,000 in March 2000 to 6,000 in April 2020, before returning to 26,000 in June 2020 after three months.[24] However, social landlords in Scotland said that this

Figure 8.1: Monthly transactions, residential property worth over £40,000, UK, seasonally adjusted, April 2005–December 2021

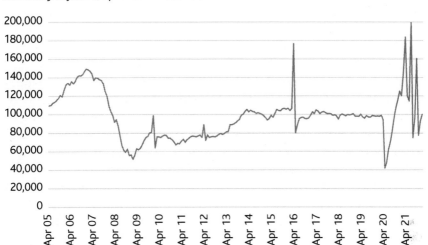

Note: The figures for October–December 2021 are provisional. The spike in 2016 was due to an increase in stamp duty on second homes, indicating the impact the tax can have on transactions
Source: ONS 2022b, Table 3

contributed to a large increase in the number of people in temporary accommodation, a significant backlog in getting empty homes in to use, and a considerable loss of income ... Arguably, a major lesson from the pandemic is the critical importance of continuing to let homes, especially to those people experiencing homelessness.[25]

These landlords commented that 'unlike the housing sales market', which was provided with a stamp duty holiday, they had no policy support to increase transactions.[26] In 2019, there were 1,160,000 people on council waiting lists in England. In 2020, this had dropped to 1,146,000, probably due to administrative disruption, but by 2021, the number had increased to 1,188,000, 2% above 2019, although there was a lot of local variation in policy and numbers.[27]

Some restrictions by lenders

FCA researchers noted that there had been less research on mortgage markets in the pandemic than employment, consumption and investment, despite the significance of home ownership, housing debt and housing wealth. Lender concern about high, increasing or uncertain risk is one element of housing system 'resilience'.

The number of new loans made by mortgage lenders dropped dramatically in the second quarter of 2020. Numbers of loans fell most in areas with the lowest prices, including Scotland, Northern Ireland and Wales. However, the number and value of loans then recovered and returned to the upward trends established after the GFC. In July–September 2021, lenders made £76 billion of loans, back to the level just after the peak in 2007.[28]

However, the type of new loans did change. In March 2020, lenders moved fast to reduce their risk from new loans, in effect making access to home ownership more difficult and costly for lower-income, low-saving or higher-risk households. This worked against policy efforts, such as Help to Buy (see Chapter 2), which was still responding to lending changes from the GFC, and pandemic policy including lower interest rates and the stamp duty holiday. In the first month of the pandemic, lenders cut the number of mortgage products on offer by 60%, especially the number with a Loan-to-Value (LTV) of 90% or more. The interest rate charged for new also increased slightly.[29] In October–December 2020, almost no 90–95% mortgages were agreed in the UK. Stephens et al suggested that higher LTV ratios were being used to ration the supply of homes during the period with lower transactions (Figure 8.1), as well as to reduce risk.[30] By April–June 2021, there had been a partial recovery in high LTV mortgages, but they remained scarce and were more expensive than they had been before the pandemic (Figure 8.2).

The Help to Buy policy (see Chapter 2) was still in place, and while between March 2019 and March 2020, 51,000 homes were bought using Help to Buy, over the pandemic year between March 2020 and March 2021, 56,000 homes were bought using the scheme.

Figure 8.2: Proportion of new mortgage loans with different loan-to-value ratios, UK, 2007–21

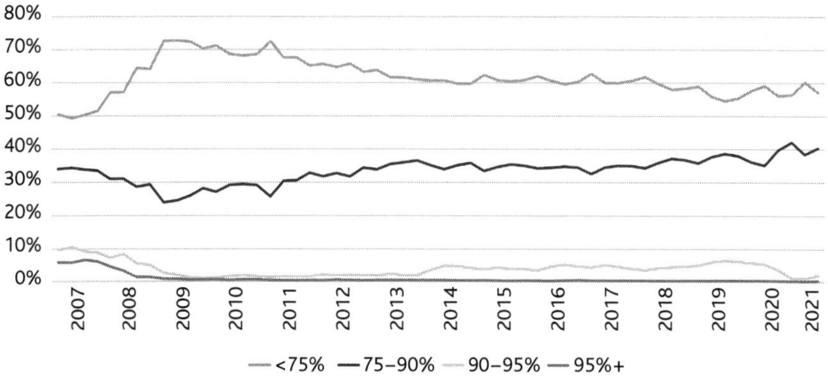

Source: FCA 2021d

However, in February/March 2021, a 31-year-old said "I feel like life has been ultimately put on hold ... I haven't been able to move out from my parents; because I can't get a mortgage". A 31-year-old who had a less-well-paid job after redundancy said "banks are making it extremely difficult for first time buyers ... which is disheartening given all the years I have been saving for this goal". A woman aged 50 with a son said the situation was "very unfair as he has been saving for years and this has made it very difficult for him to leave home".

However, existing mortgaged owners were partly protected from pandemic shock. The speedy introduction of mortgage holidays (see Chapter 7) prevented or at least postponed home loss and hardship for some existing mortgages owners affected by the pandemic, as well as some borrowers already in trouble (see Chapter 5). Because of the action of the Bank of England in reducing its base rate (see Chapter 3) and carrying out £450 billion of quantitative easing in 2020,[31] the interest rate for mortgages with less than 75% LTV reduced immediately, favouring borrowers or remortgagers with equity, who were typically older and with higher incomes.[32]

House price increases

In July 2020, the OBR's central estimate was that house prices would fall by 8%, with a range from 3% to 16%.[33] The early phases of the pandemic created enormous uncertainty for individuals, organisations and markets. Experience with previous recessions, including the GFC, and available data on C17th, C19th and the SARS epidemics suggested that house prices would fall.[34] However, despite generalised uncertainty and loss of income for large fractions of the population, house prices showed first 'apparent resilience',[35] then growth over 2020, and more growth over 2021.[36] This makes the pandemic recession 'a very odd recession'.[37] In March 2020, the average UK house price was £233,000 (including all type of homes). This changed little while transactions dropped (Figure 8.1), and then rose steadily, reaching a peak in June 2021 when the first stage of the stamp duty holiday ended and then rising again to £270,000 by September 2021, amounting to an annual rate of 11% over the pandemic (Figure 8.3). Not only was this a surprise, given the impact of the pandemic on many jobs and incomes, but it was also a change in trend after slowing price growth from 2016, resulting in no growth at all in early 2020.[38]

Why did the massive social and economic shock of the pandemic not affect house prices? 'Pent-up demand' after the brief closure of the market has been suggested, but is clearly insufficient.[39] House prices and house price growth were protected by pandemic policy, which boosted confidence, incomes and demand among the relevant part of the population. According to the OBR and other observers, the key policies were lowered interest rates, mortgage

Figure 8.3: Average nominal UK house prices, 2007–2020

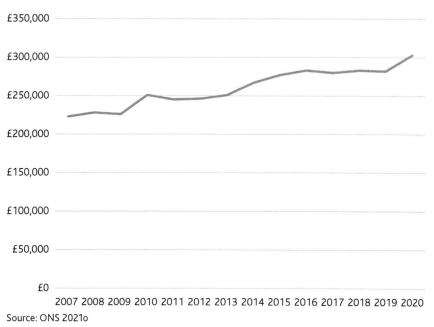

Source: ONS 2021o

holidays, the repossession moratorium and furlough from March 2020, the stamp duty holiday from July 2020, quantitative easing over 2020, extra savings for some over 2020–21, and the continuation of Help to Buy to 2021.[40] In addition, new supply was slightly more insufficient than before.[41] McCord et al described the housing market context during 2020–21 as 'artificial'.[42] If so, it was only somewhat more artificial during the pandemic than before the pandemic. Most countries in the EU, the USA, Canada and Australia all also experienced unexpected pandemic house price increases, although within nations, areas with higher infection rates and big tourism industries fared less well.[43]

Over 2020-21, the average UK home increased in value by £37,000, dwarfing the value of furlough, the SEISS, and UC and LHA uplifts to households (see Chapter 7). As in normal times, house price increases had an uneven impact and contributed to further wealth inequality between owners and renters. In addition, the pandemic created a new premium on indoor and outdoor space and less dense locations. This was widely termed the 'race for space', although Cheshire et al pointed out that there was a race for stamp duty holiday, as savings were biggest for higher-cost homes, up to £500,000. These patterns were also seen in other countries.[44] In May 2020, a woman aged 19 said: "This time has given me the chance to think more about the future. I'm considering a career change, and/or a move out of [the city]."[45] A woman aged 62 said her daughter and son-in-law had "changed their thinking about their quality of life going forward" and were planning to move from Manchester to Shropshire. A 62-year-old who had sold their home in London to downsize and relocate said "COVID-19 seems to have had the effect of increasing house prices in our area of Wales ... we are now resorting to the possibility of a building plot". In February/March 2021, a 50-year-old commented "I can't sell my flat in London because it has no outside space". Another said "flats aren't selling. In Northern Ireland there was a 'clear premium' over 2020–21 for 'larger housing in healthier and wealthier areas, which may serve to reinforce housing market inequalities'.[46] From February 2020 to February 2021, UK prices grew fastest for detached houses and in the least urban areas. Average prices actually fell in some inner London boroughs,[47] although rare centrally located detached homes showed big rises, due to walkability and some very high incomes.[48] My own home, a small ex-council flat in a high-rise block in inner London, appears to have lost about 20% of its value. Similarly, private rents fell in inner urban areas (for example, by 8% in inner London in 2020), but rose in suburban areas.[49]

The implications for inequalities

Housing is the main source of household wealth, more important than pensions, savings (see Chapter 7) or other assets. Increases in house values increase household wealth for home owners, particularly those with most equity, and they tend to increase inequalities in wealth between households and individuals.[50] The IFS found that wealth increased between 2019/20 and 2020/21 for people on above-average and average incomes. Because of the overall size of home ownership and its spread among income groups, wealth also increased for some people on below-average incomes. However, overall, wealth inequality increased.[51] House price increases had been sustained through a long list of expensive public policies. Thus, this increase in wealth inequality had been created by public policy and paid for with public money.

Pandemic effects of employment and housing market uncertainty, depleted savings, increased house prices and the end of the stamp duty holiday added to pre-existing barriers to home ownership for some, one element of the pre-pandemic housing crisis (see Chapter 2).[52] The pandemic had a big effect on tenants' expectations about buying. In contrast, tenants' hopes of buying were little affected by the GFC. After several years' stability, between 2019/20 and April/May 2021, the proportion of private renters in England expecting to buy fell dramatically from 60% to 45%. The proportion of social renters expecting to buy fell from 28% to 20%, reversing all the increase since the 'reinvigoration of the Right to Buy' (see Chapter 2).[53] A 31-year-old woman said she and her husband had both been made redundant, "the savings that we had put together to buy our first home … are now mostly gone". A 31-year-old said "I'm potentially coming to a realisation that I won't own a house regardless". A woman aged 31 commented:

"Life accomplishments not only put on hold, but also set back by at least five years. Both me and my partner [were] made redundant due to COVID-19, burnt through savings due to UC not covering bills, rent or food. Going forward, no job prospects. No way to release savings to buy a house, can't afford children."

Summary and conclusions

This chapter returns to the key questions set out in Chapter 1.

1) How prepared was the UK housing system for the COVID-19 shock?

The UK housing system, its homes and households were not prepared for the COVID-19 shock, because no UK institutions or sectors were prepared, including central government and the NHS. The explanations for this are dealt with in more detail elsewhere.[1]

When the pandemic struck, more people in the UK had the spacious homes that would enable safe and comfortable **staying home**, shielding and isolating than in many other countries in Europe and the world. Nonetheless, many did not have the right homes to shield and isolate successfully.

Before the pandemic, four housing problems were getting worse and were a source of inequality between income groups, ethnic groups and tenures: overcrowding, unaffordability (and low disposable income after housing costs), insecurity and homelessness.

UK households had high rates of employment, but large proportions of households were paying housing costs from work income that was insecure in normal times or about to become so, many households had no savings and the housing safety net had been weakened. A total of 22% of the population was in poverty after housing costs, and destitution and foodbank use were at record levels.

Before the pandemic, a housing 'crisis' for people on low incomes, some renters, hidden households and homeless people coexisted with good conditions affordability and equity growth for many. In normal times, overcrowding, unaffordability, insecurity and homelessness could be seen as problems of welfare, wellbeing and justice. In the pandemic, these were even more significant: they could expose those affected and others to risk of infection and death, as well as to the effects of abnormal income shocks.

In some senses, the UK political, economic and housing systems were more resilient to the income and GDP shock from the pandemic in 2020 than they had been at the time of the GFC in 2008, because of the experience gained at that time and reforms carried out afterwards. However, one lingering result of the GFC was that the UK government perceived the emergency role of housing policy as a tool for emergency economic policy rather than as a source of public health, living standards and wellbeing.

Expert advice for emergency preparedness and response was not drawn from the widest range of methods, disciplines or nations, and appeared to lack input from people with an understanding of households, housing and home.

2) How big was the impact of the pandemic on household and home?

The pandemic had significant impacts on households and home. For context, in 2020, the UK population was 66.8 million people, including 52.7 million adults, and 27.8 million households. The population of England was 56.3 million people, including 44.3 million adults, and 23.3 million households.[2]

Staying home

- In the first UK lockdown (March–June 2020), **the majority of the UK population at home** for 23 hours a day.[3]
- In the first UK lockdown, **21.4 million** UK adults did not leave their homes at all for five or more days a week.[4]
- In April and June 2020, **19.7 million adults in England were working at home**.[5]
- By September 2021, **11.7 million people in the UK had been furloughed and were at home**.[6]
- In June/July 2020, **9.5 million households in England had at least one extra person at home during the day** compared to normal.[7]
- **4.5 million extra people in the UK became unpaid carers** in their or others' homes[8] (see Chapter 6).
- **UK average house prices grew by 11% a year during the pandemic**, from £233,000 in March 2020 to £270,000 in September 2021 (see Chapter 8).
- In 2020, **42,000 more people died at home** in the UK compared to the historic average[9] (see Chapter 4).

Health

- In 2020, **58.5 million people in the UK lived with others**, increasing the risk of COVID-19 infection at home.[10]
- From March to December 2020, **29 million people in England were at home with symptoms** they would normally have taken to their GPs.[11] From February 2020 to January 2021, **28 million people in England**

were at home with symptoms or conditions for which they would normally had received hospital treatments.[12]

- **7.9 million households in England had more than one person, but did not have a spare bedroom for a household member to shield or isolate in if needed, while 5.5 million households did not have anywhere they could sleep alone.**[13]
- **By January 2022, an estimated 5.2–7.8 million COVID-19 infections had occurred at home** (see Chapter 5).
- By June/July 2020, **6 million households with more than one person had someone who had been asked to isolate (at least once),** creating a risk of infection for other household members.[14]
- From May 2020 to March 2021, **9.2 million people in England were contacted by NHS Test and Trace or local tracing teams and were asked to isolate at home.** At least another 2.5 million should have been contacted but were not reached.[15] Another 10.0 million were contacted between April 2021 and March 2022.[16]
- Up to 3.7 million people in England were defined as **'clinically extremely vulnerable' and recommended to 'shield' at home,** of which 3.4 million were being supported by household members, friends or family.
- A total of **1.7 million CEV people in England lived with others,** and were at risk of infection at home.[17]
- In June/July 2020, **4.0 million households in England had someone in them shielding**[18] (see Chapter 6).
- Before the pandemic, **0.8 million households in England were overcrowded,** putting members at greater risk of in-home transmission,[19] and during the pandemic, the number doubled (see Chapter 4).
- By July 2021, **500,000 people had long COVID.**[20]
- Between April and December 2020, **454,000 fewer people were transferred to hospital after 999 calls than in normal times** (see Chapter 4).
- By January 2022, **an estimated 38,000–58,000 died people within 28 days of a positive COVID-19 test after being infected at home** (see Chapter 5).
- By May 2020, at least **266 deaths from COVID-19 among rough sleepers in England had been prevented** by the provision of emergency self-contained accommodation[21] (see Chapter 7).

Income

- By September 2021, **11.7 million people in the UK had been furloughed, losing 20% of their income.**[22]
- **The Trussell Trust provided 2.5 million food parcels in the UK in** 2020/21.[23]

- Between March and June/July 2020, **2.8 million renting households in England fell behind with rent for the first time.**[24] **A total of 1.5 million renting households in England had been in arrears in March 2020, but fell further behind.**[25]
- **A total of 1.9 million households in the UK had applied for a mortgage holiday.**[26]
- Between March and August 2020, **1.0 million mortgaged home owners started claiming UC** in Great Britain.[27]
- Between March and August 2020, **0.8 million new renting households started claiming UC** to help pay their rent in Great Britain.[28]
- **A total of 970,000 self-employed construction workers received help from the SEISS**[29] (see Chapter 8).

Housing security

- Some **32,000 fewer households in England had their homes repossessed** in March–December 2020 than in the same period in 2019, while **23,000 fewer households had their homes repossessed** in 2021 than in 2019.[30]
- By September 2020, **37,000 former rough sleepers, night shelter users and people at risk of rough sleeping in England had been helped** into emergency accommodation, settled accommodation or intermediate housing.[31]
- A total of **13,000 fewer households became homeless in England because of mortgage and rent arrears than usual, and 11,000 fewer because the landlord wanted to sell or relet.**[32]
- A total of **13,000 more households became homeless in England because friends and family were no longer willing to house them, 3,000 more because of domestic abuse and 1,000 more because of other relationship breakdown.**[33]
- A total of **10,000 more households were in temporary accommodation after being accepted as homeless in England in** July–September 2020 compared to January–March 2020[34] (see Chapter 7).

3) Were household and home implicated in infections and deaths?

Household and home were implicated in infections and deaths, and in inequalities in infections and deaths.

An estimated 26–39% of all infections took place at home, potentially leading to an estimated 38,000–58,000 deaths within 28 days of a positive COVID-19 test. Infections at home were more likely in some households than others.

Where you lived within the UK in 2020/21– by region, local authority and type of settlement – was very important in determining individual risk of infection and death. However, there was relatively little variation in policy response, even between the UK nations.

Who you lived with was also an important factor in determining individual risk of infection and death. Larger households, those with vulnerable members and people working or studying outside the home were higher risk.

People's ability to **stay home**, and to shield and isolate when required, was affected by factors outside their control, including the size and facilities of their homes, and the need to pay housing costs.

These housing differences contributed to inequalities in infection and death, including differences by ethnicity and income or area deprivation. Shielding the most vulnerable at home came at a high cost to shielders and their households, and was only partly effective.

UK pandemic policies overlooked the risk of infection at home and within households, despite the availability of potential policies suggested by authoritative sources or tried in other countries. The fact that infection at home was overlooked contributed to the total number of infections and deaths, and to inequalities in infections and deaths.

However, overlooking the role of housing in health and health inequalities is not just an emergency problem. In normal times, housing problems are linked to tens of thousands of deaths annually. The pandemic inequalities in COVID-19-linked deaths rates by region and neighbourhood deprivation were little different from inequalities in death rates by region and neighbourhood deprivation in normal times.

4) Did household and home influence the impact of COVID-19 restrictions and supports?

Household size, occupancy home size and facilities, affordability and cost affected the experiences of **staying home**, including COVID-19 risk and other risks. They also affected the ability to **stay home** and shield or isolate.

Housing tenure, affordability and cost affected the impact of work income loss on household income, living standards and ability to pay for housing and avoid repossession.

Policies to mitigate the effect of pandemic income loss had significant limitations. The loss of income from furlough was difficult for the substantial minority of households with already-low income and unaffordable housing. Millions were not covered by emergency policies. Home owners found that UC would not help with housing costs. Renters who lost income for more than a short time and could not negotiate rent holidays accrued debts that many of them would be unable to pay. Despite a ministerial promise, pandemic policy, lender and landlord forbearance, using savings and family and friends, people did lose their homes because of COVID-19. Others kept their homes, but at the cost of months of worry and hardship, expending the resources and goodwill of family and friends, and eating into savings and future plans. Others moved into sharing. By the start of 2022, the predicted tsunami of legal repossessions had not occurred, but this was partly because repossessions had been postponed by law, delayed in the court system, dispersed across time and avoided due to resilience provided by family and friends, hardships, or because landlords and tenants have come to resolutions which may not be fair or legal on either side.

5) Has the pandemic changed the pre-existing inequalities in and caused by the housing system?

The pandemic has highlighted pre-existing inequalities in housing quality, size, location, affordability and security, and has also increased their significance. It has highlighted weaknesses in the housing safety net, including the fact that owners cannot claim housing costs on UC, that the LHA leaves many low-income renters paying their rent from income intended for other basic needs, the insecurity of some renters and the shortage of affordable housing. It has also highlighted the importance of the emergency housing system provided by family and friends.

Some pre-pandemic housing inequalities had grown:

- inequalities between tenures in employment rates and income;
- inequalities between tenures and between ethnic groups in overcrowding;
- inequalities in access to home ownership
- inequalities in housing wealth and thus household wealth between tenures, incomes and regions
- inequalities in mental health, including between household and housing groups, including inequality in loneliness between household types, and inequalities in the extent to which life seemed worthwhile by tenure; and
- inequalities in wellbeing between outright owners and others.

It is also likely that inequalities in satisfaction with home have grown because the pandemic has had particularly negative health, income and wellbeing effects on the groups who had the lowest pre-pandemic satisfaction: overcrowded households, households with Black, Bangladeshi and Pakistani HRPs, renters, lone parents and young people (see Chapters 2 and 3).

Because family resources are unequally distributed, increased reliance on familial welfare and family housing is inherently likely to increase inequalities – for example, between families and friends who have space and money to provide emergency housing, and those who do not.

New inequalities linked to home have developed between one-person households and others, larger and smaller households, households with members working outside the home and others where all could **stay home**, households with people who were shielding and others, people who were officially CEV and those who were vulnerable but less so, those covered by emergency COVID-19 income policies, and those included and excluded from help with housing costs. The pandemic has brought the 'housing crisis' of affordability (see Chapter 2) to some who had previously been protected, such as private renters, social renters and mortgaged owners in employment which previously appeared secure, and to some not covered by emergency income policies (Chapter 3).

By the start of 2022, all the pre-pandemic housing problems – overcrowding, unaffordability, insecurity and homelessness – remained. Despite the success of pandemic policies, the numbers of people sleeping rough and the number of homeless family households remained broadly unchanged. Improvements in housing conditions (see Chapter 2) are likely to have paused or reversed, due to disruption to maintenance, and inequalities may have grown.

6) What can be learnt from the pandemic about the housing system, household and home?

The pandemic has highlighted and apparently increased the continuing, often underrecognised, role of family and friends (as opposed to the state, the market and the voluntary sector) in providing income, material help, care, support and housing. Individuals, families and friends were a key source of the overall resilience of the UK in the face of pressure caused by the pandemic.

It has also both highlighted and increased the role of family and friends in the provision of housing, especially for younger adults, and in homelessness emergencies. Emergency housing to avoid infection, homelessness, unaffordable housing and loneliness in the pandemic was provided largely by friends and family.

As in housing, many argued that care was in 'crisis' before the pandemic. The pandemic has highlighted adult social care in care homes, because of the high death rates there, and the deficiencies in government policy and support. However, it has also highlighted the even greater role of the family in social care. At least temporarily, it has led to a further domestication and informalisation of care, taking place in the carer's or care recipient's home.

The pandemic has highlighted the problems with the concept of the 'household', as usually defined, as the household generally forms only part of any individual's social network important for wellbeing and resources. By emphasising the household as the basis for social contact, support and care, emergency regulations overlooked and disrupted significant links between households, which caused material and emotional hardship.

The pandemic has highlighted the fact that even in normal times, the meaning of 'home' can be negative, as a place of constraint, conflict and harm for some, and mixed emotions for many.

The pandemic has also reminded us of the distinction between policymaking and implementation. While some laws, policy or funding can transform institutions and public behaviour overnight, others are ignored. Results vary from overnight transformation to very little. Policymakers' assumptions about behaviour and potential for change may be wrong. Drastic changes in the activity of institutions and the public are possible.

The pandemic has highlighted the significance of rental income in incomes of some middle-aged and older people, and has subjected it to political and pandemic risk from market closure and loss of tenant income. Emergency policy has raised a question about whether non-self-contained accommodation will be satisfactory for homeless people in future.

Pandemic policy of raising the value of UC by what to better-off households may sound like a modest £20 a week, and lifting the LHA (help for low-income private renters) emergency policy on rough sleeping reduced COVID-19 infections and deaths, demonstrated that poverty can be reduced. Pandemic policy also demonstrated that homeless people can be rehoused rapidly in large numbers. However, both these facts were already well established through experience and research. It has taken a pandemic to make these changes, but they were only made on a temporary basis.

Housing and home could be central to building back better, and recovery policies could address some longstanding weakness of the housing system. However, this seems unlikely in practice.

7) Will the pandemic have lasting impacts on household and home?

In May 2020, a man aged 62 said: "If we simply revert to business as normal, it will all have been for nothing. We need to use this rest to change direction."

In early 2022, while hopefully the rate of UK COVID-19 deaths had peaked, the pandemic was an unfinished process, and some of the major effects were still ongoing. Nonetheless, some potential lasting impacts of the pandemic to date could be identified. In November 2021, only 12% of people said they would return to living exactly as they had before the pandemic.[35] Similarly, institutions and policies were unlikely to be 'built back the same', even if they were not necessarily to be 'built back better'. In addition, effects of the pandemic would 'wash away', by overlapping with new events and processes, such as rising inflation.

The pandemic changed the way in which homes are used, and some of these changes are likely to persist. Higher rates of working at home are likely to persist for some types of jobs, leading to lasting higher relative demand for larger homes and homes in less densely populated locations.[36]

The pandemic changed the size and shape of some households, and rates of household headship among younger and older people, and some of these changes are likely to persist.

The pandemic is likely to have lasting impacts on the housing careers of some individuals and groups of people. These include younger people who experienced disrupted education, early careers, partnering and housing, some older people who moved for care and support and may not return to independent housing, and to people of all ages who may have accrued debts or experienced damage to their long-term earnings through loss of work, forced early retirement, caring responsibilities, long COVID and other long-term illness.

Backlogs of tasks, likely to take several years to address, built up in several areas of public services. These include a substantial backlog of medical appointments, tests and operations, which will take years to clear. They also include a backlog of social housing lettings, a backlog of repairs to homes in all tenures, a backlog of rent arrears, a backlog of housing repossession cases, spent housing purchase deposits and other savings to be built up again. Pandemic policy squeezed out most other domestic policy in 2020/21, leaving a backlog in implementation and development of housing policy. The Conservative party's 2019 manifesto pledges to increase housing output and reduce homelessness became more difficult to implement, or became completely out of reach.

In addition, the pandemic depleted the resilience of institutions, business and communities, by depleting funds, savings, material, capacity for work, for innovation, workforce and volunteer energy. These resources will need to be rebuilt before they can be used again. The same applies to individuals and family and friends' resources and capacity for care and support.

The experiences of the pandemic are likely to result in lasting change in terms of the meaning of home and psychological relationships with homes, both for better and worse.

Appendix: The data from people aged 19, 31, 50, 62 and 74

Most of the quotations from individuals (in double speechmarks) in the book come from data provided by people aged 19, 31, 50, 62 and 74 in 2020. They participate in five different birth cohort studies, which track people born in a certain year through their lives. The studies are the 2000 Millennium Cohort Study, the 1989–90 Next Steps Study, the 1970 Birth Cohort Study, the 1958 Birth Cohort Study, and the 1946 National Survey of Health and Development.

All participants in these studies were asked to complete extra surveys during the pandemic. In May 2020 and February/March 2021, respondents were asked to provide written answers online in their own words to an open-ended question about their pandemic experiences (see Chapter 1). In May 2020, this question was answered by 12,738 people across Britain – 57% of the people who answered the whole COVID-19 survey (and 21% of the total in the cohort studies). In February/March 2021, the open-ended question was answered by 12,168 people – 43% of those who answered the COVID-19 survey (and 31% of the total in the cohort studies). Thus, the responses are likely to overrepresent people who were able to respond online, and for whom the impact of COVID-19 was salient. There were higher response rates from female and older participants.

I did not draw a sample of the total 24,000 responses to analyse, but instead searched all responses using terms related to housing issues, such as 'home', 'room' and 'landlord'. This approach obviously oversamples respondents for whom housing was a salient issue, but it is acceptable when combined with data to show how widespread different housing situations and concerns were in the period.

In May 2020, the average answer had 113 words. The commonest substantive words used by respondents were 'work', 'family', 'time' and 'home', except for those aged 74, whose most frequent words were 'family', 'time' and 'life' and 'friends'.[1] In the anonymity of the survey, many respondents revealed difficult and sensitive events, experiences and feelings. In May 2020, a woman aged 50 commented at the end of her answer "that was actually really cathartic, as I keep a brave face on for my family!:)".

In the book, respondents are generally referred to only by their age and gender. People born between 2000 and 2002 are referred to as aged 19. Parents of people born between 2000 and 2002, whose exact age was unavailable, are referred to as 'middle-aged' men and women. I have retained the original spelling and abbreviations, and have tried to ensure that quotes do not contain potentially identifying information.

I am very grateful to the Centre for Longitudinal Studies (CLS) at the UCL Social Research Institute for the use of these data and to the UK Data Service for making them available. However, neither CLS nor the UK Data Service bears any responsibility for the analysis or interpretation of these data.

Notes

Chapter 1

1   WHO 2020a
2   Calvert and Arbuthnott 2021
3   https://covid19.who.int/
4   Liu et al 2020
5   Boddington et al 2020
6   BBC 2020g
7   Kelly 2020
8   BBC 2020b
9   Quoted in Calvert and Arbuthnott 2021: 218
10   Tooze 2021
11   Farrar with Ahuja 2021: 206
12   Farrar with Ahuja 2021: 9
13   Calvert and Arbuthnott 2021
14   Tooze 2021
15   Farrar with Ahuja 2021: 40
16   Calvert and Arbuthnott 2021: 226
17   Farrar with Ahuja 2021: 224–225
18   Farrar with Ahuja 2021: 12
19   Tooze 2021
20   IMF 2020
21   Calvert and Arbuthnott 2021: 204
22   OBR 2021
23   Calvert and Arbuthnott 2021
24   IMF 2021; OBR 2021
25   Mackie and Smith 2020; Earley 2021; Stephens et al 2021
26   Jasonoff et al 2021: np
27   *The Lancet Public Health* 2020
28   Kraatz 2018; Stephens et al 2021
29   Squires and White 2019: 167
30   Mackie and Smith 2020
31   Stiglitz 2020
32   HSC/STC 2020c
33   Smart 2021
34   Qureshi 2020: 1
35   HDC/STC 2020b: Q823
36   Tooze 2021
37   Preece et al 2021
38   Burchardt 2020
39   Social Housing Resilience Group 2021
40   DCLG 2017
41   UCL 2021
42   Hammond 2021: 32
43   Gray, quoted in Barker and Heath 2020
44   UCL 2021
45   Carpentieri et al 2020

Chapter 2

1. SAGE 2020a:23
2. Randall et al 2011
3. ONS 2021d
4. Randall et al 2011: 147
5. Bramley et al 2018: 9
6. ONS 2021d
7. Bear et al 2020:24, Kaur Bhogal in Bear et al 2020
8. BBC 2020a
9. ONS 2021d
10. ONS 2021b
11. ONS 2021b: Tables 7, 8
12. Bramley et al 2018
13. ONS 2021w
14. Hills 2007
15. DLUHC 2021d: Table FA5401
16. Lelkes and Zolyomi 2009
17. DLUHC 2021d: Table DA3203 (SST3.4)
18. Eurostat EU-SILC ILC_MDHO06A and MDHO01A
19. Bradshaw et al 2008, Davis et al 2021
20. Tudor Hart 1971 ; Cookson et al 2021
21. Tunstall et al 2013
22. Moser and David 2008
23. OBR 2021
24. Cheshire et al 2021: 15
25. Apergis 2021
26. Mackie and Smith 2020: 6
27. HMRC 2021c
28. DLUHC 2021e: Release Table 1
29. Gershuny and Sullivan 2019
30. ONS 2021i
31. Gershuny 2018
32. HMT 2021
33. DCLG 2017
34. Prisk 2012
35. DLUHC 2021d: Table FA1422
36. DCLG 2012
37. Bradshaw et al 2008
38. DLUHC 2021d: Table FA122
39. Eurostat EU-SILC Table ILC_LVHO50B
40. Eurostat EU-SILC survey Table ILC_LVHO05Q
41. Barton and Wilson 2021
42. MHCLG 2020e Table AT1.12
43. Bourquin et al 2019
44. Clarke et al 2016
45. Data from FES/HBAI StatXplore (Household income threshold – after housing costs (60% of median income (AHC) in latest prices)
46. Francis-Devine 2021
47. Stephens et al 2020: Table 122
48. ONS 2020e
49. Stephens et al 2020: Table 121

[50] MHCLG 2021c: Figure 1.5
[51] Judge and Pacitti 2021b
[52] Hirsch 2019
[53] Legally owed a 'main duty', meaning help to secure housing, usually temporary accommodation followed by a social rented or private tenancy
[54] Fitzpatrick et al 2019
[55] DLUHC Live table 775
[56] Scottish Government 2020
[57] NAO 2017
[58] Fitzpatrick et al 2019
[59] Fitzpatrick et al 2017: viii
[60] Thunder and Bovill Rose 2019
[61] DLUHC 2021a
[62] Fitzpatrick et al 2019
[63] Conservative Party 2017, 2019
[64] Tunstall 2016
[65] DLUHC 2021a
[66] Benfer et al 2021
[67] De Hollander and Staatsen 2003
[68] Leather and Morrison 1997; Revell and Leather 2000; de Hollander and Staatsen 2003; Marmot Review Team 2010, 2011
[69] Marsh et al 2000; Wilkinson 1999; Douglas et al 2003; Marmot Review Team 2010; Pollack et al 2010
[70] Piddington et al 2013
[71] Nicol et al 2015; HMT 2021
[72] ONS 2018
[73] ONS 2020c
[74] Marsh et al 2000; Pevalin et al 2017
[75] Reeves et al 2016
[76] Marmot et al 2010, 2020
[77] Tooze 2021: 36
[78] Grenfell Tower Inquiry 2019; House of Commons Housing Communities and Local Government Committee 2020
[79] MHCLG 2021c: Tables 1–4
[80] Stephens et al 2021
[81] Fitzpatrick et al 2021
[82] ONS 2021o
[83] Bank of England 2022
[84] Bracke et al 2020
[85] DLUHC 2021e: Release Table 1
[86] Stephens and Blenkinsopp 2020
[87] DLUHC Live Table 104
[88] HoC Public Accounts Committee 2019: 3
[89] Stephens et al 2021: 25
[90] Dowell-Jones and Buckley, 2017: 1, in Stephens et al 2021
[91] Ostry et al 2016
[92] Tunstall 2016
[93] OBR 2021
[94] Stephens et al 2019
[95] Bottery and Ward 2021
[96] Farrar with Ahuja 2021: 92

97 Quoted in Calvert and Arbuthnott 2021: 93
98 Calvert and Arbuthnott 2021: 88
99 Davis et al 2020: 5
100 Bottery and Ward 2021
101 OBR 2022
102 OBR 2021
103 Stephens et al 2021
104 DWP 2021d
105 Fitzpatrick et al 2020b
106 Bhattacharjee and Lisauskaite 2020
107 Eurostat EU-SILC survey MDES04
108 MHCLG 2020e Table AT1.19
109 ONS 2020e Tables 1, 7
110 ONS 2021r
111 DLUHC 2021d: Table FA1301 (S11)
112 MoJ 2022: Table 1
113 MoJ 2022
114 Parkin and Wilson 2016
115 Clarke et al 2017
116 Clarke et al 2015
117 Chartered Institute of Housing Wales 2016
118 MoJ 2022
119 Stephens and Leishman 2017: 1040
120 DLUHC 2021c
121 Cromarty 2019
122 Charlesworth et al 2020
123 Clarke et al 2015
124 Charlesworth et al 2020
125 Clarke et al 2015
126 Richardson 2020
127 Poggio and Whitehead 2017
128 Wilcox et al 2017
129 NAO, quoted in Lupton and Collins 2015
130 JRF 2022
131 Esping-Andersen 1990
132 Isakjee 2017
133 ONS 2021c
134 Hill et al 2021
135 Fitzpatrick et al 2019
136 MHCLG 2020c
137 MHCLG 2020c
138 MHCLG 2021b
139 MHCLG 2021b

Chapter 3

1 For example, Horton 2020; Calvert and Arbuthnott 2021; Farrar with Ajuja 2021; Hammond 2021; HSC/STC 2021a; Jasonoff et al 2021; Tooze 2021
2 Farrar with Ahuja 2021
3 Calvert and Arbuthnott 2021
4 BBC 2020a
5 Jombert et al 2020: 1

6   Calvert and Arbuthnott 2021
7   Hammond 2021
8   Tooze 2021
9   SAGE 2000b
10 Karlinsky and Kobak 2021
11 ONS 2020a, 2021g
12 Aburto et al 2021
13 ONS 2020d
14 Alinsky and Kobak 2021
15 ONS 2020b
16 EMG/NERVTAG 2020: 2
17 UKHSA 2020
18 ONS 2021a: Tables 1i, 3d, 4d, 5d; NISRA 2021
19 Hammond 2021: 36
20 ONS 2020a
21 ONS 2021h
22 NRS 2021b: Table 5
23 NISRA 2021
24 Middle Super Output Areas, with an average population of 8,000
25 ONS 2021s
26 Historic England 2018
27 ONS 2021h: Table 1
28 ONS 2020c; NRS 2021b: Table 9; NISRA 2021. Data for England and Wales are for 1 March–31 July 2020, Scotland for 2020 and Northern Ireland for 1 March 2020–31 January 2021. Data for adjacent deciles for England were averaged to create figures for quintiles.
29 Office for Health Improvement and Disparities 2021
30 Marmot 2010, 2020
31 HSC/STC 2021b: Q912
32 ONS 2021j
33 Census 2011, accessed via https://www.nomisweb.co.uk/sources/census_2011
34 Francis-Devine 2021
35 ONS 2021e
36 Hammond 2021: 17
37 ONS 2021h
38 NRS 2021b: Table 9; NISRA 2021
39 ONS 2021k
40 Islam et al 2021
41 Clift et al 2020
42 ONS 2021p
43 ONS 2021m: Table 2
44 ONS 2021g
45 NRS 2020
46 ONS 2021q: Table 1
47 Lo et al 2021
48 ONS 2021g
49 ONS 2021o
50 Hodgson et al 2020
51 Shah et al 2020
52 Huang et al 2020
53 WHO 2020b
54 DHSC 2020a

55 Farrar with Ahuja 2021
56 WHO 2021
57 Chan et al 2020
58 Quoted in Calvert and Arbuthnott 2021: 141
59 Calvert and Arbuthnott 2021
60 Farrar with Ahuja 2021
61 DHSC 2020a
62 DHSC/PHE 2020
63 Calvert and Arbuthnott 2021
64 DHSC 2020a
65 EMG/NERVTAG 2020; PHE 2021
66 Le Page and McNamara 2021
67 For example, Horton 2020; Hammond 2021; Farrar with Ahuja 2021; Calvert and Aburthnott 2021; HSC/STC 2021a; Tooze 2021
68 HSC/STC 2021b: 32
69 HSC/STC 2021b: 36
70 HSC/STC 2021b: 32
71 HDC/STC 2021
72 STC 2020 136: Q883
73 Jasnonoff et al 2021
74 Inside Housing 2020
75 DoH 2007; PHE 2017
76 SPI-B 2020
77 EMG/SPI-B 2021
78 Farrar with Ahuja 2021: 95
79 HSC/STC 2021d: Q1011
80 Boyd 2020
81 Calvert and Arbuthnott 2021
82 DHSC 2020a
83 Quoted in Farrar with Ahuja 2021: 97
84 Farrar with Ahuja 2021: 100
85 Calvert and Arbuthnott 2021; HSC/STC 2021b
86 HSC/STC 2021b: 38
87 Hodgson et al 2020
88 Johnson 2020b
89 Calvert and Arbuthnott 2021
90 Tooze 2021
91 PHS 2021
92 Hodgson et al 2020
93 Calvert and Arbuthnott 2021: 145
94 Benmelech and Tzur-Ilan 2021, Bank of England 2022
95 IMF 2021
96 Farrar with Ahuja 2021
97 Hodgson et al 2020
98 Campbell Tickell 2020
99 Calvert and Arbuthnott 2021: 226
100 Calvert and Arbuthnott 2021: 218
101 Dunn et al 2021
102 Tatlow et al 2021
103 Dunn et al 2021
104 Tatlow et al: 21

[105] Calvert and Arbuthnott 2021
[106] HSC/STC 2021b
[107] Institute for Government 2021
[108] Fancourt et al 2021
[109] Hale et al 2021
[110] Mackie and Smith 2020: 6
[111] Tatlow et al 2021: 2

Chapter 4

[1] ONS 2021a: Table 1
[2] ONS 2021x
[3] Judge and Pacitti 2021a: 5
[4] ONS 2021b: Tables 1.1, 2.1
[5] ONS 2020aa: 5
[6] ONS 2021b: Table 5
[7] Quoted in BBC 2020c
[8] MHCLG 2020a: Table 29a, b
[9] MHCLG 2021a: Tables T25b, T26
[10] DLUHC 2021a: Table T24b
[11] MHCLG 2020a: Table 30
[12] Bear et al 2020: 10
[13] Zilanawala et al 2020
[14] ONS 2021b: Table 6
[15] MHCLG 2020a: Tables T27, T28, T29
[16] ONS 2021c
[17] ONS 2021d: Table 7
[18] Zilanawala et al 2020
[19] ONS 2021aa: Table 5
[20] Fitzpatrick et al 2021
[21] MHCLG 2020d: Table FA2601
[22] Calvert and Arbuthnott 2021; see also South Hams 2021
[23] Fancourt et al 2021
[24] Long et al 2020: 4
[25] Appleton 2020
[26] Kearns et al 2020
[27] Calvert and Arbuthnott 2021: 240
[28] ONS 2020b
[29] Fancourt et al 2021
[30] Fancourt et al 2021
[31] Crossley et al 2021b
[32] ONS 2020nits: Table 9a
[33] Fancourt et al 2021
[34] MHCLG 2020a: Table T11k
[35] MHCLG 2020a: Table T11b
[36] Lenhard 2020: 1
[37] MHCLG 2020f, DLUHC 2021g
[38] DLUHC 2021a: Table T40i
[39] MHCLG 2020f: Annex Table 1.18; DLUHC 2021a: Table T40a
[40] DLUHC 2021a: Table T40e
[41] MHCLG 2020f: Annex Table 1.18; MHCLG 2020a: Table T42i; DLUHC 2021a: Table T40i

42 Fancourt et al 2020
43 ONS 2021i
44 Fancourt et al 2020
45 ONS 2021i
46 Fancourt et al 2020
47 MHCLG 2020a: Table T02a
48 ONS 2020g: Table9a
49 DLUHC 2021a: Table T02a
50 MHCLG 2020a: Table T12Ae
51 DfE 2021b: Table 1b
52 ONS 2021i
53 Preece et al 2021: 11
54 ONS 2021i
55 MHCLG 2020a
56 ONS 2021i
57 ONS 2021i
58 Eurostat EUSILC ILC_LVHO01
59 Gurney 2020
60 Gurney 2020, 2021
61 Gurney 2021: 7
62 Fancourt et al 2020
63 Yalcin and Duzen 2021: np
64 Byrne 2020: 351
65 Taylor et al 2020
66 Yalcin and Duzen 2021: np
67 National Voices 2020: 3
68 Taylor et al 2020: np
69 ONS 2022a: Table 6
70 Dorling and Arundel 2020
71 Emili 2020: 146
72 Johnson 2021
73 National Voices 2020: 9

Chapter 5

1   Census 2011: Table KS405EW, from www.nomis.web
2   Tsai and Wilson 2020:e187
3   Edge et al 2020: np
4   Kirby 2020: 447
5   Quoted in Edge et al 2020: np
6   Fitzpatrick et al 2020a
7   Cromarty 2020
8   Kirby 2020
9   Some non-UK citizens have the condition of 'No Recourse to Public Funds' ('NRPF') put on their leave to enter or remain in the UK, which means they are unable to claim most benefits, including housing benefit, or to access many services
10 Cromarty 2020; Machin 2022
11 Heath 2020b
12 Fitzpatrick et al 2020a: vi
13 Thomas and Mackie 2021
14 MHCLG 2020z
15 MHCLG 2020b

16 Fitzpatrick et al 2021: 24
17 Heath 2021a
18 Fitzpatrick et al 2020a
19 Fitzpatrick et al 2021
20 Fitzpatrick et al 2020a: vi
21 Mackie and Smith 2020
22 Fitzpatrick et al 2020a: 9
23 Wilmore 2021
24 Heath 2021b
25 Quoted in Heath 2021a
26 Heath 2020b
27 Fitzpatrick et al 2019
28 Rosenthal et al 2020
29 Dorney-Smith et al 2020: 191
30 MHCLG 2020d
31 MHCLG 2020f
32 MHCLG 2020d
33 MHCLG 2020d
34 Gurney 2020
35 SAGE 2020b
36 SPI-B 2020: 1
37 SPI-B 2020: 2; Beale et al 2021
38 DHSC/PHE 2020
39 Hammond 2021: 7
40 Hammond 2021: 32
41 HSC/STC 2020a: Q724
42 Huang et al 2020
43 Chan et al 2020
44 Farrar with Ahuja 2021
45 Qui et al 2020; Yang et al 2020; Zhu et al 2020, Li et al 2020
46 Liu et al 2020
47 Pfefferle et al 2020
48 Nande et al 2021: np
49 Zhu et al 2020
50 Lopez-Bernal et al 2020
51 Thompson et al 2020
52 Fung et al 2021
53 Madewell et al 2020
54 Fung et al 2021: np
55 Fung et al 2021; Madewell et al 2021
56 Thompson et al 2020
57 Farrar with Ahuja 2021
58 Calvert and Arbuthnott 2021
59 Boddington et al 2020: 15
60 Lopez-Bernal et al 2020
61 Singanayagam et al 2021
62 Lopez-Bernal et al 2020: np
63 Lai et al 2021
64 Lopez-Bernal 2020
65 SAGE 2020: 3
66 SAGE 2020: 23

[67] Beale et al 2021
[68] NHS Test and Trace 2021
[69] EMG/SPI-B 2021: 3
[70] Singanayagam et al 2021
[71] Calculations need to take into account the fact that one-person households had no in-household transmission and that multi-person households had different numbers of people
[72] SAGE 2020a: 6
[73] SAGE 2020a: 2
[74] SAGE 2020a
[75] Shadmi et al 2020
[76] SPI-B 2020: 1
[77] EMG/SPI-B 2020: 2
[78] MHCLG 2020a; Fancourt et al 2020
[79] Aldridge et al 2021: 9
[80] ONS 2021o
[81] Shah et al 2020
[82] McConnell 2020
[83] SAGE 2020a
[84] HSC/STC 2020i: Q337
[85] SPI-B 2020: 6
[86] SPI-B 2020: 1
[87] House of Commons Library 2021
[88] Quoted in House of Commons Library 2021
[89] DLUHC 2021d: Table DA1101 (SST1.1)
[90] Dunn et al 2020; Hodgson et al 2020
[91] Glynn et al 2020: 2751
[92] Fung et al 2021: np
[93] SPI-B 2020: 13
[94] EMG/SPI-B 2020
[95] World Health Organization 2020
[96] EMG/SPI-B/SPI-M 2021
[97] PHE 2021
[98] PHE 2021
[99] EMG/SPI-B 2021
[100] Bear et al 20020: 24
[101] SPI-B 2020
[102] EMG/SPI-B 2020: 2
[103] EMG/SPI-B 2021: 7
[104] PHE 2021
[105] Original source withdrawn
[106] HSC/STC 2020i: Q337
[107] NHS 2017
[108] Qui et al 2020
[109] Yang, et al 2020: 31
[110] Hammond 2021: 7
[111] Farrar with Ahuja 2021
[112] Tooze 2021
[113] SAGE 2020a
[114] Smith et al 2021b
[115] Farrar with Ahuja 2021; HSC/STC 2020j: Q475
[116] HSC/STC 2020i: Q337

[117] SAGE 2020a: 3
[118] HSC/STC 2020a: Q724
[119] Denford et al 2020
[120] EMG/SPI-B 2021
[121] PHE 2021b
[122] Boddington et al 2020: 15
[123] Edge et al 2021: np
[124] LB Newham 2021
[125] HSC/STC 2021c
[126] HSC/STC 2021b: Q1387
[127] SPI-B 2020: 6
[128] SAGE 2020a
[129] Shah et al 2020: 7
[130] SAGE 2020a: 24

Chapter 6

[1] PHS 2021
[2] NHS Digital 2020a
[3] NHS Digital 2021a
[4] BBC 2020d
[5] PHS 2021
[6] ONS 2020h; Tatlow et al 2021
[7] PHS 2021
[8] MHCLG 2021a: Table T06a
[9] Bear et al 2020
[10] Carers UK 2020b: 9
[11] ONS 2020h
[12] NHS Digital 2020b
[13] PHS 2021
[14] Hodgson and Peytrignet 2021
[15] MHCLG2020b and MHCLG 2021a: both Table T06b
[16] HSC/STC 2020g
[17] Calvert and Arbuthnott 2021
[18] Original source removed
[19] NHS England 2021c
[20] Hansard, 26 February 2020, vol 672, col 331
[21] Johnson 2020a
[22] NAO 2021
[23] Prime Minister's Office 2020; Dunn et al 2021
[24] Dunn et al 2021
[25] Ferguson and Kennedy 2021
[26] https://coronavirus.data.gov.uk/
[27] NAO 2021
[28] HSC/STC 2021d
[29] MHCLG 2020a: Table T05f
[30] ONS 2022a: Table 1a
[31] DfE 2021a
[32] ONS 2020h
[33] MHCLG 2020a: Tables T17d, e, f, g
[34] ONS 2020h
[35] HSC/STC 2020f: 6

36 HSC/STC 2020e
37 Benton and Power ud
38 National Voices 2020: 9
39 HSC/STC 2020f
40 ONS 2021y: Table 5.1
41 Farrar with Ahuja 2021
42 Smith et al 2021b
43 NAO 2021
44 Fancourt et al 2021
45 ONS 2021y: Table 2.1
46 Smith et al 2021b
47 Smith 2021b
48 Smith et al 2021b
49 ONS 2021y: Table 2.1
50 Fancourt et al 2021
51 Smith et al 2021b
52 ONS 2021y: Table 6.1
53 Brewer and Patrick 2021: 18
54 CPAG 2018
55 Calvert and Arbuthnott 2021
56 HSC/STC 2021d: Q1014
57 DHSC 2020b
58 Prime Minister's Office 2020
59 ONS 2021y: Table 6.1
60 LB Newham 2021
61 NHS Test and Trace 2022: Table 22
62 Farrar with Ahuja 2021; Hammond 2021; HSC/STC 2021a
63 HSC/STC 2020i: Q335
64 SAGE 2020a: 23
65 HSC/STC 2020j: 78
66 SAGE 2020a: 24
67 HSC/STC 2020j: 78
68 See MHCLG 2020a
69 ONS 2020h
70 MHCLG 2020a and MHCLG 2021a: both Tables T06c
71 ONS 2020h
72 ONS 2020h
73 ONS 2020h
74 United Nations Office on Drugs and Crime 2015
75 Prison Reform Trust 2020
76 ONS 2020h
77 Hansard, 26 February, vol 672, col 330
78 Mikolai et al 2020: 2
79 ONS 2020h
80 ONS 2020h
81 MHCLG 2020a
82 Tudor Hart 1971
83 Eurostat EUSILC Table ILV_LVHO5Q
84 Hansard, 26 February, vol 672, col 330
85 SPI-B 2020: 5
86 ONS 2021y: Table 5.3

[87] EMG/SPI-B 2021
[88] ONS 20212a: Table 5
[89] HSC/STC 2020d: 1
[90] Smith et al 2021a: 3
[91] Smith et al 2021a
[92] ONS 2020h
[93] PHS 2021
[94] ONS 2021q: Table 1
[95] Byrne 2020: np
[96] DHSC 2020a; PHE 2021a; WHO 2021
[97] ONS 2021v
[98] WHO 2020c: 1
[99] Hammond 2021: 9
[100] Zilanawala et al 2020
[101] SPI-B 2020: 6
[102] Hammond 2021: 40
[103] NHS England 2021d
[104] NHS 2020s; Hammond 2021: 24
[105] Calvert and Arbuthnott 2021
[106] ONS 2021l
[107] Calvert and Arbuthnott 2021; HSC/STC 2021b
[108] Quoted in Calvert and Arbuthnott 2021: 394
[109] HSC/STC 2021b: Q867
[110] Hammond 2021: 34
[111] NHS England 2021a
[112] ONS 2021: live tables 8, 9, 10, 11,12
[113] ONS 2020h
[114] Warner et al 2021
[115] Fancourt et al 2020
[116] Sunstein 1996
[117] ONS 2020h
[118] Hammond 2021
[119] Sunstein 1996
[120] ONS 2021u: Figure 3
[121] NRS 2021a: Table 3
[122] ONS 2021s
[123] NRS 2021a: Table 3
[124] ONS 2021u: Figure 3
[125] ONS 2020c
[126] ONS 2021n: Figure 4
[127] ONS 2020c
[128] ONS 2021n: Figure 4
[129] Gurney 2020
[130] NRS 2021a: Table 3
[131] ONS 2021s
[132] Marie Curie 2021: np
[133] Steward 2000: 108
[134] Marie Curie 2021
[135] Quoted in Carers UK 2020b: 10
[136] Gurney 2021
[137] ONS 2022a: Table 8

138 Fancourt et al 2021
139 ONS 2022a: Table 8
140 Evandrou et al 2021
141 ONS 2020f
142 Pierce et al 2020: 1
143 Banks and Xu 2020: 5
144 Banks and Xu 2020: 3
145 Gurney 2021
146 ONS 2020f
147 ONS 2020f; Pierce et al 2020
148 Pierce et al 2020
149 MHCLG 2020a: Tables 34Aa, Ba, Ca, Da, Ea; MHCLG 2021a: Tables 30Aa, Ba Ca, Da, Ea; DLUHC 2021a: Tables 29Aa, Ba, Ca, Da, Ea
150 Banks and Xu 2020, Pierce et al 2020: 8
151 MHCLG 2020a: Tables 34Aa, Ba, Ca, Da, Ea; MHCLG 2021a: Tables 30Aa, Ba Ca, Da, Ea; DLUHC 2021a: Tables 29Aa, Ba, Ca, Da, Ea
152 Bear et al 2020: 24
153 Fancourt et al 2021
154 Fancourt et al 2020
155 Evandrou et al 2021
156 MHCLG 2020a: Table 34; MHCLG 2021a: Table 30; DLUHC 2021a: Table 29
157 NAO 2018, Dunn et al 2020, HSC/STC 2020c
158 ONS 2013
159 Carers UK 2020b
160 Carers UK 2019
161 DWP StaXplore CA: Cases in payment: Cases from May 2018
162 ONS 2018; HMT 2021
163 NAO 2018
164 HSC/STC 2020g
165 Carers UK 2020b
166 Whitley et al 2021
167 Carers UK 2020b
168 Carers UK 2020b
169 Bear et al 2020: 47
170 Carers UK 2020b
171 MOD 2020; HoC Defence Committee 2021
172 Carers UK 2020a
173 Carers UK 2020b
174 Sunstein 2021
175 NAP 2018
176 Whitley et al 2021
177 HSC/STC 2020f
178 HSC/STC 2020gg
179 Carers UK 2020a
180 FCA 2021c
181 Bear et al 2020: 8
182 Dunn et al 2020a: 25
183 HSC/STC 2021d: 2
184 Bear et al 2020: 4
185 SAGE 2020a: 23
186 PHE 2020f

187 Carers UK 2020a: 19
188 Dunn et al 2020
189 HSC/STC 2021d
190 SAGE 2020a: 23
191 Carers UK 2020a
192 HSC/STC 2020h: 1

Chapter 7

1 DLUHC 2021a: Table T04b
2 Benmelech and Tzur-Ilan 2021
3 Tooze 2021: 12
4 Hale et al 2021
5 Crossley et al 2021a
6 Summer 2018
7 Crossley et al 2021a
8 HMRC 2021a
9 HMRC 2021a
10 DLUHC 2021a: Table T50a
11 Powell et al 2021
12 DLUHC 2021a: Tables T50a–i
13 MHCLG 2020a: Table T03b; MHCLG 2021a: Table T31a
14 OBR 2021; ONS 2021z
15 Powell et al 2021
16 Blundell et al 2022
17 Crossley et al 2021b
18 Cowie 2020
19 Chancellor Rishi Sunak, quoted in Mackley et al 2021: 3
20 OBR 2021
21 DWP 2021e
22 Davis et al 2020
23 Patrick and Lee 2021
24 Judge 2020
25 DWP 2021b
26 HMRC 2021b
27 BBC 2021
28 BBC 2021
29 NAO 2020
30 www.excludeduk.org
31 DWP 2021d: Table 2_1db
32 MHCLG 2019
33 MHCLG 2020a
34 Watson and Bailey 2021: 8
35 MHCLG 2020a: Tables FA1422 and DA1101
36 MHCLG 2021a: Table T03a
37 Brewer and Patrick 2021
38 ONS 2022a: Table 8
39 DWP 2021f: Table 6.2
40 Crossley et al 2021b, ONS 2022e
41 Crossley et al 2021b
42 FCA 2021c
43 FCA 2021c

44 Fancourt et al 2020
45 Crossley et al 2021
46 Crossley et al 2021: 4
47 DWP 2021d: Table 3.5db; ONS 2022d: Tables 1.3c, 1.3d
48 DWP 2021d: Table 2.1ab; ONS 2022d: Table 1.2c
49 ONS 2022d: Table 1.2b
50 ONS 2022d: Table 1.3a
51 Bundell et al 2022: np
52 Mackley et al 2021: 6
53 Davis et al 2020: 2
54 Blundell et al 2022
55 Bell and Judge 2021; Judge et al 2021a
56 Davis et al 2021
57 Brewer and Patrick 2021
58 FCA 2021c
59 Bhattacharjee and Lisauskaite 2020; Fitzpatrick et al 2020b
60 Bhattacharjee and Lisauskaite 2020
61 DWP 2021d: Table 9.1a; ONS 2022d: Table 1.3c
62 Trussell Trust 2021
63 Trussell Trust 2021
64 DEFRA 2021; Lasko-Skinner and Sweetland 2021
65 Blundell et al 2022: np
66 DWP 2021d: Tables 4.7db, 6.11db; ONS 2022d: Tables 1.6d, 1.4e
67 FCA 2021c
68 MHCLG 2020a: 3
69 FCA 2021c
70 Crossley et al 2021; OBR 2021
71 Albuquerque and Varadi 2022
72 MHCLG 2020e Table AT 1.19
73 MHCLG 2021a: Table T38
74 DLUHC 2021a: Table T36
75 DLUHC 2021a: Table T36
76 Crossley et al 2021a
77 DLUHC 2021d
78 Tunstall 2021
79 MHCLG 2020g Table AT209; MHCLG 2020f Table AT2.4; MHCLG 2020a: Table T26b, T27b; MHCLG 2021a: Tables T22b, T23b; DLUHC 2021a: Tables T21n, T22b
80 Judge and Pacitti 2020
81 MHCLG 2021a
82 MHCLG 2021a: Table T36b
83 MHCLG 2020g: Tables AT209, AT2.4; MHCLG 2020a: Tables T26b, T27b; MHCLG 2021a: Tables T22b, T23b; DLUHC 2021a: Tables T21n, T22b
84 Usually mortgaged owners: CPAG 2018
85 MHCLG 2021a: Table T14b
86 FCA 2021c
87 MHCLG 2021a: Table T36b
88 MHCLG 2020a
89 For example, housing costs made up more than 25% of income for more than half of renters before the pandemic (see Chapter 2), leaving 75% or less disposable for other spending. If a typical renter was furloughed, rent would take up 31% or more of furlough income, and the amount remaining for other spending would be 49% or less of the former

disposable income. In other words, if all earners in the household were put on furlough, typical renters would have to deal with at least a 35% drop in disposable income

90 MHCLG 2021a: Table T36b
91 SHE home ownership Table AT209, SHE private renters AT2.4, MHCLG 2020a: Tables T26b, T27b; MHCLG 2021a: Tables T22b, T23b; DLUHC 2021a: Tables T21n, T22b
92 Derricourt et al 2021
93 DLUHC 2021a: Table T44b
94 DLUHC 2021a: Tables T44a–i
95 MHCLG 2020
96 Tunstall 2021
97 Judge and Pacitti 2020
98 MHCLG 2021a
99 MHCLG 2020a: Tables T26b, T27b; MHCLG 2021a: Tables T22b, T23b; DLUHC 2021a: Tables T21n, T22b
100 MHCLG 2021a: Table T36b
101 Social Housing Resilience Group 2021
102 Heath 2020c
103 DLUHC 2021a: Table T44b
104 MHCLG 2021a: Table T30a
105 MHCLG 2021a: Table T36b
106 Wilson et al 2020
107 https://twitter.com/robertjenrick/status/1243299372894486535?lang=en
108 Fitzpatrick et al 2021: 9
109 Albuquerque and Varadi 2022
110 Fritsche 2021: 4
111 FCA 2021a
112 Wilson et al 2020
113 FCA 2021b
114 MHCLG 2020a: Tables T17d, e, f, g
115 Albuquerque and Varadi 2022
116 FCA 2021c
117 FCA 2021c
118 Albuquerque and Varadi 2022
119 FCA 2021b
120 MoJ 2022: Tables 2, 5
121 MoJ 2022: Tables 2, 5
122 FCA 2020
123 Wilson 2021
124 Barker 2021b
125 Watson and Bailey 2021
126 House of Commons Library 2021
127 Nande et al 2021
128 Watson and Bailey 2021: 6
129 Soaita 2021
130 Albuquerque and Varadi 2022
131 DWP 2021a
132 https://twitter.com/robertjenrick/status/1243299372894486535?lang=en
133 MHCLG 2020
134 Judge 2020
135 DLUHC 2021a: Table T18a
136 Heath 2020a

137 DLUHC 2021a: Table T18a
138 FCA 2021c: 96
139 Judge et al 2021b
140 Campbell Tickell 2020
141 Judge et al 2021b
142 Barker 2021a
143 Barker 2021a
144 For example, Lovett 2020; Mackie and Smith 2020
145 https://twitter.com/robertjenrick/status/1243299372894486535?lang=en
146 MoJ 2022
147 Leifheit et al 2021
148 Nande et al 2021
149 MHCLG 2021b
150 For example, Mackie and Smith 2020
151 Burchardt 2020
152 Watson and Bailey 2021: 10
153 MHCLG 2021b
154 Fitzpatrick et al 2020a
155 MHCLG 2021b
156 Gurney 2020
157 Quoted in Fitzpatrick et al 2021: 27
158 MHCLG 2021b
159 MHCLG 2021b
160 Heath 2020b
161 Fitzpatrick et al 2020a: 5
162 Lewer et al 2020
163 Thomas and Mackie 2021
164 Hippisley-Cox et al 2020
165 ONS 2021s
166 Fitzpatrick et al 2020a: 7
167 DHLUC 2021b
168 Fitzpatrick et al 2020a: 6
169 CHAIN 2020, 2021
170 Fitzpatrick et al 2020a
171 Fitzpatrick et al 2020a: 15
172 Baptista et al 2021
173 Albuquerque and Varadi 2022
174 Baptista et al 2021
175 Barker 2021c
176 Heath 2021c
177 Barker 2021c
178 Baptista et al 2021
179 Tunstall 2019
180 Baptista et al 2021
181 Tunstall 2019

Chapter 8

1 Judge et al 2021a
2 Stephens et al 2021: 7
3 Fritsche 2021
4 Jenrick 2020

5   OBR 2021: 55
6   DLUHC 2021f: Table 120
7   ONS 2022f
8   Judge and Pacitti 2021a: 1
9   DLUHC 2021f: Table 118
10 Powell et al 2021
11 HMRC 2021b
12 Scanlon et al 2021: 2
13 Judge et al 2021a; Scanlon et al 2021
14 Seely 2020
15 Judge et al 2021a
16 Mackie and Smith 2020
17 Seely 2020; Judge et al 2021a
18 Judge et al 2021a
19 Bricongne et al 2021
20 Bracke et al 2020
21 Bricongne et al 2021
22 OBR 2021; ONS 2022b
23 Cheshire et al 2021
24 Social Housing Resilience Group 2021
25 Social Housing Resilience Group 2021: 5
26 Social Housing Resilience Group 2021: 37
27 DLUHC livetable 600
28 Bank of England/FCA 2021
29 Bracke et al 2020
30 Stephens et al 2021
31 IMF 2021
32 Judge and Pacitti 2021a
33 OBR 2020
34 McCord et all 2021
35 Gustaffson 2020: 1
36 OBR 2021
37 Judge and Pacitti 2021b
38 According to the Nationwide index of all home sales (including Buy to Let), in Bracke et al 2020
39 For example, Stephens et al 2021
40 OBR 2021; Cheshire et al 2021; Fritsche 2021; McCord et al 2021; Scanlon et al 2021
41 Cheshire et al 2021; McCord et al 2021
42 McCord et al 2021
43 Fritsche 2021; Judge et al 2021a; McCord et al 2021
44 McCord et al 2021
45 Carpentieri et al 2020: 18
46 McCord et al 2021
47 Judge and Pacitti 2021b
48 Cheshire et al 2021
49 Cheshire et al 2021
50 Bear et al 2020
51 Crossley et al 2021b: 3
52 OBR 2021
53 2019/20 English Housing Survey Section 1 Households Annex Table 1.21; MHCLG 2021a: Table T39; DLUHC 2021a: Table T48b

Chapter 9

1. Hammond 2020
2. ONS 2021b; ONS 2021j
3. Fancourt et al 2020
4. Fancourt et al 2020
5. ONS 2022a: Table 1a
6. Powell et al 2021
7. MHCLG 2020a: Table T12Ac
8. Carers UK 2020b
9. ONS 2021n
10. ONS 2021d
11. NHS Digital 2021b
12. NHS Digital 2021a, 2022
13. MHCLG 2020a: Table T07k
14. MHCLG 2020a: Table T07k
15. NHS Test and Trace 2021
16. NHS Test and Trace 2022: Table 12
17. ONS 2020h
18. MHCLG 2020a: Table T06a
19. MHCLG 2020e Live table FA1422
20. ONS 2021l
21. Lewer et al 2020
22. Powell et al 2021
23. Trussell Trust 2021
24. MHCLG 2020a: Table T38a
25. MHCLG 2020a: Table T38a
26. FCA 2021b
27. DWP 2021f
28. DWP 2021f
29. HMRC 2021b
30. MoJ 2022
31. Fitzpatrick et al 2021
32. Fitzpatrick et al 2021
33. MHCLG 2021a: Table TA1
34. MHCLG 2021a: Table TA1
35. Fancourt et al 2021
36. OBR 2021; Stephens et al 2021

Appendix

1. Carpentieri et al 2020

References

Almost all the sources in the references can be found online, and in most cases are available for free. All web sources were last accessed in March 2022. Some articles were first published as 'pre-prints', before peer review and formal journal publication. The pre-print references are retained here even when articles have later been published in journals, so that the date of first availability is clear.

Aburto, J.M. et al (2021) 'Estimating the burden of the COVID-19 pandemic on mortality, life expectancy and lifespan inequality in England and Wales: A population-level analysis', *Journal of Epidemiology and Community Health*, 75:735–740, 19 January, online

Albuquerque, B. and Varadi, A. (2022) *Staff Working Paper No. 963: Consumption effects of mortgage payment holidays: Evidence during the Covid-19 pandemic*, London: Bank of England

Aldridge, R.W. et al (2021) 'Household overcrowding and risk of SARS-CoV-2: Analysis of the Virus Watch prospective community cohort study in England and Wales', *medRxiv*, 25 May

Alinsky, A. and Kobak, D. (2021) 'Tracking excess mortality across countries during the COVID-19 pandemic with the World Mortality Dataset', *eLife* 10:e69336.

Apergis, N. (2021) 'The role of housing market in the effectiveness of monetary policy over the Covid-19 era', *Economics Letters*, 200: 109749

Appleton, N.S. (2020) 'The bubble: A new medical and public health vocabulary for COVID-19 times', *Somatosphere*, 3 May

Bank of England (2022) *Interest rates and bank rate*, London: Bank of England

Bank of England/FCA (Financial Conduct Authority) (2022) *MLAR statistics: Detailed tables March 2022*, 3 March

Banks, J. and Xu, X. (2020) *The mental health effects of the first two months of lockdown and social distancing during the Covid-19 pandemic in the UK*, 8 June, IFS Working Paper W20/16 London: IFS

Baptista, I et al (2021) *COVID-19 impact on social protection and social inclusion policies in Europe: An analysis of policies in 35 countries*, Brussels: European Social Policy Network, European Commission

Barker, N. (2021a) 'L&Q's operating surplus increases 10% during pandemic while services struggle', *Inside Housing*, 19 August

Barker, N. (2021b) 'NI government extends longer eviction notice periods until May 2022', *Inside Housing*, 31 August

Barker, N. (2021c) 'Welsh government to introduce £10 million grant scheme for struggling private renters', *Inside Housing*, 30 June

Barker, N. and Heath, L. (2020) 'Council with highest COVID-19 death rate brands illness a "housing disease"', *Inside Housing*, 29 May

Barton, C. and Wilson, W. (2021) *What is affordable housing?* House of Commons Briefing No. 07747, 19 April, London: House of Commons

BBC (2020a) *Coronavirus: Woman in 70s becomes first virus fatality in UK*, BBC Online, 5 March

BBC (2020b) *Coronavirus: Stay at home to stay safe, 1.5 million advised*, BBC Online, 22 March

BBC (2020c) *Coronavirus: Can couples meet up?*, BBC Online, 24 March

BBC (2020d) *Thousands more in Wales told to shield from coronavirus*, BBC Online, 5 May

BBC (2020e) *Coronavirus: Prof Neil Ferguson quits government role after 'undermining' lockdown*, BBC Online, 6 May

BBC (2021) *Covid: Who are the workers 'excluded' from support?*, BBC Online, 27 January

Beale, S. et al (2021) 'Relative perceived importance of different settings for SARS-CoV2 acquisition in England and Wales: Analysis of the Virus Watch Community Cohort', *medRxiv*, 16 June

Bear, L. et al (2020) *A right to care: The social foundations of recovery from Covid-19.* London: Covid and Care Research Group LSE Anthropology, LSE

Bell, T. and Judge, L. (2021) *Lockdown lessons: What 2020 has to teach us about the difficult weeks ahead*, London: Resolution Foundation

Benfer, E.A. et al (2019) 'Eviction, health inequity, and the spread of COVID-19: Housing policy as a primary pandemic mitigation strategy, *Journal of Urban Health*, 98:1–12

Benmelech, E. and Tzur-Ilan, N. (2021) 'The determinants of fiscal and monetary policies during the COVID-19 crisis', NBER Working Paper 27461, Cambridge, MA: NBER

Benton, A. and Power, A. (2020) *Community responses to the Coronavirus pandemic: How mutual aid can help*, CASE Report 134, London: CASE, LSE

Bhattacharjee, A. and Lisauskaite, E. (2020) 'Covid-19 impacts on destitution in the UK', *National Institute Economic Review*, No. 253, August

Blundell, R. et al (2022) *Inequality and the COVID-19 crisis in the United Kingdom*, IFS Working Paper W22/01, London: IFS

Boddington, N.L. et al. (2020) 'COVID-19 in Great Britain: epidemiological and clinical characteristics of the first few hundred (FF100) cases: A descriptive case series and case control analysis', *medRxiv*, 18 May

Bottery, S. and Ward, D. (2021) *Social care 360*, London: The King's Fund, 6 May

Bourquin, P. et al (2019) *Why has in-work poverty grown?* IFS Working Papers No. W19/12, London: IFS

Boyd, I. (2020) 'We practised for a pandemic, but didn't brace', *Nature*, 580:9, 30 March

Bracke, P. et al (2020) *Mortgage market disruptions*, FCA Occasional Paper 57, London: FCA, October

Bradshaw, J. et al (2008) 'Housing: The saving grace in the British welfare state?', in S. Fitzpatrick and M. Stephens (eds), *The future of social housing*, London: Shelter, pp 7–25,

Bramley, G. et al (2018) *Scoping project to investigate the alternatives for including non-household populations in estimates of personal wellbeing and destitution: Final 3 Interim Research Report to Joseph Rowntree Foundation and ONS*, Edinburgh: Heriot-Watt University

Brewer, M. and Patrick, R. (2021) *Pandemic pressures: Why families on a low income are spending more during Covid-19*, London: Resolution Foundation

Bricongne, J-C., Meunier, B. and Pouget, S. (2021) *Scraping housing prices in real-time: The COVID-19 crisis in the UK*, Working Paper #824, Paris: Banque de France, August

Burchardt, T. (2020) *Does COVID-19 represent a 'new Beveridge' moment, a crisis that will wash away, or a call to action? Report of a roundtable discussion on theories of welfare,* SPDO research note 2, London: CASE, LSE, 9 June

Byrne, M. (2020) 'Stay home: Reflections on the meaning of home and the COVID-19 pandemic', *Irish Journal of Sociology*, 28(3): 351–55

Calvert, J. and Arbuthnott, G. (2021) *Failures of state: The inside story of Britain's battle with Coronavirus*, London: Mudlark

Campbell Tickell (2020) *Housing chief executive COVID-19 WhatsApp digest*, 18 March, updated 24 March

Carers UK (2019) *Facts about carers: Policy briefing August 2019*, London: Carers UK

Carers UK (2020a) *Caring behind closed doors (April 2020)*, London: Carers UK

Carers UK (2020b) *Caring behind closed doors: six months on: The continued impact of the coronavirus (COVID-19) pandemic on unpaid carers*, London: Carers UK

Carpentieri, J. et al (2020) *In their own words: Five generations of Britons describe their experiences of the coronavirus pandemic. Initial findings from the COVID-19 Survey in Five National Longitudinal Studies* , London: UCL Centre for Longitudinal Studies

CHAIN (2020) *Rough sleeping in London (CHAIN reports)*, London: GLA

CHAIN (2021) *Rough sleeping in London (CHAIN reports)*, London: GLA

Chan, J. F.-W. et al (2020) 'A familial cluster of pneumonia associated with the 2019 novel coronavirus indicating person-to-person transmission: A study of a family cluster', *The Lancet*, 395: 514–523, 24 January

Charlesworth, Z. et al. (2020) *Evidencing the link between the Local Housing Allowance freeze and homelessness*, London: LGA

Cheshire, P. et al (2021) *The pandemic and the housing market: A British story,* COVID-19 Analysis Series, London: CEP, LSE, March

Clarke, A. et al. (2015) *How do landlords address poverty?* York: JRF

Clarke, A. et al. (2017) *Poverty, eviction and forced moves* York: JRF

Clarke, S. et al (2016). *The housing headwind: The impact of rising housing costs on UK living standards*, London: Resolution Foundation

Clift, A.K. et al (2020) 'Living risk prediction algorithm (QCOVID) for risk of hospital admission and mortality from coronavirus 19 in adults: National derivation and validation cohort study', *BMJ*, 371: m3731

Conservative Party (2017) *Forward, together: Our plan for a stronger Britain and a prosperous future*, London: Conservative Party

Conservative Party (2019) *Get Brexit done: Unleash Britain's potential. The Conservative and Unionist Party manifesto 2019*, London: Conservative Party

Cookson, R. et al (2021) 'The inverse care law re-examined: A global perspective', *The Lancet*, 397(10276): 828–38

Cowie, J. (2021) 'The number of our tenants on Universal Credit has more than doubled', *Inside Housing*, 9 August

CPAG (Child Poverty Action Group) (2018) *Welfare benefits and tax credits handbook 2018/19*, London: CPAG

Cromarty, H. (2020) *Coronavirus: Support for rough sleepers (England)*, Briefing paper No. 09057, House of Commons Library, 27 November

Crossley, T.F. et al (2021a) 'The heterogeneous and regressive consequences of COVID-19: Evidence from high quality panel data', *Journal of Public Economics*, 193:104334, January

Crossley, T.F. et al (2021b) *A year of COVID: The evolution of labour market and financial inequalities through the crisis*, IFS Working Paper 21/39, London: IFS, 10 November

Davis, A. et al (2020) *A minimum income standard for the United Kingdom in 2020*, York: JRF

Davis, A. et al (2021) *A minimum income standard for the United Kingdom in 2021*, York: JRF

DCLG (Department for Communities and Local Government) (2012) *Allocation of accommodation: Guidance for local housing authorities in England*, London: DCLG

DCLG (2017) *Fixing our broken housing market*, London: HMSO

DEFRA (Department for Environment, Food and Rural Affairs) (2021) *United Kingdom food security report 2021*, 22 December, London: DEFRA

Denford, S. et al (2021) 'Preventing within household transmission of COVID-19: Is the provision of accommodation to support self-isolation feasible and acceptable?', *BMJ Public Health*, 21(1): 1641), 8 September

Derricourt, R. et al (2021) *New year, same arrears: How the pandemic is leaving private renters with unmanageable debt*, London: Citizens Advice

DfE (Department for Education) (2021a) *Autumn term 2020/21: Pupil absence in schools in England: autumn term 27 May*, London: DfE

DfE (2021b) *Week 48 2021: Attendance in education and early years settings during the coronavirus (COVID-19) pandemic 30 Nov*, London: DfE

DHSC (Department of Health and Social Care) (2020a) *Coronavirus (COVID-19) action plan*, London: DHSC, 3 March

DHSC (2020b) *New payment for people self-isolating in highest risk areas*, London: DHSC, 27 August

DHSC/PHE (Public Health England) (2020) *New guidance for households with possible COVID-19 infection*, 17 March

DLUHC (Department of Levelling up, Housing and Communities) (2021a) *Rough sleeping snapshot in England: Autumn 2020*, London: DHLUC, 25 February

DLUHC (2021b) *Household resilience study: Wave 3*, London: DLUHC, 21 October

DLUHC (2021c) *English Housing Survey 2020 to 2021: Headline report*, London: DLUHC, 9 December

DLUHC (2021d) *English Housing Survey livetables*, London: DLUHC

DLUHC (2021e) *Help to Buy (equity loan scheme): Data to 30 June 2021*, London: DLUHC,

DLUHC (2021f) *Live tables on housing supply: net additional dwellings*, London: DLUHC, 25 November

DLHUC (2021g) *English Housing Survey Household Resilience Study, Wave 3 April-May 2021,* London: DLUHC

DoH (Department of Health) (2007) *Exercise Winter Willow: Lessons identified*, London: DoH

Dorling, J. and Arundel, R. (2020) 'The home as workplace: A challenge for housing research', *Housing, Theory and Society*, 39(1): 1–10

Dorney-Smith, S., Williams, J. and Gladstone, C. (2020) 'Health visiting with homeless families during the COVID-19 pandemic', *Journal of Health Visiting*, 8(5)

Dowell-Jones, M. and Buckley, R. (2017) 'Reconceiving resilience: A new guiding principle for financial regulation?', *Northwestern Journal of International Law and Business*, 37(1): 1–33

Dunn, P. et al (2020) *Briefing: Adult social care and COVID-19: Assessing the policy response in England so far*, London: Health Foundation

DWP (Department of Work and Pensions) (2021a) *Use of Discretionary Housing Payments: April to September 2021*, London: DWP, 16 December

DWP (2021b) Benefit Cap (UC Point in Time Caseload), London: DWP, Accessed via StatXplore

DWP (2021c) Households on Universal Credit dataset, London: DWP, Accessed via StatXplore

DWP (2021d) Households below average income data, London: DWP, Accessed via StatXplore

DWP (2021e) Benefit and pension rates 2021 to 2022, London: DWP, 21 December

DWP (2021f) Income dynamics: Income movements and the persistence of low income, London: DWP, 26 August

Earley, A. (2021) *Housing systems, their institutions and their resilience: Preliminary literature review*, Glasgow: UK Collaborative Centre for Housing Evidence

EMG/NERVTAG (2020) *SARS-CoV-2 transmission routes and environments SAGE*, 22 October, London: Government Office for Science

EMG/SPI-B (2020) *Mitigating risks of SARS-CoV-2 transmission associated with household social interactions SO922*, 26 November, London: SAGE

EMG/SPI-B/SPI-M (2021) *Reducing within- and between-household transmission in light of new variant SARS-CoV-2*, 15 January, London: SAGE

Esping-Andersen. G. (1990) *The three worlds of welfare capitalism*, Princeton: Princeton University Press

Evandrou, M. et al (2021) 'Changing living arrangements and stress during COVID lockdown: Evidence from four birth cohorts in the UK', *SSM-Population Health*, 13:100761, 24 February

Fancourt, D. et al (2020) *COVID-19 Social Study: Results releases 1–27*, London: UCL

Fancourt, D. et al (2021) *COVID-19 Social Study: Results Releases 28–88*, London: UCL

Farrar, J. with Ahuja, A. (2021) *Spike: The virus vs the people: The inside story*, London: Profile Books

FCA (Financial Conduct Authority) (2020) *Mortgages and coronavirus: Our guidance for firms*, London: FCA, 12 December

FCA (2021a) *Mortgages and coronavirus: Information for consumers*, 25 March

FCA (2021b) *Coronavirus linked forbearance: Key findings*, 15 April

FCA (2021c) *Financial Lives 2020 survey: The impact of coronavirus: Key findings from the FCA's Financial Lives 2020 survey and October 2020 COVID-19 panel survey 11 February 2021*, London: FCA

FCA (2021d) *Statistics on mortgage lending: Q2 2021 edition*, London: FCA

Ferguson, D. and Kennedy, S. (2021) *Coronavirus: Self-isolation and Test and Trace support payments*, CBP-9015 Housing of Commons Library, 26 July

Fitzpatrick, S. et al (2017) *The homelessness monitor: England 2017*, London: Crisis

Fitzpatrick, S. et al (2019) *The homelessness monitor: England 2019*, London: Crisis

Fitzpatrick, S. et al (2020a) *The homelessness monitor England 2020: COVID-19 crisis response briefing*, London: Crisis

Fitzpatrick, S. et al (2020b) *Destitution in the UK 2020*, York: JRF

Fitzpatrick, S. et al (2021) *The homelessness monitor: England 2021*, London: Crisis.

Francis-Devine, B. (2021) *Poverty in the UK: Statistics: CBP7096 trends by country and region,* London: House of Commons Library, 26 Oct

Fritsche, C. (2021) *The expected impact of COVID-19 on the housing market*, Streiflicht VWL, No. 5, Essen: Hochschule für Oekonomie und Management, KompetenzCentrum für angewandte Volkswirtschaftslehre

Fung, H.F. et al (2021) 'The household secondary attack rate of severe acute respiratory syndrome Coronavirus 2 (SARS-CoV-2): A rapid review', *Clinical Infectious Diseases*, 73(Suppl 2):S138–S145, 1 August

Gershuny, J. (2018) *Gender symmetry, gender convergence and historical work-time invariance in 24 countries*, Oxford: Centre for Time Use Research, University of Oxford

Gershuny, J. and Sullivan, O. (2019) *What we really do all day: Insights from the Centre for Time Use Research*, London: Pelican

Glynn, J.R. et al (2020) 'Covid-19: Excess all cause mortality in domiciliary care', *BMJ*, 370: m2751

Grenfell Tower Inquiry (2019) *Grenfell Tower Inquiry: Phase 1 report. Report of the public inquiry into the fire at Grenfell Tower on 14 June 2017*, London: Grenfell Tower Inquiry

Gurney, C. (2020) *Out of harm's way? Critical remarks on harm and the meaning of home during the 2020 Covid-19 social distancing measures*, Glasgow: UK Collaborative Centre for Housing Evidence, 8 April

Gurney, C. (2021) 'Dangerous liaisons? Applying the social harm perspective to the social inequality, housing and health trifecta during the Covid-19 pandemic', *International Journal of Housing Policy*, Ahead of print, 6 September

Gustaffson, M. (2020) *Under water: How big will the negative equity crisis be, and who is at risk, in the aftermath of the coronavirus crisis?*, London: Resolution Foundation

Hale, T. et al (2020) *Oxford COVID-19 government response tracker*, Oxford: Blavatnik School of Government

Hammond, P. (2021) *Dr Hammond's Covid casebook*, London: Private Eye Productions Limited

Heath, L. (2020a) 'Coronavirus WhatsApp group reveals rent arrears and furloughing among biggest concerns for CEOs', *Inside Housing*, 31 March

Heath, L. (2020b) 'Rough sleeping in lockdown 2.0: Is the government's "Everyone In" policy on the way out?', *Inside Housing*, 20 November

Heath, L. (2020c) 'Social housing arrears 40% higher in areas with tighter local restrictions, survey shows', *Inside Housing*, 12 December

Heath, L. (2021a) 'Charities warn thousands at risk of returning to the streets as "Everyone In" hotels close', *Inside Housing*, 8 July

Heath, L. (2021b) 'GLA keeps two "Everyone In" hotels open as Home Office delays hamper move-on process', *Inside Housing*, 19 July

Heath, L. (2021c) 'Welsh renters given six-month notice periods until end of year', *Inside Housing*, 23 September

Hill, K. et al (2021) *Staying home and getting on: Tackling the challenges facing low to middle income families where young adults live with their parents*, Loughborough: Centre for Research in Social Policy

Hills, J. (2007) *Ends and means: The future roles of social housing in England*, CASE report 24: London, CASE, LSE

Hirsch, D. (2019) *A minimum income standard for the United Kingdom in 2019*, York: JRF

Historic England (2018) *An Introduction to 'Thankful Villages' – The Historic England blog* (heritagecalling.com)

HMRC (HM Revenue and Customs) (2021a) *Coronavirus Job Retention Scheme statistics*, London: HMRC, 4 November

HMRC (2021b) *Self-Employment Income Support Scheme (SEISS) Statistics: July 2021*, London: HMRC

HMRC (2021c) *UK Stamp Tax statistics*, London: HMRC, 1 October

HMT (HM Treasury) (2021) *GDP deflators at market prices, and money GDP October 2021 (Budget and Spending Review)*, 28 October

Hodgson, K. and Peytrignet, S. (2021) *Who was advised to shield from COVID-19? Exploring demographic variation in people advised to shield*, London: The Health Foundation, 21 January

Hodgson, K. et al (2020) *Briefing: Adult social care and COVID-19: Assessing the impact on social care users and staff in England so far*, London: Health Foundation, July

De Hollander, A.E.M. and Staatsen, B.A.M. (2003) 'Health, environment and quality of life: an epidemiological perspective on urban development', *Landscape and Urban Planning*, 65(1–2): 53–62

Horton, R. (2020) *The COVID-19 catastrophe: What's gone wrong and how to stop it happening again*, Cambridge: Polity

House of Commons Defence Committee (2021) *Manpower or mindset: Defence's contribution to the UK's pandemic response*, Sixth Report of Session 2019–21 HC 35, London: House of Commons Defence Committee

House of Commons Housing Communities and Local Government Committee (2020) *Cladding: progress of remediation: Second Report of Session 2019–21*, London: House of Commons

House of Commons Public Accounts Committee (2019) *Help to Buy equity loan scheme* 17 December, London: House of Commons

HSC/STC (2020a) *Oral evidence: Coronavirus: Lessons learnt, HC 877, Mark Walport*, 2 December, London: HSC/STC

HSC/STC (2020b) *Oral evidence: Coronavirus: Lessons learnt, HC 877, Patrick Vallance*, 9 December, London: HSC/STC

HSC/STC (2020c) *LL0061 – Coronavirus: Lessons learnt Witnesses – Carers Trust*, London: HSC/STC

HSC/STC (2020d) *CLL0064 – Coronavirus: Lessons learnt Witnesses – British Geriatrics Society*, London: HSC/STC

HSC/STC (2020e) *CLL0067 – Coronavirus: Lessons learnt Witnesses – Versus Arthritis*, London: HSC/STC

HSC/STC (2020f) *CLL0048 – Coronavirus: Lessons learnt Witnesses – Blood Cancer UK*, London: HSC/STC

HSC/STC (2020g) *LL0053 – Coronavirus: Lessons learnt Witnesses – Voluntary Organisations Disability Group*, London: HSC/STC

HSC/STC (2020h) *EIC0931 – Written evidence submitted by the LSE COVID and Care Research Group*, London: HSC/STC, 20 December

HSC/STC (2020i) *Oral evidence: Coronavirus: Lessons learnt, Dominic Harrison*, London: HSC/STC, 10 November

HSC/STC (2020j) *Oral evidence: Coronavirus: Lessons learnt, HC 877, Dido Harding*, Lonon: HSC/STC, 10 December

HSC/STC (2021a) *Coronavirus: Lessons learnt to date: Sixth Report of the Health and Social Care Committee and Third Report of the Science and Technology Committee of Session 2021–22*, London: House of Commons

HSC/STC (2021b) *Oral evidence: Coronavirus: Lessons learnt, HC 877, Simon Stevens*, Lonon: HSC/STC, 26 January

HSC/STC (2021c) *CLL0120 – Coronavirus: lessons learnt: Written evidence: Sudbury and Lavenham Hotels Forum*, London: HSC/STC, 23 June

HSC/STC (2021d) *Oral evidence: Coronavirus: Lessons learnt, HC 95 Dominic Cummings*, London: HSC/STC, 26 May

Huang, C. et al (2020) 'Clinical features of patients infected with 2019 novel coronavirus in Wuhan, China', *The Lancet*, 395(10223):497–506

Inside Housing (2020) 'A timeline of the 18 housing ministers since 1997', 13 February

Institute for Government (2021) *Timeline of UK coronavirus lockdowns, March 2020 to March 2021*

International Monetary Fund (IMF) (2020) *World economic outlook update, June 2020: A crisis like no other, an uncertain recovery*, Washington DC: IMF

International Monetary Fund IMF (2021) *Policy responses to Covid-19: Policy tracker: United Kingdom*, Washington, DC: IMF

Isakjee, A. (2017) *Welfare state regimes: A literature review*, IRIS Working Paper Series, No. 18/2017, Birmingham: University of Birmingham

Jarvis, C. et al (2020) *Comparison of mean contacts for Tier 4 and non-Tier 4 areas in England from CoMix social contact survey: Report for survey week 38 for SPI-M-O and SAGE*, 21 December

Jasonoff, S. et al (2021) *Comparative Covid response: Crisis, knowledge, politics*, Ithaca: Cornell/Harvard Kennedy School

Johnson, B. (2020a) *Prime Minister's statement on COVID-19: 12 March 2020*

Johnson, B. (2020b) *Prime Minister's statement on coronavirus (COVID-19): 16 March 2020*

Johnson, B. (2021) *Prime Minister's speech to the 2021 Conservative Party Conference*, 6 October

Jombert, T. et al (2020) 'Inferring the number of COVID-19 cases from recently reported deaths', *MedRvix*, 13 March

JRF (2022) *UK poverty 2022: The essential guide to understanding poverty in the UK*, York: JRF

Judge, L. (2020) *Coping with housing costs during the coronavirus crisis: Flash findings from the Resolution Foundation's coronavirus survey*, London: Resolution Foundation, 30 May

Judge, L. and Pacitti, C. (2020) *The Resolution Foundation Housing Outlook*, London: Resolution Foundation

Judge, L. and Pacitti, C. (2021a) *The Resolution Foundation Housing Outlook, Quarter 1*, London: Resolution Foundation

Judge, L. and Pacitti, C. (2021b) *The Resolution Foundation Housing Outlook, Quarter 2*, London: Resolution Foundation

Judge, L. et al (2021a) *The Resolution Foundation Housing Outlook, Quarter 3*, London: Resolution Foundation

Judge, L. et al (2021b) *The Resolution Foundation Housing Outlook, Quarter 4*, London: Resolution Foundation

Karlinsky, A. and Kobak, D. (2021) 'Tracking excess mortality across countries during the COVID-19 pandemic with the World Mortality Dataset', *Epidemiology and Global Health*, 30 June

Kearns, M. et al (2020) 'How big is your bubble? Characteristics of self-isolating household units ("bubbles") during the COVID-19 Alert Level 4 period in New Zealand: A cross-sectional survey', *BMJ Open*, 11(1): 1–11

Kelly, J. (2020) 'Coronavirus: The 'good outcome' that never was', BBC Online, 25 April

Kraatz, J.A. (2018) 'Innovative approaches to building housing system resilience: A focus on the Australian social and affordable housing system', *Australian Planner*, 55(3-4): 174–185

Lai, S. et al (2020) 'Effect of non-pharmaceutical interventions to contain COVID-19 in China', *Nature*, 585: 410–13

The Lancet Public Health (2020) 'The coronavirus pandemic puts societies to the test', 5(5): e235

Lasko-Skinner, R. and Sweetland, J. (2021) *Food in a pandemic*, London: Demos

LB Newham (2021) *COVID-19 Advice and support,* London: London Borough of Newham

Leather, P. and Morrison, T. (1997) *The state of UK housing: A factfile on dwelling conditions*, Bristol: Policy Press

Leifheit K.M. et al (2021) 'Expiring eviction moratoria and COVID-19 incidence and mortality: Evidence from a natural experiment', *American Journal of Epidemiology*, 190(12): 2503-2510, 1 December

Lenhard, C. (2020) 'Whose responsibility? COVID-19 in a homeless shelter in the UK', *Social Anthropology*, 20: 10

Le Page, M. and McNamara, A. (2021) 'Alpha Covid-19 variant (B.1.1.7)', *New Scientist*, updated 8 September

Lewer, D. et al (2020) 'COVID-19 among people experiencing homelessness in England: A modelling study', *The Lancet Respiratory*, 8(12):1181-1191, 23 September

Li, F. et al (2021) 'Household transmission of SARS-CoV-2 and risk factors for susceptibility and infectivity in Wuhan: A retrospective observational study', *The Lancet Infectious Diseases*, 21(5): 617–628

Liu, T. et al (2020) 'Cluster infections play important roles in the rapid evolution of COVID-19 transmission: A systematic review', *International Journal of Infectious Diseases*, 99: 374–380

Lo, C.-H. et al (2021) 'Race, ethnicity, community-level socioeconomic factors, and risk of COVID-19 in the United States and the United Kingdom', *E-Clinical Medicine*, 38, August

Lopez-Bernal, J. et al (2020) 'Transmission dynamics of COVID-19 in household and community settings in the United Kingdom', *MedRxiv*, 22 August

Lovett, S. (2020) 'Coronavirus: Private renters facing "tsunami of evictions" once lockdown ends, charity warns', *The Independent*, 5 May

Machin, R. (2021) 'COVID-19 and the temporary transformation of the UK social security system', *Critical Social Policy*, 41(4): 1–12

Mackie, P. and Smith, B. (2020) *Housing policies and the COVID-19 pandemic: A perspective from the Wales Knowledge Exchange Hub*, Glasgow: CaCHE, 5 October

Mackley, A. et al (2021) *Opposition Day Debate: Universal Credit and Working Tax Credit*, Debate Pack No. 2021/0138, London: House of Commons Library, 15 September

Madewell, Z.J. et al (2021) 'Factors associated with household transmission of SARS-CoV-2: An updated systematic review and meta-analysis', *JAMA Network Open*, 4(8):e2122240

Marie Curie (2021) *Caring for a friend or family member dying at home*, London: Marie Curie

Marmot, M. et al (2010) *Fair society, healthy lives: The Marmot Review.* London: 2010

Marmot, M. et al (2020) *Marmot Review 10 years on*, London: UCL, Institute of Health Equity

Marsh, A. et al (2000) *Home sweet home? The impact of poor housing on health*, Bristol: Policy Press

McConnell, D. (2020) 'Balancing the duty to treat with the duty to family in the context of the COVID-19 pandemic', *Journal of Medical Ethics*, 46: 360–363

McCord, M., Lo, D., McCord, J., Davis, P., Haran, M. and Turley, P. (2021) 'The impact of COVID-19 on house prices in Northern Ireland: Price persistence, yet divergent?', *Journal of Property Research,* Ahead of print: 1-12

MHCLG (2019) *English Private Landlord Survey 2018: Main report,* London: MHCLG

MHCLG (2020a) *Household Resilience Study: Wave 1 tables,* London: MHCLG

MHCLG (2020b) *Dame Louise Casey writes to Local Authority homelessness managers and rough sleeping coordinators,* London: MHCLG, 23 April

MHCLG (2020c) *English Housing Survey 2018 to 2019: Sofa surfing and concealed households – fact sheet,* London: MHCLG

MHCLG (2020d) *Housing Secretary sets out plan to re-start housing market,* London: MHCLG, 12 May

MHCLG (2020e) *English Housing Survey 2019/20 Headline report,* London: MHCLG

MHCLG (2020f) *2019/20 English Housing Survey: Private rented sector report,* London: MHCLG

MHCLG (2020g) *English Housing Survey data on owner occupiers, recent first time buyers and second homes,* London: MHCLG, 9 November

MHCLG (2020h) *English Housing Survey 2019 to 2020: Headline report tables,* London: MHCLG

MHCLG (2020i) *2019/20 English Housing Survey: Social rented sector report,* London: MHCLG

MHCLG (2021a) *Household resilience study wave 2 tables,* London: MHCLG, 2 April

MHCLG (2021b) *Statutory homelessness in England: financial year 2020–21: Detailed local authority tables, financial year 2020–21,* London: MHCLG, 9 September

MHCLG (2021c) *English Housing Survey, 2019 to 2020: Feeling safe from fire,* London: MHCLG, 8 July

Mikolai, J. et al (2020) *Household level health and socio-economic vulnerabilities and the COVID-19 crisis: An analysis from the UK,* St Andrews: University of St Andrews and ESRC Centre for Population Change, 5 May

MOD (Ministry of Defence) (2020) *COVID Support Force: The MOD's contribution to the coronavirus response 23 March updated 11 June,* London: MOD

MoJ (Ministry of Justice) (2022) *Mortgage and landlord possession statistics: October to December 2021,* 11 February

Moser, C. and Davis, A.A. (eds) (2008) *Assets, livelihoods, and social policy,* New Frontiers in social policy series. Washington, DC: World Bank Publications

Nande, A. et al (2021) 'The effect of eviction moratoria on the transmission of SARS-CoV-2', *MedRxiv,* 19 January

NAO (National Audit Office) (2017) *Homelessness,* London: NAO

NAO (2018) *Adult social care at a glance,* London: NAO

NAO (2020) *Implementing employment support schemes in response to the COVID-19 pandemic,* HC 862 16 October, London: NAO

NAO (2021) *Test and Trace in England – progress update: Report by the Comptroller and Auditor General Session 2021–22,* 25 June 2021 HC 295, London: NAO

National Voices (2020) *Stories of shielding: Life in the pandemic for those with health and care needs*, London: National Voices, October

NHS Digital (2020a) *Coronavirus (COVID-19) shielded patient list*, Leeds: NHS Digital, 16 July

NHS Digital (2020b) *Coronavirus shielded patient list open data set, England by disease group*, Leeds: NHS Digital, 16 July

NHS Digital (2021a) *Provisional monthly hospital episode statistics for admitted patient care, outpatient and Accident and Emergency*, Leeds: NHS Digital, 11 March

NHS Digital (2021b) *Appointments in General Practice December 2020*, Leeds: NHS Digital, 28 January

NHS Digital (2022) *Provisional monthly hospital episode statistics for admitted patient care, outpatient and Accident and Emergency*, Leeds: NHS Digital, 10 March

NHS Test and Trace (2021) *NHS Test and Trace (England) statistics: 31 December 2020 to 6 January 2021*

NHS Test and Trace (2022) *NHS Test and Trace statistics 28 May 2020 to 2 March 2022: Data tables*

Nicol, S. et al (2015) *The cost of poor housing to the NHS*, Watford: BRE

NISRA (2021) *Covid-19 related deaths in Northern Ireland - January 2021*, Belfast: NISRA, 25 February

NRS (National Records of Scotland) (2020) *Deaths involving coronavirus (COVID-19) by ethnic group: Data*, Edinburgh: NRS

NRS (2021a) *Deaths involving coronavirus (COVID-19) in Scotland: Data deaths involving coronavirus (COVID-19) in Scotland, week 41*, Edinburgh: NRS

NRS (2021b) *Age-standardised death rates calculated using the European standard population*, Edinburgh: NRS

OBR (Office for Budget Responsibility) (2020) *Fiscal sustainability report July 2020,* London: OBR

OBR (2021) *Economic and fiscal outlook 2021 27 October CP545,* London: OBR

OBR (2022) *Brexit analysis, 9 February,* London: OBR

Office for Health Improvement and Disparities (2021) *Life expectancy*, London: OHID, 16 December

ONS (Office for National Statistics) (2013) *2011 Census analysis: Unpaid care in England and Wales, 2011 and comparison with 2001*, London: ONS

ONS (2018) *Household satellite account, UK: 2015 and 2016*, London: ONS

ONS (2020a) *The different uses of figures on deaths related to COVID-19 published by DHSC and the ONS*, London: ONS, 28 April

ONS (2020b) *Coronavirus and crime in England and Wales: August 2020*, London: ONS, 28 August

ONS (2020c) *Analysis of death registrations not involving coronavirus (COVID-19), England and Wales: 28 December 2019 to 10 July 2020*, London: ONS, 7 September

ONS (2020d) *Comparisons of all-cause mortality between European countries and regions: January to June 2020*, London: ONS, 3 July

ONS (2020e) *Dataset: Household income, spending and wealth in Great Britain*, London: ONS, 22 October

ONS (2020f) *Coronavirus and depression in adults, Great Britain: June 2020*, London: ONS, London: ONS, 18 August

ONS (2020g) *Dataset: Coronavirus and the social impacts on NUTS2 areas in Great Britain*, London: ONS, 27 November

ONS (2020h) *Coronavirus and shielding of clinically extremely vulnerable people in England: 9 July to 16 July 2020*, London: ONS, 5 August

ONS (2021a) *Coronavirus (COVID-19) Infection survey dataset*, London: ONS, 12 February

ONS (2021b) *Families and households: Dataset*, London: ONS, 2 March

ONS (2021c) *Dataset: Young adults living with their parents*, London: ONS, 3 March

ONS (2021d) *Families and households statistics explained*, London: ONS, 3 March

ONS (2021e) *Dataset: Subnational estimates of dwellings by tenure, England*, London: ONS, 5 May

ONS (2021f) *Deaths involving Coronavirus (COVID-19) by occupation (those aged 20 to 64 years), in the first and second waves of the pandemic, England, deaths registered between 9th March 2020 and 7th May 2021,* London: ONS

ONS (2021g) *Updating ethnic contrasts in deaths involving the coronavirus (COVID-19), England: 24 January 2020 to 31 March 2021*, London: ONS, 26 May

ONS (2021h) *Deaths due to COVID-19 by local area and deprivation April 2021*, London: ONS, 20 May

ONS (2021i) *How people with a vaccine spent their time – one year on from the first UK lockdown, Great Britain*, London: ONS, 23 June

ONS (2021j) *Population estimates for the UK, England and Wales, Scotland and Northern Ireland: Mid-2020*, London: ONS, 25 June

ONS (2021k) *Deaths due to COVID-19, registered in England and Wales: 2020*, London: ONS, 6 July

ONS (2021l) *ONS: Short report on long COVID, 22 July 2021*, London: ONS

ONS (2021m) *Updated estimates of coronavirus (COVID-19) related deaths by pandemic wave and disability status, England: 24 January–28 February,* London: ONS, 26 July

ONS (2021n) *Excess deaths in your neighbourhood during the coronavirus (COVID-19) pandemic,* London: ONS, 3 August

ONS (2021o) *UK House Price Index: September 2021,* London: ONS, 17 November

ONS (2021p) *Data set: Pre-existing conditions of people who died due to COVID-19, England and Wales,* London: ONS, 23 November

ONS (2021q) *Dataset: All data relating to Coronavirus (COVID-19) case rates by socio-demographic characteristics, England: 1 Sep–25 Jul,* London: ONS

ONS (2021r) *Dataset: Households by housing tenure and combined economic activity status of household members: Table D,* London: ONS, 1 December

ONS (2021s) *Deaths of homeless people in England and Wales: 2020 registrations,* London: ONS, 1 December

ONS (2021t) *Dataset: Coronavirus (COVID-19) Infection Survey: England,* London: ONS London: ONS, 3 December

ONS (2021u) *Deaths registered weekly in England and Wales, provisional: Week ending 3 December 2021,* London: ONS

ONS (2021v) *Coronavirus (COVID-19) in the UK,* London: ONS, 4 December

ONS (2021w) *Census 2021: Communal establishments,* London: ONS

ONS (2021x) *Comparisons of all-cause mortality between European countries and regions: 2020,* London: ONS, 19 March

ONS (2021y) *Dataset: Coronavirus and self-isolation after testing positive in England 1 February to 13 February 2021,* London: ONS

ONS (2021z) *Table A02 SA: Employment, unemployment and economic inactivity for people aged 16 and over and aged from 16 to 64 (seasonally adjusted),* London: ONS

ONS (2021aa) *Dataset: Households by size, regions of England and UK constituent countries, 2015 to 2020,* London: ONS

ONS (2022a) *Coronavirus and the social impacts in Great Britain, Dataset,* London: ONS, 21 January

ONS (2022b) *Monthly property transactions completed in the UK with value of £40,000 or above,* London: ONS, 22 March

ONS (2022c) *Deaths registered weekly in England and Wales, provisional,* London: ONS, 15 March

ONS (2022d) *Households below average income: For financial years ending 1995 to 2021,* London: ONS, 31 March

ONS (2022e) *Household income inequality, UK: financial year ending 2021,* 28 March, London: ONS

ONS (2022f) *GDP monthly estimate, UK,* London: ONS, 20 November

Ostry, J.D., Loungani, P. and Furceri, D. (2016) 'Neoliberalism: Oversold?', *Finance and Development*, 53(2): 38-41

Patrick, R. and Lee, T. (2021) *Advance to debt: Paying back benefit debt – what happens when deductions are made to benefit payments?*, London: Nuffield Foundation, 7 January

Perry, B.L. et al (2020) 'Pandemic precarity: COVID-19 is exposing and exacerbating inequalities in the American heartland', *PNAS*, December, 118(8): 1–6

Pevalin, D.J. et al (2017) 'The impact of persistent poor housing conditions on mental health: A longitudinal population-based study', *Preventative Medicine*, 105:304–310

Pfefferle, S. et al (2020) 'Low and high infection dose transmission of SARS-CoV-2 in the first COVID-19 clusters in Northern Germany', *medRxiv*, 16 June

PHE (Public Health England) (2017) *Exercise Cygnus report: Tier One command post-exercise pandemic influenza 18 to 20 October 2016*, London: PHE

PHE (2020a) *Guidance on shielding and protecting people who are clinically extremely vulnerable from COVID-19' Updated 31 May (previous version 1 May)*, London: PHE

PHE (2020b) *Disparities in the risk and outcomes of COVID-19*, London: PHE

PHE (2021a) *Stay at home: guidance for households with possible or confirmed coronavirus (COVID-19) infection*, London: PHE [now withdrawn]

PHS (Public Health Scotland) (2021) *COVID-19 Shielding Programme (Scotland) rapid evaluation*, 27 January

Piddington J. et al (2013) *FB62 Housing in the UK: National comparisons in typology, condition and cost of poor housing*, Bracknell: IHS BRE Press.

Pierce, M. et al (2020) 'Mental health before and during the COVID-19 pandemic: A longitudinal probability sample survey of the UK population', *The Lancet Psychiatry*, 21 July

Poggio, T. and Whitehead, C. (2017) 'Social housing in Europe: Legacies, new trends and the crisis', *Critical Housing Analysis*, 4(1): 1–10

Powell, A. et al (2021) *Coronavirus Job Retention Scheme: Statistics No. 9152*, London: House of Commons Library, 23 November

Preece, J. (2021) 'Urban rhythms in a small home: COVID-19 as a mechanism of exception', *Urban Studies*, doi.org/10.1177/00420980211018136

Prime Minister's Office (2020) *New package to support and enforce self-isolation*, London: Prime Minister's Office, 20 September

Prisk, M. (2012) Speech at the Council of Mortgage Lenders conference, QEII Conference Centre, London, 7 November

Qui, Y. et al (2020) 'Epidemiological analysis on a family cluster of COVID-19', *Chinese Journal of Epidemiology*, 12: 506–09

Qureshi, Z. (2020) *Tackling the inequality pandemic: Is there a cure?* Washington, DC: Brookings Institution

Randall, S. et al (2011) 'Cultural constructions of the concept of household in sample surveys', *Population Studies*, 65(2): 217–29

Reeves, A. et al (2016) 'Reductions in the United Kingdom's government housing benefit and symptoms of depression in the low-income households', *American Journal of Epidemiology*, 184(6): 421–429

Revell, K. and Leather, P. (2000) *The state of UK housing conditions (2nd edition): A factfile on UK housing conditions and housing renewal policies*, York: JRF

Richardson, H. (2020) 'No DSS' letting bans 'ruled unlawful' by court, BBC News online, 14 July

Rosenthal, D.M. et al (2020) 'Impacts of COVID-19 on vulnerable children in temporary accommodation in the UK', *The Lancet*, 31 March

SAGE (2020a) *Housing, household transmission and ethnicity*, London: SAGE, 26 November

SAGE (2020b) *SAGE 16 minutes: Coronavirus (COVID-19) response, 16 March 2020*, London: SAGE, 29 May

Scanlon, K. et al (2021) *Lessons from the stamp duty holiday*, London: LSE London, July

Scottish Government (2019) *Housing statistics 2019: Key trends summary*, Edinburgh: Scottish Government

Seely, A. (2020) *Stamp Duty Land Tax (Temporary Relief) Bill 2019–21,* House of Commons Library Research Briefing London: House of Commons, 23 July

Shadmi, E. et al (2020) 'Health equity and COVID-19: global perspectives', *International Journal of Equity and Health*, 19(1): 104

Shah, A.S.V. et al (2020) 'Risk of hospital admission with coronavirus disease 2019 in healthcare workers and their households: Nationwide linkage cohort study', *BMJ*, 371:m3582

Singanayagam, A. et al (2021) 'Community transmission and viral load kinetics of the SARS-CoV-2 delta (B.1.617.2) variant in vaccinated and unvaccinated individuals in the UK: A prospective, longitudinal, cohort study', *The Lancet Infectious Diseases*, 222(2), 28 October

Smart, G. (2021) 'In full: Gavin Smart's opening address to Housing 2021', *Inside Housing*, 7 September

Smith, C.A. et al (2021a) 'Critical weakness in shielding strategies for COVID-19' *ArXiv*, 15 September

Smith. L.E. et al (2021b) 'Adherence to the test, trace, and isolate system in the UK: results from 37 nationally representative surveys', *BMJ*, 372:n608, March

Soaita, A.M. (2021) *Renting during the COVID-19 pandemic in Great Britain: The experiences of private tenants*, Glasgow: CaCHE

Social Housing Resilience Group with HouseMark Scotland/Scotland's Housing Network (2021) *The impact of COVID-19 on the social housing sector in Scotland and comparisons with the whole of the UK – August 2021*, Glasgow: SFHA

South Hams District Council (2021) *Coronavirus: Open letter to second home owners*, March

SPI-B (2020) *SPI-B Evidence Review for MHCLG Housing Impacts Paper*, London: SAGE, September

Squires, G. and White, I. (2019) 'Resilience and housing markets: Who is it really for?', *Land use policy*, 81: 16–174

STC (Science and Technology Committee) (2020) *Oral evidence: UK science, research and technology capability and influence in global disease outbreaks, HC 136,* 10 June

Stephens, M. and Blenkinsopp, J. (2020) 'Help with housing costs', in M. Stephens, J. Perry, P. Williams, G. Young and S. Fitzpatrick (eds), *UK Housing Review 2020*, Coventry: Chartered Institute of Housing, pp 93–100

Stephens, M., O'Brien, P. and Earley, A. (2021) *Resilience in the housing system: The mortgage and housebuilding industries from the global financial crisis to COVID-19: Interim report*, Glasgow: CaCHE

Steward, B. (2000) 'Living space: The changing meaning of home', *British Journal of Occupational Therapy*, 63(3): 105–10

Stiglitz, J, (2020) 'Conquering the great divide', *Finance and Development*, September: 17–19

Sunstein, C.R. (1996) *Health-health tradeoffs*, Coase-Sandor Institute for Law & Economics Working Paper No. 42, Chicago: University of Chicago Law School

Tatlow, H. et al (2021*) Variation in the response to COVID-19 across the four nations of the United Kingdom BSG-WP–2020/035 Version 2.0 April*, Oxford: Blavatnik School of Government

Taylor, L. et al (2020) ''It's like going to the regular class but without being there': A qualitative analysis of older people's experiences of exercise in the home during Covid-19 lockdown in England', *International Journal of the Sociology of Leisure*, 4: 177–192

Thomas, I. and Mackie, P. (2021) 'A population level study of SARS-CoV-2 prevalence amongst people experiencing homelessness in Wales, UK', *International Journal of Data Science*, 5(4):1695

Thompson, H. et al (2020) *Report 38: SARS-CoV-2 setting-specific transmission rates: a systematic review and meta-analysis*, London: Imperial College COVID-19 Response Team, 27 November

Tooze, A. (2021) *Shutdown: How COVID-19 shook the world's economy*, London: Allen Lane

The Trussell Trust (2021) *Trussell Trust data briefing on end-of-year statistics relating to use of food banks: April 2020–March 2021*, Salisbury: Trussell Trust

Tudor Hart, J. (1971) 'The inverse care law', *The Lancet*, 27 February

Tunstall, R. (2016) 'Housing', in R. Lupton et al (eds), *Social policy in a cold climate: Policies and their consequences since the crisis*, Bristol: Policy Press, pp 125–145

Tunstall, R. (2019) 'Housing and shelter', in D. Scott (eds), *Manifestos, policies and practice: An equalities agenda*, London: UCL/IoE Press, pp 130–54

Tunstall, R. (2021) 'The deresidualisation of social housing in England', *Housing Studies*, 39(2): 1–21

Tunstall, R. et al (2013) *The links between housing and poverty*, York: JRF

UCL (University College London) Centre for Longitudinal Studies) (2021) *COVID-19 Survey in Five National Longitudinal Cohort Studies: Millennium Cohort Study, Next Steps, 1970 British Cohort Study and 1958 National Child Development Study, 2020–2021* [data collection], *3rd Edition*, UK Data Service, SN: 8658

UKHSA (UK Health Security Agency) (2020) *COVID-19: Epidemiological definitions of outbreaks and clusters in particular settings*, London: UK Health Security Agency, 7 August

United Nations Office on Drugs and Crime (2015) *The United Nations standard minimum rules for the treatment of prisoners (the Nelson Mandela Rules)*, Vienna: UNODC

Warner, M. et al (2021) 'Socioeconomic deprivation and ethnicity inequalities in disruption to NHS hospital admissions during the COVID-19 pandemic: A national observational study', *BMJ Quality and Safety*, 25 November

Watson, A.R. and Bailey, N. (2021) *The pandemic arrears crisis: Private landlord perspectives on the temporary legislation impacting the private rented sector*, Glasgow: CaCHE, 8 November

Whitley, E. et al (2021) 'Tracking the mental health of home-carers during the first COVID-19 national lockdown: evidence from a nationally representative UK survey', *Psychological Medicine*, 1-10

WHO (2020a) *WHO timeline COVID-19*, Geneva: Switzerland, 27 April

WHO (2020b) *Report on mission to Wuhan*, Geneva: Switzerland, 24 February

WHO (2020c) *Home care for patients with COVID-19 presenting with mild symptoms and management of their contacts*, Geneva: Switzerland, 17 March

WHO (2021) *Rolling updates on coronavirus disease (COVID-19)*, Geneva: Switzerland

Wilcox, S. et al (2017) *UK housing review 2017 Briefing paper*, Coventry: Chartered Institute of Housing

Wilmore, J. (2021) 'Homelessness fell in early 2021, but charities issue warning as measures come to an end', *Inside Housing*, 22 July

Wilson, W. (2021). *Coronavirus: Support for landlords and tenants*, Briefing Paper No. 08867, House of Commons Library, 10 January

Wilson, W. et al (2020). *Mortgage arrears and repossessions (England)*, Briefing Paper No. 04769, London: House of Commons Library, 17 November

Yalcin, M.G. and Guzen, N.E. (2021) 'Altered meanings of home before and during COVID-19 pandemic', *Human Arenas*:1:13

Yang, M.-C. et al (2020) 'A three-generation family cluster with COVID-19 infection: Should quarantine be prolonged?', *Public Health*, 185: 31–33

Zilanawala, A. et al (2020) *Household composition, couples' relationship quality, and social support during lockdown: Initial findings from the COVID-19 Survey in five National Longitudinal Studies*, London: UCL Centre for Longitudinal Studies

Zhu, Y. et al (2020) 'A meta-analysis on the role of children in Severe Acute Respiratory Syndrome Coronavirus 2 in household transmission clusters', *Clinical Infectious Diseases*, 72(12): e1146–e1153

Index

Note: References to figures and photographs appear in *italic* type; those in **bold** type refer to tables.